*Lessons
in the
Correllian
Tradition*

Photo © Debbe Tompkins

. . . .

About the Author

Rev. Donald Lewis-Highcorrell (Illinois) is the CEO of Witch School International, the largest online school of Witchcraft and Wicca. He is also the long-seated First Priest and Chancellor of the Correllian Nativist Tradition and principal author of the tradition's degree materials. Rev. Lewis-Highcorrell co-founded the Pagan Interfaith Embassy, where he serves as a Pagan Interfaith Ambassador to the United States. He is currently the studio head of Magick TV and producer and host of *Living the Wiccan Life*.

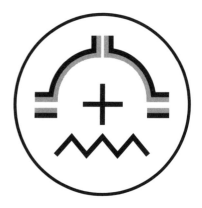

The Correllium, above, is the symbol of the Highcorrell family and the Correllian Tradition as a whole. The Correllium represents the oneness of being and is usually explained in this way: at the top, the Vault of Heaven is represented by (usually) a double line representing the elements of air and fire (light). At the center, a cross represents the element of earth and the four directions. At the bottom, a wave represents the element of water. The circle encompassing all is Spirit. The Correllium has its origin as a personal vision symbol and was later used in the manner of a familial crest.

witch school

First Degree

Rev. Donald
Lewis-Highcorrell

Lessons
in the
Correllian
Tradition

Llewellyn Publications
Woodbury, Minnesota

Second Printing, 2009
SECOND EDITION
(first edition ©2005 Witchschool.com)

Book design by Rebecca Zins
Cover design by Kevin R. Brown
Interior priest and priestess
illustrations from Dover Publications;
other interior artwork by
Llewellyn Art Department

**Library of Congress
Cataloging-in-Publication Data**
Lewis-Highcorrell, Donald.
   Witch school first degree: lessons in the Cor-
rellian tradition / Donald Lewis-Highcorrell.—
2nd ed.
      p. cm.
   ISBN 978-0-7387-1301-4
   1. Wicca—Textbooks. I. Title.
   BP605.W53L49 2008
   299'.94—dc22
                        2007050898

Llewellyn Publications
A Division of Llewellyn Worldwide, Ltd.
2143 Wooddale Drive,
Dept. 978-0-7387-1301-4
Woodbury, MN 55125-2989
www.llewellyn.com

Printed in the United States of America

• • • •

Other Books by
Rev. Donald Lewis-Highcorrell

Witch School Second Degree

Witch School Third Degree

Witch School Ritual, Theory & Practice

This book is dedicated to Reverend Traci Logan Wood, chief priestess of Holy City Temple, Chicago, without whose persistent encouragement and support it would not have been possible. Many thanks to her for continual aid and patience.

Contents

Greetings,

I am very pleased to be able to present this new, revised edition of my Correllian Tradition lessons. The creation of these materials took many years, and the new edition has taken many months, but at last I feel that we can call them completed. I think it is particularly appropriate that this new edition, long in the working, has been completed at the dawn of the year 7 Aquarius (AD 2007), with its numerical emphasis on spirituality and learning.

Of course, because people's needs and circumstances are in a constant state of change, it is only reasonable to assume that there will, in the future, be additions to these materials, but I think we can regard the basic form of Correllian Degree education to be established.

When I began writing these materials, the Correllian Tradition was a tiny familial tradition of Witchcraft. What I mean by Witchcraft in this usage is a relatively unorganized Pagan religious practice involving magic and spiritualism.

Preface

In my writings, I have always treated the term Wicca as synonymous with the word Witchcraft as it is defined above. This is what I was taught, and treating these terms as equal has been common practice for many in the United States, especially during the period when I was learning. Many people now use a much more limited definition of Wicca, confining the term to the Gardnerian-Alexandrian traditions; however, it is important for students to realize that this is not how the word Wicca will be used in these writings.

The Correllian Tradition considers itself to be Nativist—a word roughly synonymous with Pagan. In 1579 Pisces (AD 1979), the elders of the tradition decided it was a form of Wicca—again, thinking of the term as synonymous with Witchcraft as described above. The wisdom of this is now questionable, and the decision certainly has been subject to a great deal of criticism by people who note the many differences between Correllianism and Gardnerian-Alexandrian Wicca. Nonetheless, the tradition has styled itself "Wiccan" ever since, and it will continue to do so until and unless the elders decide differently.

Ultimately, however, we consider Correllianism to be something unto itself: "a lens through which all things may be seen." Though influenced by the movements it has grown up among and at times identified itself with, the Correllian understand-ing of the Universe is, ultimately, simply Correllian.

In setting forth the Correllian understanding in writing, it has always been my intention that the materials should be available to all seekers, whether Correllian themselves or not. I do not believe that we are given spiritual insight so that we can hoard it for ourselves or hold it back from others who could benefit. If a better understanding of Spirit makes one a better person, then sharing spiritual understanding should make a better world.

I hope that you find this new edition of the Correllian Tradition lessons interesting and useful in your personal spiritual journey.

May the blessing be upon you,

Rev. Donald Lewis-Highcorrell
FIRST PRIEST AND CHANCELLOR,
CORRELLIAN NATIVIST TRADITION

So you want to be a witch?

What is all this witchcraft stuff, anyway? Does being a witch mean you can point your finger and make things happen? Does it mean you can learn to fly on a broom and turn people into toads?

Well, not quite.

Witchcraft, or WICCA,[i] is a religion. Wicca is not primarily about magic, although it does use magic. Wicca is about your place in the Universe and your evolution as a spiritual being. Wicca is about moving forward on your personal spiritual journey—about learning, growing, and becoming the most you can be. As a religion, Wicca is a way of understanding and interacting with Deity and the Universe. It is a life-affirming path of growth and expansion.

Wicca is based on reverence for Nature and her cycles and respect for the earth and

. . . .

i   Terms that may be unfamiliar to readers or that require extra explanation will be set in SMALL CAPS in the text and explained in a glossary entry at the end of each lesson.

Introduction

all her creatures. Wicca teaches us to revere the natural forces of the Universe and allow us to see them reflected in the world around us, in every person and thing.

Wicca has great reverence for Deity, who for us has both a Mother and Father aspect. Wiccans approach Deity through many names and forms—both masculine and feminine, and drawn from all over the world and from every age. We often compare Deity to a diamond with many facets: each name or image for Deity is like one facet of the diamond. Each facet may be considered separately, and all are beautiful in themselves, but yet they all are aspects of a single stone.

Wicca believes that Deity comes to each person in the way that is best understood by that person, and that this occurs differently for different people. Wicca believes that the relationship between a person and Deity is highly individual, personal, and subjective. Not everyone will have the same understanding of Deity, because not everyone is in the same situation or able to understand from the same level or perspective. Because each person is different, no one has the right to judge another person's relationship with Deity.

This is why we respect all the names and forms that have been used to honor Deity through the centuries: Deity needs them all in order to come to all people in the way they can best understand.

The most common way for Wiccans to approach Deity is in the form of the TRIPLE GODDESS, whose three forms are Maiden, Mother, and Crone, and whose symbol is the moon. Her consort is THE GOD, who rules the cycles of the solar year and is called, among other things, "Lord of the Dance." His symbol is the sun. These two forms of Deity are viewed as POLARITIES, or opposing but complementary powers, like the Eastern concept of yin and yang.

Wicca has a very strong moral base. By "moral," we mean treating each other in an honorable and loving manner. Wicca has only one law on which all of its traditions agree: "DO AS YOU WILL, BUT HARM NONE." In other words, how you dress and who you sleep with is not our business—those issues are not what we mean by "morality." But a moral person doesn't hurt other people, and this is the criterion for all moral action. Whenever you act, ask yourself, "Am I harming anyone?" If you are, you are acting wrongly.

Wicca is a Pagan, or Native, religion. The word *Pagan* means "from the countryside" and reflects the fact that Pagans follow indigenous, native religions rather than "book" religions. Pagan religions have been built up over millennia as a result of people's observations and experiences; they are living, growing religions that can and do change when change is needed. Pagan religions revere the natural forces and cycles of life, and it is from observation of and interaction with these forces and cycles that their beliefs developed.

Wicca is wholly unrelated to the book religions: Judaism, Christianity, Islam, and Satanism. The book religions are all descended from the supposedly historical bargain between Abraham and Jehovah, which is recorded in their Bible. The book religions all share common elements: belief in a final Day of Judgment, in a jealous and vengeful God, in the basic sinfulness of humanity (called Original Sin), in the superiority of the male sex, and in the idea of Hell, a place of eternal torture. Most of the book religions believe in the infallibility of their book, the Bible (and its related books, the Talmud, the Koran, and the Satanic Bible). Though these books were written by humans, the book religions claim they were written by God—this is the hallmark of the book religions. Absolutely *none* of these ideas are shared by Wicca. The book religions have a totally separate origin from the Pagan religions, as well as a very different history.

• • • •

Wicca as a Spiritual Path

In taking these lessons, you must understand that you are not just learning some interesting things about magic and Pagan religion, you are undertaking a spiritual journey. If you apply the things you are taught and persevere in your studies, your efforts will change you on the deepest levels of your being. You will learn about parts of yourself that you may never have known existed (your Higher Self, your astral body, your chakras, and your aura, to name only a few), master psychic skills you've only read about or seen in movies (clairvoyance, divination, psychometry, and many more), and learn how to use magic to take control of your very destiny. You will develop strengths you did not now know you have, and you will, in time, face your deepest fears—and vanquish them.

Wicca is a path of transformation and growth that will challenge you and lead you to a renewed and enriched existence. Of course, you won't necessarily get all of this just from reading these lessons. You will have to do the work, and you will need to continue your studies beyond just the First Degree to master all of this. But the lessons contained here will build a strong base from which to grow.

• • • •

What Will You Get from These Lessons?

If you complete this course of twelve lessons, you will be eligible to apply for initiation into the First Degree of Correllian Nativist Wicca. The First Degree is the lowest degree of membership in the clergy of a WICCAN TRADITION. Wicca is composed of many traditions, most of which—but not all—recognize each other's initiations. If you choose to take the First Degree initiation—and you are not obligated to—you will become a priestess or priest of the CORRELLIAN TRADITION. The Correllian Tradition is a SYNCRETIC and highly philosophical tradition of Wicca, one that stresses the inherent unity of all Pagan traditions and the synchronicity of all spiritual paths. We believe that Deity is in all things and that therefore all paths can lead to Deity.

Wicca is not an exclusive religion. Because we believe that all paths lead to Deity, we do not believe that one must belong to any given faith or tradition to be a good person or to grow spiritually. Nor is it necessary to belong to only one. Being a Correllian initiate does not mean you cannot also be an Isian, Druidic, or Dianic initiate as well—or an initiate of any other tradition you might wish to study or join. You must, however, respect our tradition as a member and follow Correllian practices in Correllian temples—but what you do in other places is your own business. Your private beliefs and conscience are your own affairs, and we have no desire to dictate them to you. Wicca is about learning to make your own choices, and the Wiccan traditions exist to provide a framework in which to learn and grow. Wicca seeks to open your thinking, not limit it.

• • • •

So You Still Want to Be a Witch?

Now, do you still think you want to be a witch?

If you think you want to be a Wiccan, you should know a few more things. To be a Wiccan is to move at one with Deity. To be a Wiccan is to honor Nature and all that is in her, to acknowledge the life in all things and be in harmony with that life. To be a Wiccan is to work with the seen as well as the unseen; to learn the magical secrets of stones, plants, and animals; to speak to the faeries and the spirits and to hear their replies. To be a Wiccan is to use every tool available to grow, learn, and become the best person you can be. To be a Wiccan is to use magic, meditation, and ritual to overcome all limitations, all fears, and all imperfections and to move always in harmony with Deity, always to the good, and always in accordance with your Highest Self.

This is what it is to be a Wiccan. If, knowing these things, you still want to be a Wiccan, then these lessons will help you make a good beginning.

Lessons for the First Degree

Traditionally, it takes a minimum of a year and a day to achieve a Wiccan degree. Sometimes it takes much longer. These lessons have been formulated with this dictum in mind, and as such they are meant to be done at the rate of one per month. Twelve lessons, then, will require at least a year to complete. This schedule allows the student plenty of time to digest the information in each lesson, which ranges quite widely in nature.

A brief outline of the twelve lessons is as follows:

Lesson I: Magic

The first lesson is about magic: what it is, what it is not, and how to use it.

Lesson II: Cosmology

This lesson talks about the nature of Deity, Universal energy, and the soul.

Lesson III: Personal Power

This lesson explains the psychic tide and the Wheel of the Year and what these have to do with you.

Lesson IV: The Altar

This lesson talks about the altar and how and why to build and use your own.

Lesson V: The Airts

This lesson tells about the four quarters, the elements, and all of their magical associations.

Lesson VI: The Circle of Art

This lesson talks about the nature of ritual and its uses.

Lesson VII: Invocation

This lesson talks about the nature of "the gods," how to interact with them, and how to identify or choose your own special patron.

Lesson VIII: Garb

This lesson provides information about magical tools and clothing.

Lesson IX: Symbols, Omens, and Divination

This lesson, as you might imagine, is about how to interpret symbols and omens.

Lesson X: Basic Energy Work

This lesson shows you how to work with the spiritual energy of the body and of other living things.

Lesson XI: Herbs, Oils, and Incense

This lesson deals with the history, nature, and uses of oils and incense.

Lesson XII: Stones and Crystals

The final lesson introduces you to the rich world of stones and crystals.

· · · ·

Each lesson will have several parts:

- The lesson itself
- Exercises—to develop your psychic and magical skills
- Spell for the lesson—to give you experience with a variety of useful magical techniques and rituals
- God for the lesson—to acquaint you with Wiccan ideas of Deity and some of Deity's many forms
- Glossary for the lesson—to explain terms that may be unfamiliar; these terms will have appeared in small caps within the lesson
- Study questions for the lesson—to make sure you understand the concepts that have been presented

· · · ·

The Correllian Tradition

So what is the Correllian Nativist Tradition exactly, and what makes it different from other Wiccan traditions? Usually when people ask this, they are expecting to hear a liturgical answer—some special beliefs or ritual forms that are unique to Correllianism.

Correllianism does put an unusually strong emphasis on the philosophical aspects of Wicca and on the spirituality and inner mysteries of the Wiccan religion, but liturgically our beliefs do not especially differ from those of other Wiccan tradi-

tions. Rather, it is our unique attitudes toward the Pagan community and its future that tend to set us apart.

The Correllian Tradition is dedicated to the advancement of the Pagan people. We believe strongly in the need for increased communication and cooperation between Pagans everywhere, from all traditions.

We stress the importance of the Pagan clergy as teachers and facilitators, as well as the need for a strong public presence. The Correllian Tradition emphasizes celebratory as well as initiatory Wicca and is strongly committed to accessible public ritual.

· · · ·

Tradition Leadership

The leading bodies of the Correllian Tradition include the Witan Council, which is made up of all temple heads, elders, and officers of the tradition, and the Correllian Council of Elders, which includes the heads and officers of the tradition and its most respected members.

The first priestess and first priest are considered to be liturgical joint heads of the tradition, and they function as heads of the Correll Mother Temple. The chief administrator of the tradition is the chancellor, who represents and is empowered to act for the tradition's leadership as a whole. In addition to the chancellor, first priestess, and first priest, the tradition's leadership includes the first elder, who is responsible for primarily ceremonial duties, particularly in regard to the succession.

• • • •

Glossary for the Introduction

Correllian Tradition—Correllianism is highly philosophical and syncretic in its views, believing that Deity comes to the individual from within and that religion exists to help that process, not replace it. Correllianism believes that all of the indigenous, or Pagan, religions of the world are equally worthy and share fundamental concepts that are universal in nature, while at the same time manifesting external differences appropriate to their respective cultural origins. It also believes that Pagan religions must stand together and acknowledge each other's worth. In previous years, Correllian Wicca was called Nativist Wicca, and it is still formally termed Correllian Nativist Wicca.

"Do as you will, but harm none"—The Wiccan Rede, considered the oldest and most sacred Wiccan "law." Many traditions have "laws" or rules of their own, but the Wiccan Rede is the only one that almost all traditions agree on. Not all traditions agree on how the word *harm* should be interpreted here.

The God—Consort of the Goddess, the God, who is represented by the sun, is lord of the cycles of life. He is seen as the god of vegetation and of the forests, but also as lord of animals. He is represented as dying and being reborn each year in a cycle with the seasons.

Polarities—The concept of polarity is the idea that the Universe is held in balance by the interaction of two equal but opposite forces. These are variously described as darkness and light, spirit and matter, yin and yang, and Goddess and God. Everything that exists is made up of both of these qualities to varying degrees.

Syncretic—Syncretism is the likening of disparate ideas in the belief that they express a common truth. In religion, syncretism is the idea that the different religions of the world all reflect the same basic truths, but in differing ways—and that these differences are essentially external rather than integral to the true meanings of the religions. Syncretism is a dominant aspect of historic and contemporary Pagan religions. The hallmark of syncretism is the likening of deities from one area to deities from another. Thus, at the dawn of human history, the Egyptians likened the southern Amon to the northern Ra, seeing them as the same deity. Similarly, the Egyptians likened Ptah, Seker, and Osiris to one another, seeing them as one—a practice that extended throughout Egyptian religion. Much later, the Romans likened the Celtic Cernunnos and Secullos, the Germanic Odin, and their own Mercury to one another, again, seeing them all as one deity. The highest expression of syncretism in the ancient world was the worship of the goddess Isis, which in later periods taught that *all* deities were expressions of the same divine power, expressed as polarities—but this was by no means an exclusively Isiac view. The short-lived Priest Emperor Elagabalus created the most concrete example of syncretism in the form of his Elagabalium, a temple raised to all gods as one.

Triple Goddess—The three forms of the Triple Goddess reflect the three phases of the moon: Maiden (waxing moon), Mother (full moon), and Crone (waning moon). The Triple Goddess is the form of the Mother Goddess most often found in Wicca and underlying most Wiccan thought. Her symbol is the moon, and she is also represented by the earth itself (often spoken of as her body), by the sea, or by the whole of the Universe. Her spirit suffuses all things.

Wicca—Wicca is a nature-based Pagan religion focused on the worship of the Mother Goddess and her consort and the observance of the cycles of nature and the universe. Wicca is highly eclectic, drawing from many sources both in its origin and in its contemporary practices. Wicca also acknowledges and seeks to develop the higher powers of the soul through the practice of magic.

Wiccan tradition—*Tradition* in the Wiccan religion is the term used to describe an individual denomination as distinct from others. There are many Wiccan traditions, including the Gardnerian Tradition, the Alexandrian Tradition, the Seax-Wicca Tradition, the North Wind Tradition, the Blackstone Tradition, and the Lothlorien Tradition, to name just a few of the larger ones. There are also many small traditions. All are equally worthy, and all, in theory at least, respect each other equally. As membership in any Wiccan tradition is wholly voluntary, it is never appropriate for a member of one tradition to pass judgment on the practices of another tradition, except in regard to whether a given practice is the right one for that member as an individual.

Study Questions for the Introduction

1. How does Deity come to a person?

2. Who has the right to decide the best way for a person to interact with Deity?

3. What is a Wiccan "tradition"?

4. What is meant by the term *polarities*?

5. What is the one "law" that almost all Wiccans agree on?

6. What is the original meaning of the word *Pagan*?

7. What are the "book" religions? How do they differ from Pagan religions?

8. Are Pagan religions and the book religions related to each other?

9. Is Wicca an exclusive religion?

10. What is the First Degree?

11. What is the minimum amount of time traditionally required to achieve the First Degree?

12. Other than Correllianism, name a Wiccan tradition.

13. How many lessons are there in this book? How long will it take to complete them?

Lesson

I

Magic

Most people who have an interest in Wicca come to it first from an interest in magic. Therefore, we will begin these lessons by talking about magic. Many people would say that magic is only a small part of the Wiccan religion, and in the sense of spellcraft, this is true. But in a broader sense, everything about Wicca is magic, because Wicca is about transformation, creation, and spiritual growth—and this, after all, is what magic is all about. But what is magic, and how does it work?

• • • •

The Theory of Magic

The Universe is composed of energy. Everything around you—everything you see, and many things you don't—is composed of energy. You, too, are composed of energy. Your body, which seems so solid, is composed of endless numbers of microscopic particles held together at the subatomic level by energy. Modern science has taught us this. But the Vedic sages of India have taught this too—for many thousands of years. In Europe, the Druids, and after them the Witches, recognized this fact as well.

Even the most solid stone is in fact composed of millions and millions of atoms and molecules orbiting each other in the endless and graceful Dance of Life. This is part of the meaning of that ancient maxim "AS ABOVE, SO BELOW," which tells us that just as we live in a vast universe filled with countless stars, so too do whole universes of a different nature exist within us, within the microscopic makeup of our being—worlds within worlds.

The electromagnetic energy that holds electrons and protons and other microscopic particles in place has had many names in different times and places: chi (Asia), mana (Polynesia), orenda (Iroquois), od (German), the Force (*Star Wars*), and psychic energy (contemporary). For the purposes of these lessons, we will call it simply "energy."

Energy is not static or inanimate; rather, it is responsive and dynamic in character. It is fluid in its movements and as such is symbolically likened to water. Yet it is also likened to light and fire, because of its effects. In more contemporary times, it has also been compared to an electric current in its qualities, though it is not so harsh or unpredictable as this. In truth, energy is unique unto itself, and only by work-

ing with it can you come to understand it. Comparisons to other substances give only a rough approximation of what it is like.

It is the shape this energy assumes that creates the pattern of the physical world we see around us—for all physical forms are structured from it. We interact with this energy every day, in every second of our lives. It constantly transforms, renews, and changes its shape within and around us. This constant change responds to and is driven by our thoughts and emotions in ways of which most of us are not aware and of which fewer still have any understanding. This energy takes its shape from us, in reaction to us, as instantly and naturally as air conforms to the surface of the earth, or water to the shape of the sea floor.

But this is an unconscious process: we don't think about it, and we're mostly unaware of it. For most of us, this daily shaping of energy occurs at the level of our unconscious beliefs and emotions and is as automatic and out of our control as our unconscious itself. Often, we do not even know what our unconscious beliefs and emotions really are, let alone how they affect us on an energetic level. When we bring our conscious mind and willpower to bear on this process, however, we create a very different situation. Now, rather than an unconscious process out of our own control, the shaping of energy—and thus of the world itself—becomes a precise and deliberate skill that lies directly in our hands.

This is MAGIC: the art of consciously focusing and controlling this all-pervasive energy. Through focused will and effort, we use universal energy to affect the things around us. As energy reacts to thought and emotion, thought and emotion can be used to control or influence it. (Energy also reacts to certain physical stimuli, but we will deal less with that aspect than with thought and emotion; yoga is an excellent forum in which to study the influence of physical stimuli upon energy.)

It must be understood that it is not from the ordinary level of our conscious mind that we do this. If it were, everyone would be doing it, and it would be easy to teach. Rather, magic is done from a higher level of consciousness: the HIGHER SELF. Scientists studying psychics have found that when a person enters a psychic trance, the person's brain waves change. Psychics in trance do not use the normal beta waves associated with ordinary consciousness, but instead use the theta and delta waves associated with sleep. This is true of a person performing an act of magic as well: we access a higher part of ourselves, a change in consciousness that shows up even in our very brain waves. Only at this level are we fully conscious, truly human.

It is not hard to reach this level, but it is hard to learn to do it at will and to be able to access it on command. This is called SHIFTING CONSCIOUSNESS, and an accomplished witch can do it in the twinkling of an eye with no external effort or trappings. The student, however, should expect to put out some effort to effect this change in consciousness, and he or she may have to work hard to master it. Also, a number of external factors may be used to help bring about this change: specific words, ritual patterns, or items such as stones or artifacts that have power in themselves or that serve to put the person "in the right frame of mind," for example. Such external trappings are KEYS that we use to help us effect this shift in consciousness to access our Higher Self. They work on a symbolic level, bypassing conscious and unconscious limitations to act directly upon the Higher Self.

There are many different ways by which magic can be performed. All of them have the same basic goal: to focus energy and direct it from a state of higher consciousness. Visualization, trance, spellcraft (using external tools such as candles, cords, and so on), ritual of various sorts, chanting and toning—all of these and many other techniques can be used to create the necessary shift in consciousness.

Which is the best way? That depends very much on the individual. Everyone is different. What serves one person best may not work at all for another. That is why it is important to study and to try as many different techniques as possible, because only you can know what will work best for you, and only by experience can you discover this. In these lessons, we will present as much useful instruction as possible and as wide a variety of techniques as possible, but in the end your growth depends upon your willingness to experiment and your ability to combine those techniques that serve you best.

• • • •

The Practice of Magic

Through magic, we influence or control the things around us; therefore, it is wise to use magic only to make these things better. The ancient rule of Wicca is "DO AS YOU WILL, BUT HARM NONE." Magic is a great power and can be a great responsibility, and you would do well to use it wisely, as everything you do comes back to you, through KARMA. Karma dictates that every action you take you will also experience, in time, from the receiving end. So, when you do something good for another, you are also doing something good for yourself, as you will eventually experience the same good as a recipient. But if you do harm, that same harm you will ultimately do to yourself. This is very important to understand and remember. You should bear it in mind in every aspect of your life, including in the magic you practice. To do harm is

not only wrong in itself, but it ultimately harms the doer.

Moreover, most Wiccans believe in the LAW OF THREE (or Threefold Law), which is to say that what you do comes back to you not only once, but multiple times. Some Wiccans believe that the number three in the Law of Three is meant to be taken literally—that the karma of our actions returns to us exactly three times. In the Correllian Tradition, we consider the number three to be symbolic of plurality in general rather than literally referring to a specific number of times. Thus, in Correllian terms, the Law of Three means that you will experience the karma of your actions as many times as needed to learn the necessary lesson.

Before you do anything that affects another, then, always ask yourself, "How would I feel if I were on the receiving end?" because in fact you will in time receive it back, for all things return to their source. But so long as you work with a pure heart and good intent, karma will be your benefactor.

There is another distinction to note between doing and receiving. The words *magic* and *psychism* describe two aspects of the same process: connecting to the Higher Self. The word *psychic* comes from the Greek *psyche* (pronounced "SIE-kee"), meaning "soul" or "spirit"—that is, the Higher Self. In magic, we use this connec-

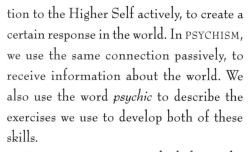

tion to the Higher Self actively, to create a certain response in the world. In PSYCHISM, we use the same connection passively, to receive information about the world. We also use the word *psychic* to describe the exercises we use to develop both of these skills.

Because magic is worked from the Higher Self, everything that helps you to connect with your Higher Self helps magic. Regular meditation and psychic exercises are valuable tools to strengthen that connection. The connection is like a muscle, and it grows stronger with use. The more you do—even if at first you do not see success—the better you will get and the easier it will be. Persistence is important.

In its opening stages, the most important thing about magic is to concentrate. Always focus as much energy as you can into what you are doing. This is rather like wishing very, very hard. This level of concentration is always an aspect of magic, but later it will begin to seem automatic for you and will not take such effort. If you are visualizing, try to see what you are visualizing as clearly as possible. Make the image as concrete and three-dimensional as you can. Visualization is one of the strongest aids to concentration.

Whatever magical working you are undertaking, by whatever method, try to put your whole being into it. The more of yourself you can put into the work, and the more energy you can focus on it, the greater the effect the magical work will have.

• • • •

Psychic Hygiene

One of the most important aspects of magical working—one that will be equally important in every magical act you ever perform—is psychic hygiene. Psychic hygiene prevents energy from becoming blocked in your body, which can make it difficult to use energy properly. Every time you do a magical work, you raise energy— that is, you focus and direct energy. When you have finished, you will still have excess energy left in your body, and this leftover energy must be released. You might guess that retaining this energy would be good, but it is not; it clogs up and causes problems. Too much of this excess energy can cause serious trouble. So always practice good psychic hygiene.

You can sometimes tell if you have excess energy after a magical working or ritual if you find yourself feeling lightheaded, off-balance, or disoriented. Also, sometimes it will manifest itself as a feeling of hyperactivity, or an inability to be still—literally, a physical feeling of excess energy. But even if you feel nothing unusual, you may still have excess energy, and you should make it a point to clear and release it as a matter of course. Another word for clearing and releasing excess energy is GROUNDING. You will find complete instructions for this in the Exercises section of this lesson. Make sure to read them.

Psychic hygiene is always important when you do magical or psychic work. You should cleanse and release both before you begin and, especially, after you finish. But this is not the only time hygiene is important. Many people on a magical path tend to pick up energy from others—usually emotional energy. Such people may find themselves picking up another person's emotions, mood, or tension level without knowing it. The same techniques of psychic hygiene can be used to release such "pickups" as well. Furthermore, because we tend to pick up from others in this way, it is important to practice PSYCHIC SHIELD-ING. Psychic shielding basically strengthens your own boundaries so that you do not pick up any energy you don't want. It's good to practice psychic shielding regularly—even daily—as it helps to strengthen the AURA, or field of spiritual energy.

· · · ·

Exercises

The Exercises section in each of these lessons will be devoted to giving you a series of exercises or meditations intended to develop your psychic and magical skills. Psychic-magical ability is rather like a muscle that grows stronger with use. The more you exercise your abilities, the more abilities you will develop. Again, psychism and magic are essentially the same thing, with psychism being receptive of spiritual influences and magic using these same skills actively to achieve specific ends.

In composing these lessons, we have assumed that you know nothing and are starting from scratch. We know that this is not true for all students and that some of you will have already acquired considerable skill and ability. If you feel your level of skill is already far beyond these exercises, then think of them as a review of the basics, or perhaps a new view of the basics. Soon enough, succeeding lessons will present you with more challenging exercises.

If you are starting from scratch and have never worked with these techniques before, practice them as much as you can. You should practice every day, and, if it is possible for you, at the same time each day. If you cannot practice at the same time each day, it is good to try to do it at least in the same part of the day—every morning, for example. This builds consistency and, believe it or not, really does make a difference to your progress.

How much you progress—and even whether you progress—depends on you. The time and effort you put in are what will determine your growth in magical ability. Like anything else, practice makes perfect.

These exercises rely heavily on VISUAL-IZATION. Visualization is a very important magical technique. In magic, our goal is to focus our energy very strongly toward the thing we want to bring about. When you visualize something, you imagine it very strongly, picturing it very clearly. When you first start visualizing, you may have to close your eyes and try very hard. It gets easier with practice, and later you will be able to do it with your eyes open. When you visualize something, try to see it as clearly and strongly as you possibly can, creating a three-dimensional image—just as if you were looking at a physical object. You do this because you are using the image, as well as the focus and concentration that go into it, to shape energy. You are not idly imagining a pretty fantasy, but actually affecting the universe on an energetic level.

Some people find it difficult to visualize. If this is true for you, then try to imagine what the energy *feels* like rather than just what it *looks* like. But even if you find it hard, don't stop trying to visualize; your ability to do so will improve with time, and the skill is of great importance.

Good Habits

As we have said, it is best to practice every day to build skill. If at all possible, it is best to practice at the same time each day. When you first begin to learn magic, it is best to practice on an empty stomach. You should wear loose, comfortable clothes (or, even better, no clothes at all), and you should select a comfortable position to work in. All of these things will help you to be psychically "open."

It is good to light one or more candles before you do your exercise. The candles will act as "batteries": when a flame burns, it gives off energy, and this extra energy will aid you in your exercise. Quartz crystal also serves to amplify the energy in this way, so it can be good to have some nearby or even to hold it during the exercise.

Some people also like to use incense to help them shift their consciousness. A few good incenses to use are sandalwood, frankincense, or lavender. You can also use an anointing oil. If you use oil, apply it to your forehead and the palms of your hands, as well as anywhere else you like.

The first exercises you will learn are two of the most important basic practices you should know: PSYCHIC SHIELDING and CLEARING AND RELEASING. These two techniques are the cornerstones of good magical practice, and their importance cannot be stressed too much. In future lessons, many other exercises will be given, but none are more important than these first two.

Psychic Shielding

Sometimes we pick up energy from other people without knowing we are doing so. Their moods or emotions may "bleed over" onto us, leaving us feeling angry, sad, tired, depressed, or whatever they are feeling—and not knowing where these emotions came from. Also, sometimes people will deliberately send negative energy to us—even though that is a very bad thing, something one should never do. Such negative energies cannot harm you as long as you don't let them in, but in daily life picking up energy is an unconscious process. For someone skilled in magic and psychism, however, this process is under one's direct conscious control. With psychic shielding, we create the boundaries that keep out unwanted energy from others while simultaneously strengthening our own aura, or spiritual energy field, and keeping it healthy.

This exercise should be done daily, either when you go to bed or when you get up, or as part of your daily psychic exercises.

Begin by putting yourself into a comfortable position and releasing all tension and anxiety. Visualize a ball of white light floating above you. Focus on the energy of the ball; know that it is full of love and strength and peace. Try hard to *feel* these qualities in the energy of the ball.

Now let the energy from the ball of light begin to flow down into you. The energy is a beautiful, clear white light. No matter how much light comes into you, the ball will remain equally strong, for its true origin is the Goddess and it is a source of boundless spiritual energy. Let the energy from the ball pour into you and flow throughout your body. Let it move out into your arms and legs and down into your fingers and toes.

Now let that light expand beyond your body. At first, see the light expand just an inch outward from your body. Now let it expand a little more—two inches, four inches, and so on. Let the light expand to form an oval around your whole body, an oval filled with clear, beautiful, loving white light from the Goddess. Let that oval of white light expand to form a perfect circle of energy around you, growing until it is about six feet across.

Now, in your mind, affirm this:

"There is one power in the universe, and I am a perfect manifestation of that power. As such, I will that the boundaries of my aura shall be strong and healthy, repelling all unwanted energy while remaining open to positive and healing energy. Safe within these boundaries, nothing can harm me, for I am filled with the strength of the Goddess. By my will, so mote it be—and it is so."

Now let the visual image of the light dissipate, but know that its protection and strength remain with you. Finally, clear and release all excess energy as instructed below.

Clearing and Releasing

Clearing and releasing of excess energy is extremely important. It is important to do this before a magical working so that your energy will flow freely. It is also important to do after a magical working so that the excess energy that may be left in your body will not cause you difficulties.

There are many signs of excess energy, among them dizziness, lack of balance, and feeling giddy or disoriented. Excess energy may also be marked by hyperactivity and/or an inability to rest or sleep after a magical working.

There are many ways that can be used to clear and release excess energy. The following is a good method for clearing energy, and the one we recommend you start with. Use this technique before a magical or psychic working to release any tension or anxiety you may be holding on to from the events of the day, so that your energy will flow freely. Use it after the working to release excess energy.

Begin by putting yourself into a comfortable position. It doesn't matter if this is sitting, kneeling, or lying down, but it should not be standing, as you may have a tendency to lose your balance until you become proficient in the technique.

Visualize—that is, imagine very strongly—a bright white light pouring down from above the top of your head, passing through your whole body, and exiting through the soles of your feet. Release all tensions, anxieties, and stresses in your being, and imagine them flowing out of you along with the white light. Let it all pour out of you. Imagine the excess energy as little bits of darkness being carried away with the light as it flows through you. When the last little bits of darkness are gone, let the light stop coming down and let the last of it flow out of you.

Another version of this practice uses the image of water rather than light. Some people find it easier to visualize water, because the image is more familiar. So if you have difficulty using light, try the version below.

Again, find a comfortable position. Imagine yourself lying in a river and visualize the water flowing through you, entering through the top of your head and exiting through the soles of your feet. Imagine the excess energy as leaves and twigs and other detritus that might fall into a river. See the water carry these things away from you. Again, when the last is gone, you are clear.

There are many other ways to do this practice as well. Some people imagine themselves standing before a beautiful lake. They imagine themselves being very dirty, and they walk into the lake until the water completely covers their head. Then they see themselves walking back out of the water, completely clean. Other techniques visualize wind blowing through the person to carry away the excess energy, or fire burning it away.

Still another technique is to imagine a long root, like the root of a tree, growing down from your root chakra (your pelvic region, loosely speaking—you'll learn more about chakras in a future lesson). Visualize this root going down into the earth. If you are indoors, see the root going down through the floor and through any lower levels of the building, then entering into the ground. Let the root go down deep into the earth. Now imagine your excess energy running down through this root to Mother Earth. When you are done, draw the root back up into yourself.

You can also use physical objects to help release energy. One of the simplest ways to do this is to put a bit of salt on the tip of your tongue or run the tips of your fingers through some salt. This will have a natural grounding effect and will eliminate any excess energy.

Another technique is to hold a piece of haematite, a stone formed from iron oxide. Haematite has a natural grounding quality and will have some effect all by itself.

But to get the best effect, hold the stone or object made from haematite and imagine the excess energy draining into it from all parts of your body. When you are finished, hold the object under a stream of cold water (such as a bathroom faucet) and imagine white light pouring through the stone as the water washes it. This cleanses the stone.

In each case, the excess energy returns to the Mother Goddess when you release it. She will recycle it, putting it to good use elsewhere. Some people like to say an affirmation when they release, such as, "I clear and release all excess energy" or "I release this energy to the Goddess to be used elsewhere." This sets a clear intent, and the affirmation can sometimes help to focus the process. It is not necessary to say the affirmation out loud.

All of these techniques are good, but we feel the white light, or alternatively the water, are preferable, because they tie into things you will learn in successive lessons, and in addition to releasing excess energy, they also exercise important psychic muscles you will need later. But as with all things, the most important aspect is that it works well for you.

• • • •
Spell for Lesson I
Ritual Bath

From our earliest beginnings as a species, we humans have recognized the healing and purifying qualities of water. Immersion in water has always been a sacred act, as cleansing to the soul as it is to the body. In ancient times, wells, lakes, and rivers were considered sacred, and people would immerse themselves in these bodies of water to release negative energy, help heal spiritual blockages or imbalances, and prepare for ceremonies. Even today Hindus immerse themselves in the sacred Ganges River as an act of both spiritual and physical cleansing.

This spell comes in the form of a ritual bath. A ritual bath is not for physical washing, but rather for meditation and to effect changes using the energy of the water and whatever may be added to it. This particular bath is for cleansing and blessing.

For this spell, you will need the following:

- Bath tub (or shower, if need be)
- A handful of salt
- A handful of dried rosemary
- A handful of dried sage
- White candles, as many as you wish
- A mirror (your bathroom mirror is fine)
- Oil

Notes: Sea salt is preferred, but any kind of salt may be used. The herbs may be added loose to the water, or you may tie them up in a square of cheesecloth for easier cleanup afterward. It is not necessary to use candles, but they are beneficial and will help to create a conducive atmosphere. If you have access to it, a fragrant anointing oil is preferred. Aromatic oils may be purchased not only at metaphysical stores, but also at bath shops or stores that carry aromatherapy products. A good oil to use would be sandalwood. If you do not have access to an anointing oil, any oil can be used, especially olive oil, which has a long history of use in sacred rituals.

To begin this spell, pick a time when you will not be disturbed. Have all of your materials together. Run a tub full of warm water. The water should be comfortable, so adjust it to your own preference. While the water is running, add the salt, rosemary, and sage. If you are using candles, light them and turn off the electric lights.

When the bath is ready, take a moment to ground and release as you learned how to do in the Exercises section of this lesson. Then make a prayer, both to ask the help of the Goddess and to help set your intent. You can use words such as these:

"O Mother Goddess, help me to cleanse myself now of all that holds me back or blocks my growth and progress. Help me as I embrace my fullest potential and I open my heart to growth."

Now get into the water. Rinse yourself thoroughly, so that every part of your body gets wet, including your face and hair.

Now lie back. Get comfortable. Let the warmth of the water soak into you. Take a few moments just to appreciate the sensation.

Now reflect upon your life. Think about every part of your life that has ever held you back in any way: every pain, sorrow, and anxiety, and every fear, hesitation, and self-imposed limitation. Review every painful memory, every event that ever hurt you. Be as thorough as you can. And as you think of each thing, make an affirmation to yourself and to the universe:

"I release this. It leaves me now."

You may say these words, or words to this effect, out loud, or you can concentrate on them silently.

Release each and every issue that holds you back. When you cannot think of any others, augment your efforts with a prayer like this:

"O Mother Goddess, look within my soul and help me to release whatever remains that I have not seen."

Now clear your mind. When thoughts come, do not respond to them, but let them drift right back out of your mind. Meditate in this way for a few minutes. Let the Goddess look inside you. Remain this way for as long as you are comfortable.

Now rise. Stand up. Think of all the things that you have released. Affirm the following:

"All that I have released, I leave behind me. May their energy return to the Mother to be reused."

So saying, step out of the tub. Do not dry off—let the air dry you as you continue the spell. Look into the mirror. Examine the face that stares back at you. Remind yourself:

"This is a good person."

Mean it. Tell yourself:

"I love this person. This is the child of the Goddess, whom she loves."

Now take up the oil. Open it, and dab out a little onto your fingers. Reach down and anoint the top of each foot with the oil. Affirm:

*"Blessed be my feet, that I
may walk in sacred paths."*

Now dab a little more oil onto your fingertips. Anoint both knees. Affirm:

*"Blessed be my knees, that
I may kneel at the altar of
the Ancient Ones."*

Now get a bit more oil for your fingertips. Anoint your pelvic region (just above your pubic area, or wherever you please). Affirm:

*"Blessed be my second
chakra, that I may bring forth
life, and art, and joy."*

Place a bit more oil on your fingers. Anoint the center of your chest and affirm:

*"Blessed be my heart, which
is formed in beauty, that I
may love and receive love."*

Now take a bit more oil. Anoint your lips and affirm:

*"Blessed be my lips, that
I may speak the Words of
Power in time to come."*

Finally, take a little more oil and anoint the very center of your forehead. Affirm:

*"Blessed be my mind's eye,
that I may see the unseen and
receive the messages of Spirit."*

Now look into the mirror and speak words to the effect of the following:

*"In the name of the Goddess,
I am blessed. Like a flower, I
shall open and grow. May all
that I have released be replaced
with the love and blessings of
the Mother. So mote it be."*

You have now finished the spell. Clear and release all excess energy in the manner you have learned.

You may feel an immediate difference from this spell. You may not. It can sometimes take days for the effects of the spell to become manifest. They deepen with time. Not every aspect you have released will necessarily disappear completely. You may have to go back and do additional healing for some. This is normal. Sometimes releasing works in layers, with each successive ritual releasing a little bit more. Above all, remember, practice makes perfect. If at first you have trouble with some aspects of this spell, such as the meditation or the concentration, do not be discouraged—practice! Skill is built through use.

• • • •

God for Lesson I
Genius/Juno

Paganism has many, many deities. Each month, this section will give you information regarding a specific deity, class of deities, or group of deities. This is to help you build a knowledgeable overview of the concept of Deity and to help you to interact with it.

In Lesson II, you will learn more about how Wiccans view Deity. Once you understand that, you will be better able to interact with the higher forms of Deity. Here in Lesson I, however, we thought we'd start closer to home, with the deity you may find easiest to understand: your own.

In Lesson I, you have been introduced to the concept of the Higher Self. This is the part of you that lies above your conscious mind. It has access to knowledge and abilities that your conscious self does not, and it is not troubled by the fears and anxieties of the material world. The Higher Self is an aspect of your soul, which is immortal and experiences many lifetimes. The Higher Self is not a separate part of yourself, but rather a different level. The Higher Self is the part of you that becomes an ancestor or a spirit guide after death, and it has that same ability now. It has knowledge and ability far beyond the conscious self, and it works always for the good. That is its nature, and it cannot do

otherwise, not because it is prevented from doing so, but simply because it would never occur it the Higher Self to do ill.

The Higher Self is also sometimes called the spirit, but this can be confusing, as the word *spirit* is used in so many ways by so many people.

Every person has a Higher Self, but most people have little contact with it. The conscious mind is separated from the Higher Self by the VEIL. One of the principal goals of a spiritual path is to part the veil and see beyond it, accessing and using the powers of the Higher Self. This is what we do in magic.

The ancient Romans called the Higher Self the Genius (masculine) or Juno (feminine). They considered the Genius/Juno to be the divine part of each individual. Every person was encouraged to be in touch with the Genius/Juno and to move in sync with it. In this way, the Romans believed that they would act from their best self, moving at one with the universe and learning the lessons life offered them with greater ease. They were encouraged to talk to their Genius/Juno and listen for its answers and to honor it with offerings and ceremonies that served to strengthen their bond to it.

Every day, the whole family would make offerings to the Genius of the head of the family, and sometimes also those of other important clan members, along with the gods who protected the household. In later times, many families also made offerings to the Genius of the emperor and sometimes the Juno of the empress. (This is the practice that horrified Christians described as "worshipping the emperor as a god.") By making these offerings, Romans believed that they were helping the person to achieve a closer bond with his or her Higher Self, and thus be a better person—because the Higher Self always acts to the good and cannot, by its nature, do otherwise. The Higher Self is rather like what some people call a guardian angel, except that instead of being outside of you, it is a part of you—a higher, better part with a clearer viewpoint.

Every year on their birthday, all of the members of the family would receive these same offerings to their Genius/Juno from the whole house. This, more than the mere marking of age, is what made the celebration of birthdays so important. It was the time to acknowledge people's highest, best self and encourage their relationship with it.

Most people also made daily offerings to their Genius/Juno in private. People would tell the Genius/Juno what they wanted to do or learn or acquire, in the hope that the Genius/Juno would help with this. These offerings commonly included something to represent each of the four elements, such as incense (for air), the flame of an oil lamp (for fire), wine (for water), and cakes (for earth).

There follows below a modern version of the ritual for honoring the Genius/Juno, which you might like to try as an aid to attunement with your Higher Self. It is perhaps different from the ancient ritual in form, but not in function. In keeping with modern custom, the term "Higher Self" is used rather than "Genius" or "Juno." This ritual can be done whenever you wish, especially on your birthday. You can do this ritual by itself or in connection with other, similar rituals you will learn to honor the ancestors and the deities.

Ritual for the Genius/Juno

You will need the following materials:

- Some incense (any kind that you particularly like)
- A candle or candles, your favorite color or any other color you like
- A glass of water, juice, wine, or other beverage
- A picture to represent your Higher Self; this can be a photograph or drawing of your physical self or a drawing representing the qualities of your Higher Self

Set up an altar using these elements. The altar can be anywhere you like, and it will be taken down when you are done (or you may leave it up to use again, if you wish). You can set it up in any way that seems good to you.

Begin by releasing. Let all of the tensions and anxieties of your day flow out of you, as has been discussed in the Exercises section of this lesson.

Now light the candle(s). Focus on the flame and concentrate. Make your mind still, so that you are not thinking of anything else but what you are doing here and now. Light the incense and say:

"I invoke You, O Higher Self."

Now try to imagine the image of your Higher Self before you. You can imagine it looking just as you look in the flesh, or as you would like to look, or you might see it as a cloud of beautiful white light or some other image that may come to you—one that you haven't thought of yourself but that the Higher Self itself has chosen. It doesn't really matter, because the Higher Self doesn't have a physical form, and you will use the image only to give you something to focus on to help you communicate with it better.

Speak to the Higher Self. The following words are only to give you a basic form; you should speak from the heart. (You can also use this invocation by itself anytime you feel a need to attune to the Higher Self.)

*"I attune to my Higher Self.
I move in harmony with my Higher
Self. I am at one with my Higher
Self. O Higher Self, I ask you to*
*help me to see and understand the
lessons of my life, give me clarity
and courage to learn them, and help
me to learn them with ease and joy.
I rededicate myself to the purposes
for which I entered this life and ask
you to guide me through them."*

Lift up the glass. Imagine a bright white light shining from it, as though it were glowing, and say:

*"O Higher Self, I offer
you this glass in token of
the love I bear you."*

Now drink the liquid. Imagine the white light entering you along with the liquid, spreading out through your chest and giving you a pleasant warmth. Then put the glass back on the altar.

Now take a few minutes and meditate while the candles and incense burn and the offering stands. Imagine your Higher Self strong and healthy and happy. Concentrate on it. In this way, you are sending the Higher Self energy and strengthening your bond to it. When you have finished, say:

*"O Higher Self, I pray that you
have enjoyed this offering. I give
you my thanks and my love."*

Now put out the incense and extinguish the candle. It is an ancient belief that you should never extinguish a candle by blowing on it. Rather, you should use a candle snuffer, pinch it out with your fingers, or extinguish it with the side of a blade. This is because blowing on the flame is considered disrespectful.

You should also wash the glass under cold running water and imagine white light flowing through it along with the water. Say:

"I cleanse you."

Concentrate on the water and white light, removing all excess energy from the glass.

. . . .

Glossary for Lesson I

"As above, so below"—The ancient maxim "As above, so below" is attributed to the Egyptian spiritual master Hermes Trismegistus, whose Emerald Tablet and other works were the standard of traditional Hermetic teaching. What is meant by this phrase is that all of creation, whether great or small, reflects the same Divine Nature, or plan. Because all things that exist are emanations of the Goddess through the God, all things naturally mirror and reflect their divine qualities. For this reason, the same truth will be discerned in a galaxy of stars and in a single grain of sand, if one is open to it. It is ultimately on this principle that all forms of divination are based.

aura—The field of spiritual energy around the body. The size, shape, and color(s) of an aura can reveal many things about the person's spiritual state.

"Do as you will, but harm none"—The Wiccan Rede, the great law of Wicca. Because what you do comes back to you—through karma—magic and all other actions should be used for constructive purposes only. Using one's actions for harm is wrong and will only bring harm back to you in the end.

grounding—Clearing and releasing excess energy to focus oneself back into the physical here and now after magical or psychic work. Grounding is done by allowing excess energy to flow out of the body so that it can be returned to Mother Earth to be used in other, more productive ways.

Higher Self—The higher portion of one's being, through which the connection to the Divine is perceived. By attuning to the Higher Self, we move in concert with the part of us that is divine and have access to its knowledge and powers. Lesson II will give more details about the nature of the Higher Self.

karma—Divine justice, or balance. Karma tells us that for every action there is a reaction. A good action will beget good. A bad action will beget bad. Everything we do comes back to us in time—sometimes in this life, sometimes in another, but all will eventually return. To satisfy karma, one must learn the lesson of the action, not merely experience it. And one will reexperience the event as many times as necessary to learn the lesson.

keys—A "key" is something we use to help induce a shift in consciousness. The key may be anything that evokes the desired mental or emotional atmosphere and makes the shift easier to accomplish. By making us feel "magical," these keys help ease us into our Higher Selves. An example of a key is candlelight, which can do much more to put us into a magical state than, say, fluorescent light.

Law of Three—Most Wiccans believe in the "Law of Three," that is, that what you do—good or bad—comes back to you multiple times. Some mean this literally as three times, while others mean it symbolically: you will repeat the experience as many times as necessary to learn the lesson it offers, and "three" here simply means "multiple times." The Correllian Tradition holds to the latter view. The true meaning of the Law of Three has nothing to do with the exact number of times something will reoccur, but rather reveals the concept

that karma is about learning rather than simply balancing out one's acts.

magic—Magic is the technique of creation. Magic is a method of creating, changing, or affecting circumstances through the manipulation of energy. Magic is accomplished through the focus of willpower and emotion, which shape energy. Magic is best used for self-improvement, prosperity, and healing.

psychic shielding—Strengthening one's aura to keep out extraneous or unwanted energies.

psychism—Magic is the art of actively using the powers of the soul. Psychism is the art of using those same powers passively, to receive information or communication from the Higher Self or from others. Magic and psychism are intimately connected, and the division between them is arbitrary, made solely to simplify understanding.

shifting consciousness—The process through which we rise from our normal thinking level of consciousness to connect with our Higher Self. It is from this higher level of consciousness that magic is practiced as a conscious act. Science has shown that our brain waves actually change when we shift consciousness in this way, creating a distinctly different state from that of our normal mind.

veil—A term describing the inability of the ordinary conscious mind to easily access the powers or memories of the soul.

visualization—The art of concentrating on or imagining something very strongly, usually as a visual image. In this way, you focus your mind and emotion to shape that which is visualized into reality.

Study Questions for Lesson I

1. Of what is the universe composed?

2. What is magic? Of what use is it to the individual?

3. What is meant by the term Higher Self?

4. What do we mean by shifting consciousness?

5. To what sorts of stimuli does energy react?

6. Give two other names for "energy."

7. What is karma?

8. What is the Law of Three?

9. What is psychic hygiene? Why is it important?

10. What is visualization?

11. What is psychism? How does it differ from magic?

12. Why is psychic shielding important?

13. If you were to fully master the art of magic and could use it to do anything you wished, what would you do?

Lesson

II

Cosmology

. . . .

God, the Universe, and Everything

There are two levels to the Wiccan understanding of Deity. The first is personal, the second universal.

On a personal level, we approach Deity as an entity with which we interact through words and actions and with whom we maintain a personal relationship. At this level, we give Deity many names and faces, and we interact with Deity through these. Most Wiccans will use a variety of names and faces for Deity in this personal sense but will have one particular form they perceive as their PATRON. They will interact with this patron deity, or in some cases patron deities, in a very personal way, seeking guidance, inspiration, and practical help in both daily life and esoteric matters.

Let us use the goddess Sekhemet as an example. Sekhemet is a goddess of Egyptian provenance, and her worship goes back to and beyond the dawn of recorded

history. Sekhemet is commonly portrayed as a woman with the head of a lioness, carrying either a scepter or a sword. Sekhemet is the patroness of magic, but also of courage and strength. A DEVOTEE of Sekhemet might hope to be inspired by her with these qualities. Does this mean that we believe Sekhemet is an entity living somewhere with the actual head of a lioness on a human woman's body? No.

But this personal sense goes deeper than that. The best analogy of how Wiccans look at Deity is in the famous example of the diamond. We think of Deity rather like an enormous diamond of many facets. Each facet is beautiful in and of itself and can be used as a way to access the heart of the diamond, but in reality each facet only provides a different but equal way of looking at the same stone. Thus, when the devotee speaks to Sekhemet, they are in reality using a personal form to access a universal power. The reason we need such personal forms is that we build our bond with Deity through emotion. All of the abstract understanding in the world will make no difference to you if you cannot connect to it emotionally; it will seem dry and empty and will strike no resonance in your being.

Since everyone's emotional nature is different—being, as we are, individuals— we Wiccans use many different images of Deity. A person who has negative feelings toward their mother may have difficulty identifying with the Mother Goddess but may find the Crone Goddess a great source of strength and comfort. A person who loves the ocean may find it much easier to connect with more aquatic Mother goddesses, such as Yemaya, than with an earthy Mother Goddess like Gaia. Both represent the same concept, but the exact approach of each image offers variety to the individual.

At no time do we perceive an individual face of Deity, such as Venus, Cerridwen, or Xochitl, as being the only face of Deity—only our individually preferred face. Also, it must be remembered that we live many lifetimes through reincarnation. Sometimes we resonate very strongly with a particular face of Deity because we have interacted with Deity through that face in previous lifetimes. Thus, we might be drawn to Isis, for example, because in previous lifetimes we have been a devotee of Isis.

The second way in which Wiccans look at Deity is universal. We acknowledge that the true nature of Deity is beyond all names and forms, and indeed perhaps beyond all mortal understanding. As our personal images of Deity are the facets, so UNIVERSAL DEITY is the diamond. Wiccans believe that any one name or form for Deity can never possibly encompass all of the nature of Universal Deity, but rather can only serve to limit our understanding of it. Because of this, we regard monotheism as an extremely primitive and limiting point of view. Rather, we use our personal images of Deity symbolically to help us understand the nature of Universal Deity, and we use myth as a tool to illustrate the qualities and processes of Universal Deity without ever imagining that a single view can encapsulate the whole nature of the Divine.

Having laid out this basic understanding of how Wiccans view Deity, let us illustrate it by presenting one of the most sacred myths of the Wiccan faith and explaining its deeper meaning.

• • • •

Introduction to the
Vangelo delle Streghe

One of the most sacred pieces of Wiccan literature is the *Vangelo delle Streghe*. This is a collection of legends preserved and passed down by generations of the ARADIAN witches of Italy. A little over a century ago, the Italian witch MADDALENA gave a copy of the *Vangelo* to the famed folklorist CHARLES GODFREY LELAND on the understanding that he would publish it.

The most important part of the *Vangelo* is the creation story it contains. This creation story is a sublime allegorical account

of the creation of the physical world and the descent of spirit into matter. The story touches on very ancient themes and is reminiscent of the Greek myth of OPHION and EURYNOME and the creation myth of the goddess CYBELE.

You must understand, however, that the stories in the *Vangelo* are meant to be understood as ALLEGORY, which is to say that these stories represent their subject symbolically, portraying it in familiar, everyday forms rather than with abstract concepts. If you try to read these stories literally, they appear rather shallow and foolish. Only by understanding that the *Vangelo's* human characters actually represent the timeless forces of Nature and the universe, and that their actions portray the cosmic processes, can you hope to get anything out of it.

Maddalena did not bother to explain this. She was willing to let people know more about the ancient Aradian Wiccan traditions, but she didn't want them to know too much. She knew that people who understood allegory would be able to read between the lines and appreciate what they found there. She is also supposed to have made certain alterations to the text, apparently for the purpose of secrecy, which leaves some confusion in the original text. But despite this, the text is of enormous value.

• • • •
Creation in the *Vangelo*

According to the *Vangelo delle Streghe*, "Diana was the first created of all creation. In Her were all things." In other words, Diana, or Goddess, is PRIMEVAL DEITY. She existed before the first beginning as CHAOS: God without form existing in a void and having within herself the seeds of all things, both spiritual and material, all mixed up without order or definition. Primeval Deity is androgynous, having both feminine (spirit or yin) and masculine (matter or yang) elements, and is sometimes portrayed as such in myth and artwork. Other times, however, Primeval Deity is portrayed as feminine, since we think of Primeval Deity in association with the Goddess—indeed as the Higher Self of the Goddess. In this sense, Primeval Deity is identified with the CRONE Goddess—the Goddess in her aged state, having existed from before the dawn of time. This is the wisest and most knowing part of Goddess, most commonly called HEKATE. This is the Goddess portrayed with greater or lesser respect as the Hallowe'en witch, with pointed hat and broom.

For endless eons, Primeval Deity existed in this amorphous and undifferentiated state in the darkness before the first creation. At first, aware of nothing, she slept, resting and recharging, gathering her energies and merely being—alone and complete in herself.

But over the course of time, Primeval Deity began to stir, to become aware. First she became aware of her own existence. In time, she began to think, to dream, to question—and to desire. She wondered, "What would it be like to feel? What would it be like to move? To take action? To be able to receive sensation? To see? To taste? To hear?"

And so for eons Primeval Deity thought, and considered, and wondered. And then:

> Out of herself, the first Darkness, she divided herself. Into Darkness and Light she was divided. The God, Her brother and son, herself and Her other Self, was the Light.

Primeval Deity divided herself—one became two. All of the physical, tangible, and volatile parts of Primeval Deity went into the God, who was the Light. The God exploded into existence out of Primeval Deity in a shower of spark and flame that we remember as the big bang, the starting point of physical creation.

All of the spiritual, ethereal, and eternal parts of Primeval Deity remained in the Goddess. In this sense, the Goddess is thought of as a continuation of Primeval Deity, since the consciousness of Primeval Deity is one of the spiritual parts that remained with her.

The God spread out in all directions through the primordial void, a blaze of light and superheated matter. In time, his fire would cool into stars, and from stars into planets. As this happens, the vibration of the matter slows and it becomes more dense, seemingly solid.

This slowing, cooling, and solidifying is described as "falling into matter." Symbolically, the God is described as having fallen into SEVEN PLANES of existence. Some people say there are more, but since the divisions are not as exact as all that, the number is not as important as the concept. Seven is the ancient number, based on the idea of the seven Ptolemaic planets (that is, the sun, the moon, and those planets visible with the naked eye). The seven planes are, from the lowest up, physical, emotional, mental, astral, soular or egoic, monadic, and divine. We will talk more about these later. The seven planes are also sometimes called the seven spheres or the seven dimensions; all refer to the same basic concept.

The *Vangelo* continues:

And when Diana saw that the light was so beautiful, the light which was Her other half, her brother the God, She yearned for it with exceeding great desire. Wishing to receive the light again into Her darkness, to swallow it up in rapture, in delight, She trembled with desire. And this trembling was the first dawn.

But the God's light fled from Her and would not yield to Her wishes. He was the light which flies into the most distant parts of heaven, the mouse which flies before the cat.

Seeing the beauty of the God—that is, of the physical universe—the Goddess was entranced with desire, and she wanted it back. She had dreamed of seeing and tasting and doing, but being separate from the God, she could do none of this. She could only observe from the outside that which she had created. The Goddess wanted the experiences she had dreamed of, and so she desired to take the created Universe back into herself . . . but it wasn't that easy.

The *Vangelo* tells how the Goddess went to the oldest part of herself, Primeval Deity, who was still within her. The *Vangelo* calls Primeval Deity "The Mothers and Fathers who were before the first creation," which emphasizes Primeval Deity's androgynous aspect. In other words, the Goddess consulted her own Higher Self. In many ancient myths—notably the story of Demeter and Persephone—this same process is shown by the Goddess entering Hekate's cave to take counsel from the eldest and wisest part of Deity.

In the *Vangelo*, Diana asks Primeval Deity how she can reunite with the God, how spirit could take matter back into itself. And the Ancient One, Primeval Deity, the Goddess's own Higher Self, answered in this way: "To rise You must fall. To become the greatest of all Goddesses, You must first become a mortal."

In other words, it was not possible for spirit simply to take matter back. If the Goddess wished to reunite with the God, to be one with matter and experience it, she had to enter into the physical world. Only in that way could the Goddess and the God reunite.

And so Diana "fell"—that is to say, she descended through the seven planes to the physical. She did this by dividing off parts of herself—the many souls—which she sent into the physical and placed into physical forms. Each soul was to lead many lifetimes, going through many physical forms in the process. Reading this now, you are one of the lifetimes of one of those souls that are part of the great Goddess. We are her children, and we are also children of the God, for our existence is the accomplishment of their union.

The *Vangelo* describes this process in extremely symbolic terms. It tells how Diana took the form of a cat (the soul entering into material form) and in this way got close to the God. Then, resuming her own form, she made passionate love to him. Then, to maintain the union of spirit and matter, the Goddess cast a spell:

> She sang a charm, and her voice was as the buzzing of bees. And then Diana sat at Her spinning wheel and began to spin

the thread of life, and the God turned the wheel.

In other words, having placed soul into matter, the Goddess used the power of sound—that is, VIBRATION—to set the universe as we know it into motion. Energy is what holds all things together, from subatomic particles to galaxies of stars. The vibration of that energy—its movement, sometimes described as its frequency—is what makes it work and determines on what level it works. The denser or more physical a thing is, the lower its vibration or frequency is said to be. The more spiritual the energy, the higher its vibration is said to be. Vibration is comparable to sound, which can be a powerful magical tool. For this reason, the vibration of the universe, at differing frequencies through each of the seven planes or spheres, is often described as the MUSIC OF THE SPHERES.

Music and song have long been used in many spiritual traditions as a means of affecting the vibration of energy. Sound can be used in this way to disperse negative or unfocused energy, to break down psychic blockages, and to create or affect specific energetic forms. Sound is a very powerful tool precisely because sound, or vibration, is the very force the Goddess used to set the Wheel of Life into motion.

Called the Goddess's "spinning wheel" in the *Vangelo delle Streghe*, the Wheel of

Life is a very ancient concept. It is represented annually by the sacred Wheel of the Year (which you will learn about in Lesson III). From this wheel, the Goddess (spirit) spins the thread of life—that is, she determines its nature and qualities, the lessons to be learned, and the things to be done and accomplished; the DESTINY, if you will. But the God (matter, or perhaps more precisely physical experience) turns the wheel. As the Goddess is the nature of life, the God is the process of living—the *movement* through the planes of existence. The Goddess is the essential nature of the universe and of life itself; she provides the Divine Spark that animates all things. But the God carries that spark forward. The God is lord of space and time—master of the temporal universe. In this aspect, he is called the Lord of the Dance, for he leads the dance of life, facilitating experience and growth.

In this way—their essence originating from the Goddess and their ability to move and grow originating from the God—the many souls descended to the physical plane. The goal of this, as stated above, was to experience—to learn and grow. Having arrived in the physical, the souls set out to learn all that the physical plane could teach them, and they then began their ascent back up through the seven planes to ultimately rejoin with the Goddess, from whence they came. Each plane has its own special lessons that are of great importance to the soul.

Though seemingly separated from the Goddess, each of these souls remains always attached to her, always a part of her—for it is through them, as part of them, that the Goddess entered into her own physical creation, the God. We are one with the Goddess, and our experiences are her experience. We are eternal and immortal as souls, never cut off from the Goddess, or spirit, only differentiated. All of the powers and abilities of the Goddess are within us and at our command if we can clear our vision enough to see and access them.

Descending through the planes of existence was like going through a curtain, or VEIL. The veil obscures our vision of the things above us. Because of the veil, we forget that we are part of the Goddess—that we are spiritual beings experiencing the physical—and we start to think that we are simply physical beings. As we ascend the planes, we are highly aware of those planes that are below us, and we perceive them fairly easily. It is much harder to perceive the planes above us. From where we are, it is difficult for us to see or communicate with the higher planes of consciousness, and it is easy to imagine that what our eyes perceive is all that exists. To progress, we must part the veil and see beyond it. The more we work magically and psychically, the thinner that veil becomes. Some people are born with the veil already very thin; these people are said to be "BORN OLD." It may seem that those who are born old don't have to work as hard to progress and that psychic and magical skills just come naturally to them. This is because they have already done the work to develop these skills in previous lifetimes.

It is generally said that we are currently on the mental plane, able to easily perceive mental, emotional, and physical energies. It is also said that we are—and have long been—in the process of moving into the astral, or intuitional, plane and thus have increasing perception of what we might loosely call psychic matters. Though we have some perception of the planes beyond this, it is difficult to see very much of them from our current perspective.

Of course, as in all things, there are a variety of points of view on the subject of the planes, or spheres, of existence. This is the Correllian view.

. . . .

X—You Are Here

As you can see, Wicca perceives the conscious mind as only a small part of a much larger being, originating from and eternally connected to the Mother Goddess. Our conscious self is normally a reflection of our physical body (first dimension), our emotions (second dimension), and our

thinking mind (third dimension). These three dimensions of our being are said to compose our LOWER SELF. It should be understood that "lower" refers to vibrational frequency and is not meant as any sort of value judgment, as all parts of the being are good and valuable. The lower the vibrational frequency, the greater the physical density.

As humans, we normally have a natural comprehension of these three aspects of our Lower Self, accepting them without question as an obvious component of our being. We all know our physical body and its reactions. We all feel our emotions, both conscious and subconscious. We are all aware of our cognitive and rational faculties. All of these are within our level of common experience and are known to us, if not always fully understood.

Above our level of common experience is our Higher Self, a concept you were introduced to in Lesson I. The Higher Self, like the Lower Self, has three levels of being. Immediately above our common perception is the astral self (fourth dimension). Also called the causal self, the astral self is the part of us that determines what things we choose to experience in a given physical life and what lessons we are trying to learn. It is from this level that the Higher Self creates the life we are living. The astral portion of the Higher Self sets the pattern of life, accepts or rejects

every potential event in that life, and can make whatever alterations the Higher Self chooses at any point during the life. This is one reason it is so important to be on good terms with our Higher Self, because by moving in sync with its choices, we make life a much easier process. The astral level, also sometimes called the intuitional or Buddhic level, is the level that we shift to when we work magic.

Above the astral is the egoic self, or soul (fifth dimension). The word *soul* is often used to describe the whole Higher Self, but specifically it refers to the fifth level of the being. The soul is the separate personality of the Higher Self, built up out of the total experience of many, many lifetimes. All of the benefits of every life lived, the outcome of every lesson learned, the knowledge of every thing seen, felt, and done is retained in the soul, and this accumulation gives it its special character that is distinct from all other souls. The soul is the organ by which the being grows and the manner in which experience and growth is retained and built upon.

Above the soul is the monad. The term *monad* comes from the Greek *monos*, meaning "single unit." The monad is the portion of the soul that is perfect in itself, just as it was when the Goddess divided it off from herself. The monad is the Divine Spark of Life that animates the being and that is conscious of itself as a portion of Deity. It

is a separate portion of the Goddess, but it is essentially the same intelligence with no differentiation. Individuated but not differentiated from the Goddess, the monad contains all of the attributes and qualities of the Divine while at the same time being separate unto itself. The monad is the motivating force of the being. Because of this, the monad moves always to the good and is incapable of doing otherwise. A perfect microcosm of Goddess, the monad remembers the time before the first creation, when all was One. The monad also remembers the reason it was separated from the Goddess, and because of this it has a natural desire to evolve and unfold until it is one with the Goddess again.

These three parts form the Higher Self, of which we become aware only through effort: the astral self, which creates our life as we live it, deciding and arranging all that happens; the soul, which stores all of these experiences and is shaped by them; and the monad, the divine part of us that sought those experiences and revels in them but that also seeks eventual union with the rest of Deity and a return to the primordial oneness.

The final level of being, above the monad, is the Goddess herself (seventh dimension). She is the single soul of the universe from whom all others ultimately come, and she is the very center of your being. All of creation branches off from her through the medium of the God. The Goddess is the life; the God is the living. The Goddess is the essence; the God is the manifestation. Every aspect of creation is endowed by both the Goddess and the God, and all is sentient in the higher levels of being, if not always in the physical.

• • • •

More About Energy

Now, as we said in Lesson I, the universe is composed of energy. All of these different parts of the being are composed of energy. You, in every level of yourself, are composed of energy, as is everything around you. Energy reacts to thought and emotion. This is why by rising to your Higher Self, specifically the astral level, you can affect and control energy—work magic. This is also why energy affects *you* and why clearing and releasing is so important.

There are other ways in which you can be affected by energy besides holding excess energy after psychic and magical work. The energy of certain times and places has an effect on people, as does the energy of certain objects, such as gemstones, to use a well-known example. By aligning with these energies and working with them, you can increase and improve your own energy—and thus your psychic and magical abilities and their results in your everyday life.

In Lesson III, you will learn more about how these energies affect you and how you can best take advantage of them to aid your personal spiritual growth.

• • • •

Exercises

As you advance through these lessons, you will be introduced to many exercises that will build your psychic energies and help you learn to control them. Many of these exercises use the CHAKRA points. Chakras are the energy centers of the body, and there are a number of them. You will receive more specific information about the chakras in future lessons. In this lesson, however, we will be using just two chakras; these are located in the palms of the hands and the soles of the feet. You can imagine these chakras as a ball of white light directly in the center of the palm of the hand or the sole of the foot. These two chakras are basic chakras that are used for bringing energy into the body and for sending it out of the body. Other chakras are more specialized.

Exercise 1

Put yourself into your comfortable position. Begin by releasing; close your eyes and imagine all of the worries and anxieties of your day just pouring out of you like water, down and out through the palms of your hands and the soles of your feet.

Now place the palms of your hands together. Imagine a ball of white light between your two palms, radiating out from where they touch. Imagine it very strongly, seeing it clearly.

Now pull your hands slowly apart. Imagine that ball of light stretching out between your hands as you separate them, becoming a beam of light between your palms. Hold this for a few seconds, longer if you can. Then, slowly, bring your hands together, shrinking the beam of light between them until they close together and it is gone.

Clear and release all excess energy as you learned to do in Lesson I. Imagine a stream of white light or water flowing through you from the top of your head and carrying all excess energy away through the soles of your feet.

Practice this until you get good at it. Then you are ready for Exercise 2.

Exercise 2

This exercise begins just like Exercise 1. Do it just the same way until you come to the point where you have created the beam of energy between your two hands. Then, instead of stopping, imagine that beam growing and expanding to form a ball of white light between your hands. Hold that image as long as you can. Then, slowly, bring your hands back together, seeing the ball shrink between them, growing smaller and smaller until by the time your hands close, the ball is gone.

Clear and release when you're done. When you get good at this, you're ready to try Exercise 3.

Exercise 3

This exercise is just like Exercise 1, except when you open your hands, instead of a beam of white light, imagine a rainbow between your hands. Every color has an effect on energy, so this will work to strengthen you on a number of levels at once.

These three exercises are not meant to replace each other, but to be done together. As you master each one, you will add the next one to your daily regimen. Always release before and after, but not between, the exercises. When you have mastered all three, this will be your regimen: release, Exercise 1, Exercise 2, Exercise 3, release again.

• • • •

Spell for Lesson II
Manifesting a Desire

This is a simple spell for manifesting something you desire. When trying to manifest a desire, there are several things you should keep in mind: always respect the rule of "harm none," what you are manifesting should not be something that belongs to another, and never ever should what you are manifesting be a person. You must always respect the free will of others. Also, you should not be too narrow in your desire. For example, if you were manifesting money, you should not ask for "ten dollars" but rather for "the money I need, at least ten dollars." Spirit may send you more than you ask for, unless you yourself have limited it. Spirit will never overrule the limitations you place on yourself; only you can remove those. Finally, when just starting out in magic, it may be advisable to start with small things. This is because magic will not work if you don't believe it will work, as energy responds to thought and emotion. If your thought is "I manifest a Cadillac" but your emotion is "I could never do this," then it won't work. By starting with simple things, you can build up in increments and be less likely to run into self-imposed limitations.

For this spell, you will need the following items:

- A candle—white is good, but so is red
- Something to light it with—nothing will screw up your magical consciousness worse than forgetting the matches and having to stop and look for them in the middle of the working
- A piece of paper
- Something to write with
- A burning dish—that is, a dish that is not going to be damaged by fire; brass incense burners work very well, but many other things do too
- Something to stir the fire with—a stick or a knife work well

Put yourself into a comfortable position. Begin by releasing all tension and anxiety. Now think about what you want to manifest. Concentrate on it and imagine clearly what it might be like to have it. Meditate on this for a while, keeping it clear in your mind.

Now write down on your paper what it is you wish. You may want to write it in a manner similar to the invocation given below. You may notice that we will use the same one rather a lot, but when something works, why mess with it?

Now light your candle. Again, release all tension before you start the actual spell. Focus for a few moments on the candle's flame. Now take your paper. You may want to fold it in half, but don't fold it up tightly, as this will retard the burning process.

Imagine a ball of white light in the center of your chest. Affirm the following:

"Behold, I connect myself to powers of the universe."

Imagine yourself rising up above your physical body, and high above the earth.

You may want to imagine looking down at the whole earth below you. Now affirm:

"There is one power in the universe, and I am a perfect manifestation of that power."

Open your eyes and take your paper. Affirm:

"There is one power in the universe, and I am a perfect manifestation of that power. And as such I will that even as this paper burns, so too shall this which I have written come to pass. May it come to me easily, and with harm to none. I will it. I draw it to me. I manifest it. I accept it. I receive it. I give thanks for it. By my will, so mote it be."

Now set the paper on fire. Imagine a ball of white light all around the paper, as clear and bright as possible. Hold the paper as long as possible, and then place it in the burning dish and let it burn until it is gone. Use a stick or a knife to lift it in the bowl so that it doesn't lie on just one side and prevent that side from burning. The speed and thoroughness with which the paper burns shall be an omen to you of how long it will take for the thing to come to you. If any part of the paper doesn't burn, take that piece and, repeating the affirmation over it, burn it again.

Now clear and release as you know to do, and do not obsess over what you have manifested. Worrying about it excessively will tend to block it, so the less you can think about it, the better. Instead, simply know that you have done it successfully and wait for it to come. If you cannot be patient, tell yourself, "I put myself into a position of love and trust, knowing that what I want shall come." Then imagine stepping over a half-step to the left.

What you have manifested may not come immediately, but it will come soon. These things take time, but you will eventually find this a very useful spell. And remember, if you're just starting out—practice makes perfect!

· · · ·

God for Lesson II
The Triple Goddess

As you have learned, Wiccans revere Deity in many forms, the principal form being the Goddess. The Goddess represents the feminine, nurturing side of Deity—intuitive, creative, magical. She is the inner nature of Deity, the origin of the external universe.

Thus, the Goddess is the Creator, the Source. The God emerges from her when she sets the universe into motion. The God is the Goddess's Divine Child, formed from her inner nature, her "Other Self," as the *Vangelo delle Streghe* puts it. The God is also the Divine Consort, whose union with the Goddess describes existence as we know it.

In this sense, the Goddess and the God are the polar forces also termed yin and yang. Yin is the feminine, spiritual, and emotive aspect of Deity that is within all things and whose presence gives all things life. Yang is the masculine, physical, and volatile aspect of Deity that manifests in motion and action and whose permutations build up the outer form of things.

In Wicca, the Goddess is primarily revered through her form as the Triple Goddess. As the God is often represented by the sun, the Goddess is often represented by the moon. The moon's three phases are taken as instructive as to the nature of her being: the waxing moon represents creation and inspiration, embodied in the Maiden Goddess; the full moon represents fruition and sustenance, embodied in the Mother Goddess; and the waning moon represents fulfillment and endings, embodied in the Crone Goddess.

The Maiden

The Maiden is the young goddess of spring and new beginnings. She is the goddess of the dawn, of youth and fresh potential. The Maiden is the goddess of art and creativity and self-expression—of beauty, intelligence, and skill. The Maiden is manifest in action and self-confidence, exploration and discovery.

The Mother

The Mother is the Goddess in her aspect as sustainer of the universe. She is the goddess of motherhood, of nurturing and providence. The universe is her child and she loves and cares for it, providing it with inexhaustible resources from within herself even as a mother nurses her infant from the lactations of her own body. Infinitely loving and compassionate, the Mother Goddess is a never-ending source of bounty for those who are open to her gifts.

The Crone

The Crone represents the Goddess in her aspect as elder. The Crone is the wise woman, the witch, the matriarch. The Crone is the goddess of death, magic, and the spirit realm. She is also the goddess of wisdom, visions, and guidance. Hers is the height of spiritual power, for she is the great sorceress who creates her will through magic. Goddess of transformation, the Crone is the destroyer who dissolves outmoded forms, allowing new growth to occur.

· · · ·
Glossary for Lesson II

allegory—Allegory is the supreme achievement of Pagan religion. It is the art of using easily understandable symbols to describe difficult or abstract concepts. In this way, for example, we describe the interaction of spirit and body, a complex and intangible concept, as the dance of Goddess and God, a concrete and easily understood image from which the higher concept can be extracted. It is allegory that allows us to speak of energy as "light," and it is allegory that allows us to speak of the universe as a divine web connecting all things. Allegory allows us to free ourselves from literality and opens the door to abstract thinking.

Aradian—Italian Wiccan tradition as exemplified by the *Vangelo delle Streghe*.

born old—People who are born with the veil very thin between the conscious self and the powers of the soul, and who can thus access the Higher Self easily with minimal or no instruction, are said to have been "born old." Talents that others must work to develop come to them easily, seemingly without effort. This is because such souls have already put out great efforts to develop these skills in previous lives, and they bring them through to the present.

chakra—Chakras are the energy centers of the body, where body and spirit most strongly connect. There are thousands of chakras in every part of the body, and these are connected to each other by meridians, or energy pathways. This is the basis of such systems of medicine as acupuncture, shiatsu, and moxidermy, which treat physical illness by applying stimulation to the chakra points. In general practice, however, most people work only with the seven major chakras, which correspond to the seven spheres of existence and the seven bodies. These are the root chakra, at the prostate in males and the paraurethral gland in females, which corresponds to the physical plane; the second chakra, at the testicles in males and the ovaries in females, which corresponds to the emotional plane; the solar plexus chakra, roughly at the navel, which corresponds to the mental plane; the heart chakra, at the heart, which corresponds to the astral plane; the throat chakra, at the throat, which corresponds to the soular or egoic plane; the third eye, at the level of the pineal gland, which corresponds to the monadic plane; and the crown chakra, at or above the top of the head, which corresponds to the Divine.

chaos—Primordial Deity; God/dess before creation; the original state that contains within itself the beginnings of all that is given form in the physical world, but in a dreamlike and undifferentiated state. Both female and male, spiritual and physical, dark and light, all bound up together, chaos is also called unity or union, among many other names. Chaos is both the starting point and the ending point of creation; it is the wholeness of Deity, from which we come and to which ultimately we shall all return, enriched by our physical experiences. Chaos is also thought of as Deity at rest, between the creation and destruction of successive universes or at the center of multiple universes.

Crone—The Goddess in her aged form. The Crone, represented by the waning moon, rules over wisdom, understanding, magic, and learning, among other things. People who do not possess wisdom often fear it, and thus the Crone Goddess is often feared as well. She is the goddess of death, who consumes all things—but only to give them transformation and rebirth. The Crone is often equated with Primordial Deity, who precedes all creation and waits to consume it (i.e., reunite with it) at the end of existence. In popular iconography, the Crone is the "Hallowe'en Witch," with her pointed hat that symbolizes the upward-spiraling cone of power,

her broomstick for sweeping away old forms of existence, and her cauldron of transformation for creating new ways of being.

Cybele—Cybele was the Phrygian form of the Great Mother, who was adopted by the Romans as mother of the gods. Cybele was worshipped by transsexual priest/esses who castrated themselves and afterward lived as women—somewhat to the horror of the conservative Romans. The myth of Cybele is very ancient, and it has its roots in the earliest times. It was taught that Cybele was the first being to exist in the universe. She was all alone and possessed the characteristics of both sexes; that is, she was both male and female at the same time. When she grew tired of being alone and desired a companion, she castrated her male parts and flung them to the earth, whereupon they became the god Attis, her son, brother, and consort. It will readily be seen that this myth is cognate to that of the *Vangelo delle Streghe*, with Cybele being the Goddess who creates the God out of herself.

destiny—Destiny refers, ultimately, to the lessons afforded one in life—the chances for growth and advancement that will be placed in our path. What we do with these lessons, of course, is our own; they can be positive or negative according to our choices, rather than follow any pre-set "destiny." But the lessons themselves are chosen and agreed on prior to birth, to try to stimulate the growth the soul needs and desires. Consequently, it can be said that life gives us opportunities that we cannot avoid or short-circuit, because we have asked for them before entering this life, but what the outcome of these opportunities might be is the result of our own choices and actions.

devotee—A devotee is a person who is attached, or devoted, to a particular patron deity. Thus, one might be a dev-otee of Hekate, or a devotee of Isis, or a devotee of Ganesha, or any of the vast number of forms of Deity.

Hekate—Hekate is the great Crone of ancient Greece, patroness of magic and wisdom, and a goddess of the spirit world. Hekate is a goddess of uncer-tain provenance, being clearly older than and outside of the Greek classi-cal pantheon. Some say she is of Myce-naean origin, the culture that precedes the classical. Others say that she is of Phrygian origin. Some equate her with Hekat, the Egyptian goddess of creative force and magic with whom Hekate was most certainly identified in Hellenistic times. Hekate was known in medieval times as Dame Hecat, in which form she was considered a patroness of Euro-pean Witchcraft.

Leland, Charles Godfrey—Folklorist and author who studied Witchcraft exten-sively at the turn of the last century and published the *Vangelo delle Streghe*.

Lower Self—That part of ourselves of which we are easily aware: the physical, the emotional, and the mental aspects of the being. Through meditation and magic, we can access our Higher Self, which includes the astral or creative level of our being, our soul, those traits that make us a distinct aspect of Deity, our monad, the level at which we are divine but separate, and ultimately the divine level, at which all is one.

Maddalena—Maddalena Talenti was an Italian Witch who worked with Charles Leland, supplying him with much information on what she represented to be traditional Italian Witchcraft. Mad-dalena met Leland in 1486 Pisces (AD 1886). Most notably, Maddalena sup-plied Leland with a manuscript, written in her own hand, that she represented as expressing the foundational myths of Italian Witchcraft. This manuscript was the *Vangelo delle Streghe*, which Leland subsequently published under the title *Aradia, or the Gospel of the Witches*. Whether Maddalena copied an older manuscript, wrote down existing oral traditions, or created the text herself is a highly debated issue. Assuming that Maddalena did not create the *Vangelo* out of whole cloth, exactly whose beliefs it represented is also a question: Maddalena claimed to represent a familial tradition that may or may not have existed and may or may not have been highly idiosyncratic compared to that of other Italian Witches. However, the *Vangelo* itself contains some very deep concepts and some very old ideas, including themes that also appear in other studies of Italian Witchcraft written both before and after the publication of Aradia. Notably, the work of Carlo Ginzburg shows many of the same themes arising in sources from the late Renaissance and Baroque eras. Neither Maddalena nor Leland himself appear to have realized some of the deeper themes in the work—or at any rate to have commented upon these. Roma Lister, a folklorist and friend of Leland's, claimed that Maddalena was actually a pseudonym for a woman whose real name was Margherita, though others have suggested that Maddalena and Margherita were two different women. In any event, Maddalena's final correspondence with Leland informs him of her impending marriage to one Lorenzo Bruciatelli and their plans to emigrate to the United States.

music of the spheres—Each of the seven planes has its own energy vibration, which in turn corresponds to a certain sound, for sound is generated by vibration. The vibration of vocal cords creates speech and song. The vibration of a drum skin produces the drumbeat. The vibration of strings produces the music of the violin or the cello. So as the energy of the spheres vibrates at a given rate, it too must create a sound. This is the theory behind the "music of the spheres." A variety of techniques have evolved from this theory to link sound with energy. They are the basis on which tuning forks, bells, and singing bowls are used for energetic healing, to give just a few examples. Another form in which vibrational sound is used in energy work involves the linking of the seven vowel sounds with the seven planes, bodies, or chakras.

Ophion and Eurynome—Eurynome is a very ancient Greek moon goddess. Her name means "far wanderer." The creation myth of Ophion and Eurynome is far older than classical Greek mythology and reveals a very different set of beliefs. Chaos was the first thing to exist: this is the primeval feminine, which resolves within itself the seeds of all things in an unmanifest state—the primordial soup, if you will. A spark of light arose from chaos, and that spark was Eurynome, the moon. She arose and danced through chaos, and where she danced became the horizon that separates sea and sky. Her dance was beautiful, and it stirred the unmanifest potential within chaos and caused others to arise as well. The north wind came into being, and it loved Eurynome and pursued her, following the steps of her dance of creation. Likewise arose the west wind, which pursued the goddess, and after that the south and the east winds. The four winds followed in the dance of Eurynome, then overtook her and surrounded her. The four winds then coalesced into the form of Ophion, the cosmic serpent, and became the lover of Eurynome. When they had finished, she took the form of a white bird and flew away. She made a nest and laid a cache of silver eggs. From these eggs were born all other things that exist. It will readily be seen that this is the same basic myth found in the *Vangelo delle Streghe*, with Eurynome and Ophion as Goddess and God, from whose union arises all creation.

patron—A patron deity is the particular goddess or god whom one feels most at home with. Some people have more than one, but usually one will predominate. Any deity that you are drawn to can be your patron deity. One's patron deity is prayed to for guidance, visions, blessing, and so on.

Primeval Deity—God/dess before creation, being both feminine and masculine, both spiritual and physical, resolving all opposites and polarities and containing within itself all things. Primeval Deity is both the origin and the destination of existence, the inner soul of all creation. Primeval Deity is most often represented as the Androgyne or the Crone.

seven planes—The seven planes, or spheres, of existence are used to describe the different levels of being that spirit, or Goddess, experiences in interaction with matter, or God. As is often the case with classifications, these seven levels are not nearly as neat as they are made to sound, but rather they overlap and blend in ways that defy category. These seven planes are sometimes described as a successive "fall" into progressive densities of matter, with progressively slower vibrations. The seven planes are these: physical, at which we experience physical form and sensation; emotional, at which we experience emotional feelings; mental, at which we experience thought and abstract concepts and understandings; astral, at which we create our existence and its conditions; soular, at which we develop those traits that make a unique part of Deity; monadic, that part of us that is divine but is separate from the whole of Deity; and divine, at which we are one with all existence.

Universal Deity—The different faces of Deity are ways of understanding Universal Deity. All of the faces of Deity in the end reflect the same universal power, as in fact do we humans, and all of the rest of creation. That universal power is infinite and beyond our power to know in its totality, so we make understandable images through which we may interface with it. That infinite power is Universal Deity—the spirit of Deity that is beyond all names and images.

Vangelo delle Streghe—An Aradian Wiccan scripture containing the creation story, the Charge of the Goddess, and a collection of other myths deriving from Italian Witchcraft. Published by Charles Leland in 1499 Pisces (AD 1899) under the title *Aradia, or the Gospel of the Witches*, the book requires serious annotation to be properly understood, but it is a cornerstone of Wiccan thought.

veil—Most people perceive easily only the so-called "lower" aspects of their being: the physical self and its sensations, the emotional self and its feelings, the mental self and its thoughts. The higher aspects of the being, from which we derive such abilities as clairvoyance, telepathy, telekinesis, and so on, most people can only access through much work and difficulty. Ordinarily, we have no conscious knowledge of them, unless we have been "born old," in which case we have worked to develop them in earlier lives. The separation between what we consciously perceive of ourselves and our higher powers is symbolically called a veil. This is because in former times an ornamental veil was often used to screen off the sanctuary of a temple from the general temple precincts. Consequently, the idea of a veil hiding something spiritually higher seemed a natural allegory.

vibration—Vibration, the movement of energy, is believed to become slower the farther down the seven planes it proceeds. The slower the vibration, the denser the matter; thus, the physical plane is the home of the densest matter with the slowest vibration while the divine plane has the least density and the fastest vibration. As energy moves upward from lower vibrations to higher ones, it generates heat. As energy slows from higher to lower vibrations, it produces coldness. You will notice this in energy working.

Study Questions for Lesson II

1. What do we mean by a "universal" view of Deity? How does this differ from a "personal" view of Deity?

2. What is Primordial Deity?

3. What do we mean when we say that to unite with the God, the Goddess "fell into matter"?

4. What is the *Vangelo delle Streghe*? Where does it come from?

5. What are the planes of existence?

6. What are the three parts of the Lower Self?

7. What are the three parts of the Higher Self?

8. What is the astral self? What purpose does it serve?

9. What is a patron deity?

10. Describe the three forms of the Triple Goddess.

11. What is the veil? Why is one "born old," and what does that mean?

12. What are the chakras?

13. What is vibration?

Lesson
III

Personal Power

In Lesson I, we learned that the universe is composed of energy and that we can influence that energy by means of magic, through the concentration of mind and emotion. In Lesson II, we learned that the universe, composed of energy, is an emanation of the Goddess in union with the God. We learned that the universe has seven planes or dimensions of existence and that we exist as a being in all seven of these at once. Those dimensions of which we are easily aware make up our Lower Self. Those dimensions we must work to connect with make up our Higher Self. In the end, we are all one, because the spirit of the Goddess is in each of us and animates us all.

We have spoken about how we can influence and direct energy through magic. But energy influences us as well. Now, in Lesson III, we will talk about how we are all influenced on a daily basis by the energies around us.

Everything that exists is composed of energy. Though it may all look solid, it is in fact a pattern of energy held intact by vibration and frequency. Affected by experience, each thing develops its own special character and attributes, which it carries forward.

This is true of objects, such as gemstones, different kinds of wood, shells, or metal. Each of these things, though existing in a denser state of matter than our own, has its own energies that can affect our energy. For example, jade interacts with our energy to promote calmness and tranquility, while amber has an energy that aids mental clarity and concentration. Rock crystal (quartz) will amplify one's psychic energy, while metal will tend to ground it.

This is also true of fragrances, such as essential oils and incenses, whose unique qualities affect our energy as well. For example, sage and rosemary have a cleansing energy, which we use to aid in purification. Sandalwood promotes spiritual opening, while cinnamon is protective in character.

Not only physical objects, but also more abstract things, such as color, affect our energy. The color red will tend to increase one's energy, but if overdone, it can also set one on edge. Blue tends to be soothing to the emotions, but too much can be depressive in character.

Specific places also have particular energies. Some locations are known to have especially powerful energy, which acts as a battery to anyone who goes there. Such places are called VORTICES and are the energy centers, or chakras, of the earth. Some of these vortices have special qualities, such as healing or psychic opening. If you visit such a vortex and work with its natural energy, you will be able to accomplish much more of whatever its special quality dictates than you might normally be able to do. For example, at a healing vortex, such as that at Bath, England, or Lourdes, France, healers will be able to manifest much greater healing powers than they might in other places around the globe. Meditations conducted at vortices known for psychic opening, such as those in Sedona, in the Southwest United States, may be able to reach much deeper levels and effect greater transformations than if carried out elsewhere. For these reasons, such vortices are considered sacred and are often the site of pilgrimages by persons seeking to benefit from the particular energy of the vortex.

Such vortices can also be artificially created, both consciously and unconsciously. Our thoughts and emotions, as we have said, affect energy. A location that is subject to a given emotion or thought pattern over a long period of time—or even a short time, if it is of extreme potency—will be imbued with that quality. Thus, a house that has seen much suffering and anger may have a "negative" energy about it, which will be felt by subsequent inhabitants and their visitors. Similarly, a place that has known great joy may tend to feel uplifting to those who live in or visit it. These artificial vortices are created unconsciously by the everyday process of living. But an artificial vortex can also be created intentionally. A temple or a place where magic is performed can be imbued with psychic energy, which can turn it into a powerful psychic vortex and which will strengthen the abilities and perceptions of all who enter. But this is a high-level working and should not be attempted until one is thoroughly familiar with energy working.

In magic, we learn to interact with all things, with a view to how they can aid us energetically. Because each of us is different, this is a subjective process, one that can be mastered only by trial and experience. But the basics can be grasped fairly easily.

You will learn more about the affects of gemstones and scents in future lessons. If you continue your studies beyond the First Degree, you will learn more about energetic vortices. But now we are going to concentrate on the effect of a still more abstract energy: time.

Like everything else, different times have different energies. Also like every-

thing else, the exact manner in which you interact with these is individual to you. To fully understand how best to relate to these energies, you must practice with them and see how you yourself attune to them. But in general, there are certain principles, and these we shall outline for you now.

· · · ·

The Psychic Tide

Time has cycles. These repeat constantly. The cycles are created by and are the effect of movement: the movement of the planet, the movement of the galaxies, the movement of energy through the planes.

These cycles range from the time it takes our planet to revolve upon its axis (twenty-four hours) to the length of the so-called GREAT YEAR (19,200 years, according to the Correllian system). All of these cycles have their own qualities, and in accordance with the ancient law "As above, so below," all reflect the processes of the universe as a whole.

When the Goddess separated the many souls from herself and sent them into the physical, they began a process of INVOLUTION, a movement downward to a place of utmost density: the physical plane. After arriving there, the many souls began a movement back upward, through the seven planes, to their original divine origin: the Goddess. This is called spiritual EVOLUTION. Together, these two processes form

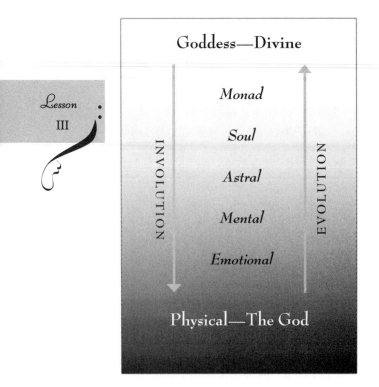

Goddess—Divine

Monad

INVOLUTION   *Soul*   EVOLUTION

Astral

Mental

Emotional

Physical—The God

a whole. Involution is the DARK HALF of the whole; it is the yin that spirals inward, contemplative and esoteric. Evolution is the LIGHT HALF; it is the yang that spirals outward, active and exoteric. All cycles possess these two parts: a Dark half and a Light half, which mirrors the cosmic order. Darkness always precedes Light, just as involution precedes evolution.

The cycles of time are known as the PSYCHIC TIDE. It is called this because the inner and outer movement of the energy is like the tide of the ocean. If the tide is in its Dark half, the energy is going inward; it is a time for contemplation, inner work-

ings, examination of the inner levels of the self, and releasing that which one has outgrown. When the tide is in its Light half, the energy is going outward; it is a time for physical manifestation, creation, and the beginning of new projects. Both halves of the tide propel one forward, each in its own way. It is a perpetual cycle of consolidation (Dark), followed by growth (Light), followed by consolidation (Dark), followed by still more growth (Light). Neither can be sustained without the other for balance.

In a twenty-four-hour period, the Dark half is night and the Light half is day. In the monthly cycle of the moon, the Dark half is the waning moon (from full moon to new moon), and the Light half is the waxing moon (from new moon to full moon). During the waning moon, we do releasing and inner work. We use this time to rid ourselves of all that limits us or holds us back. During the waxing moon, we do manifestation to bring about our goals and desires in the outer world, creating that which we desire. It is the lunar cycle that affects us most strongly as individuals.

In the yearly cycle, the Dark half is the winter and the spring, during which earth rests and refreshes herself before bringing forth new life. The Light half is the summer and fall, during which fields and forests grow and blossom to feed the creatures of the earth. In the Dark half, the energy of the earth is directed inward to replenish fertility. In the Light half, the energy of the earth is focused outward, making fertility manifest in physical form.

The yearly cycle does not affect us as strongly as the monthly lunar cycle, but it can have a noticeable effect. Particularly important are the changeover points, Bealteinne (May 1) and Samhain (November 1). At these two dates, the psychic tide is said to be at its yearly height, and the veil between the worlds at its thinnest. At these two Sabbats, psychic powers are keenest, magic is most effective, and supernatural phenomena are most frequent. You will learn more about the Sabbats under the section titled "Wheel of the Year" later in this lesson.

This same pattern is present in each ZODIACAL AGE. The zodiacal ages are divisions of time named for the signs of the ZODIAC and are linked to the so-called PRECESSION OF THE EQUINOXES. These include the Age of Aquarius, of which you may have heard, and the Age of Pisces (AD 400–1999), which has recently ended. According to the CORRELLIAN CALENDAR, the Age of Aquarius began with AD 2000 (the year 0 Aquarius).

The first several hundred years of each zodiacal age make up the Dark half. During these years, the best of the preceding age is consolidated. People create rigid structures of thought and tend to be rather introspective. The last several hundred

years of the age are the Light half; during these years, people throw off old ways of thought and try to create new ones.

By telling you this, we are not saying that you should allow yourself to be limited because you are in the Dark or Light half of any given time period. Just because the natural energies favor a certain sort of work doesn't mean that that is the only sort of work that can be performed—far from it! Rather, we say this so that you will know how to pick the *best* time for a given work, during which the natural energies of the universe will be moving in the same direction you are. Also, if you find yourself working against the natural energies—say you need to do releasing during the waxing moon—you will know that you need a stronger ritual to compensate.

The Wheel of the Year

In Lesson II, we spoke of the Wheel of Life. In the *Vangelo delle Streghe*, it is said that the Goddess spins the thread of life from the wheel while the God turns it. The God is often likened to a great serpent curled in a circle and swallowing its tail; this represents that he is the body of the wheel, that is, that the wheel turns through physical manifestation. "As above, so below": the great wheel is mirrored each year in the cycles of the seasons and the eight holidays of Wicca. As explained above, the WHEEL

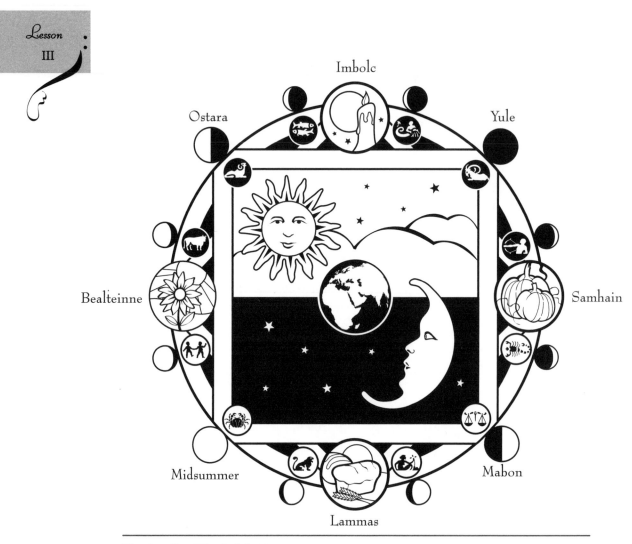

Imbolc

Ostara

Yule

Bealteinne

Samhain

Midsummer

Mabon

Lammas

The Correllian Wheel of the Year

OF THE YEAR follows the process of involution and evolution, having both a Dark and a Light half.

• • • •

Sabbats

The eight holidays are known as SABBATS. They are also simply called "festivals." The word *Sabbat* is of uncertain origin. It may be related to the word Esbat, which comes from an Old French word meaning "to frolic or celebrate." We will talk more about Esbats shortly. Also, *Sabbat* may be related to the Judeo-Christian word *Sabbath*. There is no way to know, as medieval chroniclers did not leave any clear etymological references.

The eight Sabbats are divided into two sets of four. These are the Grand Sabbats, which are feminine and dedicated to the Goddess, and the Lesser Sabbats, which are masculine and celebrate the God. The Grand Sabbats are lunar in character and in former times were tied to the lunar calendar. Some groups still reckon the Grand Sabbats by the lunar calendar, and some fix their date by other means, but most groups today celebrate them by the calendrical dates given below. The Lesser Sabbats are solar in nature and are the equinoxes and solstices of the sun, on which the solar calendar is based. As the year is divided into a Dark and a Light half, there are two Grand Sabbats and two Lesser Sabbats in each.

The eight Sabbats are as follows:

Samhain: November 1; begins the Dark half of the year (Dark)

Yule: December 20–22; celebrated on the midwinter solstice, date varies (Dark)

Imbolc: February 1 (Dark)

Ostara: March 20–22; celebrated on the vernal equinox, date varies (Dark)

Bealteinne: May 1; begins the Light half of the year (Light)

Midsummer: June 20–22; celebrated on the summer solstice, date varies (Light)

Lughnassadh: August 1 (Light)

Mabon: September 20–22; celebrated on the autumnal equinox, date varies (Light)

Each of these festivals has a particular meaning and customs, as detailed below.

Samhain

Samhain (pronounced "SOW-en" or "SOH-en"), the beginning of the ancient Celtic liturgical year, is the Festival of the Dead. At Samhain, we honor the spirit world, the spirits of our ancestors and deceased loved ones, and our spirit guides. At this time, we reflect upon our own physical mortality and the nature of change and transformation in the cycle of life and death. Samhain, celebrated on November 1, is the festival of the end of the harvest and the beginning of winter, by traditional reckoning. The word *Samhain* is Gaelic and means "summer's end." *Samhain* is pronounced "SOW-en" in Ireland and "SOH-en" or "SAH-en" in Scotland. By ancient reckoning, the day begins at sundown, which is why the Samhain celebrations begin on October 31. The nighttime portion of the festival is properly called the Oiche Shamna, or "vigil of Samhain." *Oiche Shamna* is pronounced "uh-EEK-uh HOW-nuh." Samhain is also called Hallows or Hallowmas, and the Oiche Shamna is also called Hallowe'en. The word *Hallow* means "spirit," literally "holy one."

Samhain is a lunar or Grand Sabbat, and it is sacred to the Crone Goddess, from whom the image of the Hallowe'en witch originates. The Crone has many names, including Hekate, Morgan, and Cerridwen. She is depicted as an elderly woman and is the patron of magic and of the spirit world. The Crone is the goddess of the dead, of wisdom, and of the ultimate spiritual origin of all things. In the *Vangelo delle Streghe*, the Crone is equivalent to Primeval Deity, the Goddess before the first creation.

At Samhain, the psychic tide is at a high point, so it is a good time for all sorts of magic, divination, and inner workings. Traditionally, Wiccans consider Samhain the most sacred of all festivals.

Yule

Yule is celebrated at the midwinter solstice, and by traditional reckoning it marks the high point of winter. The word *Yule* comes from the Germanic *Iul* and means "wheel." Yule celebrates winter and the rebirth of the sun god. As Yule is the shortest day of the year, it marks the sun's low ebb; after this, the sun will begin to grow stronger.

Yule is a solar Sabbat and is sacred to the Old God, the lord of winter. This ancient god has many names, including Cernunnos, Odin, Harlequin, Santa Claus, and the Holly King. This god is portrayed as an old man, majestic and often jolly. Sometimes he is shown as a king in ermine-trimmed robes; other times he is shown as a jester and called the king of fools. As the Crone is the goddess of death, the Old God is the lord of death and of the spirit world and magic. He is the god of the forest, of animals, and of the hunt. Often he is shown with antlers or horns. In this form, he is the subject of one of the oldest paintings known to exist, "Le Sorciere," a cave painting from Cro-Magnon times.

Yule is also known as midwinter and as Alban Arthan (pronounced "AL-bahn AR-than").

Imbolc

Imbolc is celebrated on February 1. Some groups, however, celebrate it on February 2. Imbolc is the festival of the beginning of spring, by traditional reckoning. It represents the renewed life of the earth after winter and the growing strength of the sun. Imbolc is a festival of light and of the dawn. It is traditional to light many candles for this festival, in order to encourage the sun to shine brighter and the earth to throw off the cold of the winter months. For this reason, Imbolc is also called Candlemas, and this is perhaps the more popular name for the festival. Because winter does not always end this early, however, the custom of the groundhog was developed as a form of sacred divination. A groundhog is released at dawn on Imbolc. If the groundhog doesn't see its shadow, it is believed that winter will end. If the groundhog does see its shadow, it is believed that winter will last six more weeks—until Ostara, the next Sabbat. This rite can also be performed with other, similar creatures, such as hamsters or guinea pigs, who are easier to handle than groundhogs.

Imbolc, a lunar or Grand Sabbat, is sacred to the Maiden Goddess, the goddess of the dawn and of fire. The Maiden Goddess has many names, including Brighid, Bride (pronounced "VREE-juh"), Eos, Aradia, and Vesta. The Maiden is not only the goddess of physical fire, but also of the fire of inspiration, the fire of creativity. Hers is the fire that is the first spark of fertility and life. In the *Vangelo*, it says that when the Goddess first beheld the beauty of the God, she trembled, and her trembling was the first dawn; that is why dawn is thought of as a goddess, and that quality of inspiration and desire for beauty is the nature of the Maiden Goddess.

Imbolc is also called Oimelc (pronounced "EE-mell"), which is Gaelic and means "lactation of ewes." Another Gaelic name for this festival is La Fheile Bride (pronounced "Law EYE-lah VREE-juh"), "the feast of Bride," honoring the goddess Brighid. The festival is also called Groundhogs' Day, because of the ritual described above.

Ostara

Ostara is celebrated at the spring equinox, when day and night are equal. It is considered the high point of the spring season, when life is bursting forward in all directions. Like Imbolc, Ostara is a festival of the dawn and of increasing life. The word *Ostara* comes from the Germanic word *Ost* or *East*, a reference to the dawn and the renewal of life. The rituals of Ostara celebrate renewed life in many forms: eggs, a symbol of rebirth, are painted in bright colors and used in sacred rites before being eaten; baby animals, especially chickens, ducks, and rabbits, are symbolic of the season; the rabbit, ancient symbol of the moon, represents the earth's renewed fertility.

Ostara is a solar Sabbat and is sacred to the Young God, lord of the rising sun and of life. He is the custodian of the growing plants and animals as well as the growing light of the sun. This god has many names, but he is particularly venerated as the Green Man, in which form he is shown surrounded by greenery and breathing it out from his lips. In this form, he is also known as Green Jack or Green George. Sometimes he is represented as a tree. Maypoles are sometimes used as part of the Ostara festivities, and these represent the phallus of the Young God.

Ostara is also known as Eostre (pronounced "EH-yoh-ster," "eh-OH-ster," or "YOH-ster"), Alban Eilir ("AL-bahn EYE-lir"), or simply Spring.

Ostara also has strong feminine connotations and is sacred to the Maiden Goddess as well as the Young God. Ostara and Eostre are both Germanic names of the Maiden Goddess as lady of the dawn.

Bealteinne

Bealteinne (pronounced "BALL-tuh-nuh" in Gaelic but "BELL-tane" in English) is celebrated on May 1. It is the beginning of the Light half of the year and the beginning of summer, by traditional reckoning. Bealteinne, the polar opposite of Samhain,

is the Festival of Life. The word comes from the Gaelic *La Bealteinne* and refers to the sacred balefires: bonfires that were lit in ancient times for the god Bel, or Belenos. Bealteinne celebrates the union of the Goddess and the God and is celebrated with great joy. Flowers are used to symbolize the divine union, and the maypole is used to represent the phallus of the God planted in the body of the Earth Mother.

Bealteinne is a lunar or Grand Sabbat, and it is sacred to the Great Mother Goddess. This goddess has many names, including Eartha, Demeter, Mati Suira Zemlya, Yemaya, and Gaia, as well as others too numerous to mention. She is the lady of life, who brings fertility to the earth, and at this time her power is on the rise as the earth brings forth an abundance of life. The Mother Goddess is the principal archetype of the Goddess.

Bealteinne is also known as Beltane, Kalenda Maia, Roodmas, Walpugis, May Day, or simply May.

Midsummer

Midsummer, as its name implies, is celebrated at the summer solstice, the longest day of the year. Midsummer is considered the high point of the summer season. Midsummer celebrates the very height of the powers of the sun and of life, but it also acknowledges that after this date the sun will begin to weaken and the days will grow shorter.

A solar Sabbat, Midsummer is sacred to the sun god, as lord of life. This god has many names, including Apollo, Balder, Lugh, Horus, Chango, and many others. He is the god of life and the physical world and is the principal archetype of the God. The celebrations of Midsummer stress the powers of light and life and rejoice in the good things the universe has to offer. Midsummer is also known as Litha (pronounced "LEE-thuh").

Lughnassadh

Lughnassadh is celebrated on August 1, though a few groups may celebrate it on August 2. The name *Lughnassadh* comes from the Gaelic *La Lughnassadh*, pronounced "Law LOO-nuh-suh," and it means "marriage of Lugh." Lugh is the Celtic god of the sun and of vegetation and the cultivated fields. The "marriage" of Lugh is the harvest, when the crops are reaped. When the harvest is completed and the last of the crops has been cut, Lugh is symbolically married to the Crone, goddess of the dead. But Lughnassadh marks the beginning, not the end, of the harvest. It is the beginning of the autumn or fall season, by traditional reckoning. Lughnassadh is the Festival of First Fruits, when thanks are given for the fertility of the

fields and the first bread baked from the new harvest is blessed.

Though Lughnassadh celebrates the death of Lugh, it is a lunar or Grand Sabbat sacred to the Mother Goddess as lady of the harvest. It is she who provides the bounty of the earth, and to her thanks are given. At Lughnassadh, the promise of Bealteinne is fulfilled by the bounty of the earth.

It is in this form, as lady of life, that the Goddess is portrayed in the famous Venus of Willendorf statuette. Some thirty thousand years old, the Venus of Willendorf shows the Mother Goddess pregnant, her bosoms heavy with milk—a testament to the fertility and life-giving qualities of the Great Mother. Lughnassadh is also called Lammas, First Fruits, and Bron Trograine.

Mabon

Mabon (pronounced "MAH-bohn") is celebrated at the fall equinox, when day and night are again equal. Mabon is the middle of the harvest and of the fall season. This is the time of the sun's denouement, its slow slide into winter and symbolic death. It is also the time of the earth's ebbing life force, as the plants of summer bear their fruit and decrease.

The name *Mabon* comes from the Celtic God Mabon, or Maponos, who died every year, to be reborn in the spring.

A solar Sabbat, Mabon is sacred to the Father God. This is the God as King and judge, lord of the tribe and elder of the community. He is the lord of balance, law, and justice, the god of honor and conscience. This is the god who willingly gives his life for the renewal of the land, as a good parent would give their life for their children, or a good leader for their people. The Father God has many names, including Zeus, Nodens, Thor, Jupiter, and many others.

Mabon is also sometimes associated with the Old God, especially in his form as Dionysus, because this is the time of the grape harvest. In this sense, Mabon honors the god of ecstasy, spiritual visions, and freedom.

. . . .

Esbats

In addition to lunar and solar Sabbats, Wiccans also celebrate Esbats. Sabbats are the big ceremonies. Sabbat ceremonies tend to be about celebrating and attuning to the season and honoring Deity. Esbats are the little ceremonies. They also honor Deity, but they are much more personal. At Esbats, groups tend to do more individual work, work geared toward the goals and growth of their members rather than cosmic phenomena.

Traditionally, Esbats are held on the nights of the new moon and the full moon.

In practice, however, groups will often choose a specific day, such as Saturday, and hold their Esbat on the Saturday night closest to the actual new or full moon. The period from new to full moon is the Light half of the month, while the period from full to new moon is Dark. The Light half of the month is used to work for things one wishes to create or accomplish. The Dark half is used to do releasing of things one wishes to let go of and to do inner work that requires looking inside oneself.

A new moon Esbat takes place at the very beginning of the moon's cycle, the start of the Light half of the month. At the new moon, one works to manifest things that will grow along with the moon as it waxes. The full moon Esbat takes place at the very end of the Light half of the month, when the moon is at the strongest point in its cycle and the energy of the monthly cycle is also at its strongest. We use that heightened energy of the full moon to give added strength to our working. Esbats are not commonly held during the dark half of the month.

These, then, are the basic points of the psychic tide: that it rises and falls during each month, reaching its highest point at full moon and its lowest point at new moon.

The psychic tide also rises and falls each year, reaching its highest points at Samhain and Bealteinne. Winter is the Dark or internal half, and summer the Light or external half of each year. The psychic tide further rises and falls during each zodiacal age, reaching its highest point at the turn of each age, such as the period we are in now (during the turn from Pisces to Aquarius). By knowing and understanding the psychic tide, you can attune to it to take advantage of its points of highest energy.

. . . .

Exercises

As usual, you should find a comfortable position in which to do your exercises. Begin by releasing, as you learned to do in Lesson I. Do Exercises 1, 2, and 3 as usual. Now you are ready for Exercise 4.

Exercise 4

Exercise 4 involves your solar plexus chakra. Chakras are energy centers in the body. There are both major chakras and minor chakras. The solar plexus chakra is a major chakra. You will learn more about chakras in future lessons.

The solar plexus chakra is located near the navel. For the purposes of this exercise, you should visualize the solar plexus chakra as being behind the navel, at the center of the body. Chakras have many levels and can be worked with at the front of the body, the middle, or along the spine. Here we will work with this chakra at the center.

Imagine a ball of yellow-white light at your solar plexus chakra. Visualize this ball of light as being clear and bright, shining out in all directions like an internal sun. If the ball of light is unclear, muddied, or dull, take a moment and concentrate on making it as clear and bright as possible.

Visualize the ball of light growing and expanding within you. Let it expand to fill your whole abdomen. Let it continue to expand until it is about three feet across. Each day as you repeat this exercise, make the ball of light expand farther. Let the ball of light expand as far as you can while still keeping the image clear.

When you have expanded the ball, hold the image in your mind for a few moments. The longer you can hold the image, the better. If possible, expand the length of time you hold the image each day, or every few days.

Now, after opening and expanding the ball of light and having held it for a time, you must close it. Imagine the ball of light slowly shrinking, back down to the spot behind your navel. The ball of light gets smaller and smaller until it disappears. Now imagine a tiny open door in the spot where the ball of light was, and see that door close. Finally, clear and release as usual.

What you have done in this exercise is open, expand, and close your solar plexus chakra. Chakras are much like the muscles of the physical body: they are strengthened by exercise. A strong solar plexus chakra will be extremely important to the exercises you will learn in future lessons.

When you can do Exercise 4 easily, add Exercise 5 to your daily regimen.

Exercise 5

This exercise will follow the preceding one. After you have closed the solar plexus chakra, you will move up to the heart chakra. The heart chakra, as you might imagine, is located in the general area of the heart. Imagine the heart chakra as being approximately at the center of the chest. As in Exercise 4, we will work with the chakra at the middle of the body rather than at the front or along the spine.

Imagine a ball of pale pink light at the heart chakra—clear, gentle pink light. If the light is muddy or dull, take a moment to imagine it clearing and brightening. Let this ball of light expand until it fills your chest.

In the center of this ball of pink light, imagine a pink rosebud. See that bud begin to open, slowly spreading its petals like the flowers one sees in time-elapse photography. Let the pink rosebud unfold until the flower is fully revealed—a large and beautiful pink rose.

From the center of this pink rose, imagine light shining out in all directions—beautiful white or yellow-white light. When this image is clear in your mind, hold it for a while. Again, it is best if you can increase the holding time each day.

Now you must close the chakra. Imagine the ball of light with the rose inside beginning to shrink—growing smaller and smaller until it disappears. And again, just as in Exercise 4, imagine a tiny open door where the ball of light was, and see that door close. To finish, as always, clear and release excess energy.

Exercise 6

Exercise 6 is a continuation of Exercise 5. When you can do Exercise 5 easily, you will replace it with this exercise.

Exercise 6 begins just like Exercise 5. Imagine a ball of pink light in the heart chakra. Expand the ball of light. Visualize a rosebud within the ball of light, and see that bud expand until it is fully opened into a rose. See beautiful white or yellow-white light shining out from the rose.

Now, at the very center of the pink rose, see a gleaming white pearl, iridescent and lovely. Imagine the pearl floating out from the rose, out of your chest, and then upward toward your face. See the pearl come to your lips, and imagine taking the pearl into your mouth and swallowing it. Visualize the pearl as it goes down your throat—all the way down past the heart chakra to the solar plexus chakra.

Now close the heart chakra as before, seeing the ball of light with the flower shrink down and disappear. Then imagine the tiny open door and close it. Now clear and release as per usual.

As you prepare for Lesson IV, your daily exercise regimen should include Exercises 1, 2, 3, 4, and 6.

More about Chakras in Exercises

There are many schools of thought about the chakras. Some of these are ancient; some are very recent. Not all of these schools of thought agree.

It is not our purpose to discuss these differences in thought at this time. In writing these lessons, we are working from a single, coherent system regarding the chakras. As with everything else, some sources will agree with us, and some sources will disagree with us. We present it as being the preferred Correllian system, not the only system.

The solar plexus chakra is of immense importance to your ability to work with these exercises. Chakras are energy centers, and they form connections that act as energy circuits in the body. The first and most important of these is the SOLAR CIRCUIT. It is called the solar circuit because it has its origin in the solar plexus chakra. The solar plexus chakra is said to be the place where the physical body connects to the higher levels of the being. The solar

plexus chakra may be viewed as a kind of internal sun producing endless quantities of energy. This energy originates from the Higher Self and provides the power by which physical life moves forward. Emanating from the solar plexus chakra, this energy then forms a circuit moving through all of the other chakras. This production and distribution of energy is constant, but it is normally unconscious. By exercising the solar plexus chakra, you are increasing the amount of energy that the chakra produces as well as gaining more conscious control over the process, which will allow you to call upon that energy as needed.

Though the solar plexus chakra produces energy, it does not usually receive it. Rather, it is the heart chakra that usually receives energy (within the solar circuit), thus the importance of exercising it. When you receive healing or additional energy from outside, it will usually enter through the heart chakra. This will be of great importance later.

. . . .

Spell for Lesson III
Image Magic

Image magic is the art of using an image of something to create or affect it. We use image magic as a key—an aid to help focus our magical intent and assist in the shift of consciousness.

Image magic is the most famous form of magic. People who know nothing else about real magic know what a "voodoo doll" is, even if they have only a limited and skewed understanding of its uses.

Image magic is also among the oldest forms of magic. It has been said, and is most likely true, that the oldest images created by humankind were made for magical purposes.

The cave paintings of Europe, made tens of thousands of years ago by the Cro-Magnon people, depict great herds of animals: mighty bison, deer, wild horses—all the quarry of ancient hunters. Painted with vivid color and amazing skill in the deep recesses of subterranean caves, these ancient paintings are almost universally accredited a magical purpose, although the exact nature of this is debated. Most believe that the paintings were used for sympathetic magic—the idea that "like affects like."

By painting the animals they wished to catch and enacting the appropriate ceremonies, ancient hunters believed they could magically ensure a successful hunt. Energy focused through ritual supplied the magic, and the image was used to direct it.

There are many ways to use image magic. For example, the image of a particular deity can be used as a key to aid communication with that deity. The image helps one to shift consciousness and to focus on the

deity, so as better to send or receive energy from that deity.

An image can be used in the same way to facilitate communication with an ancestor. In Egypt, images of the deceased were used in this way, as a key to access the spirits of the beloved dead. Symbolic offerings of food and drink were made to the image to strengthen the psychic connection of the offerant to the spirit by virtue of the focused energy put into the ceremony.

The Egyptians—as well as most other ancient peoples—believed that the better the likeness, the stronger the connection to the spirit the image represents. The nose was considered to be of particular importance. The ancients believed that if the nose of an image were damaged, its use as a key to the spirit was destroyed. This is because in PHYSIOGNOMY the nose is considered to represent the ego, or sense of self. It is for this reason that many ancient and classical statues have missing or damaged noses: the early Christians, greatly fearing Pagan images, went around smashing the noses off of them, believing that this would destroy the spiritual effectiveness of the image.

Today we know that it is not how good the likeness is but how strongly it serves to represent the essence of the deity or spirit in the mind of the observer that gives the image effectiveness as a key. We know from experience that while a beautiful work of art may give great pleasure as an image, an effective key may be created by quite simple or even abstract portrayals.

In addition to facilitating communication with deities or spirits, images can also be used to strengthen desired qualities within ourselves or in the outer world. To do this, we create an image of the quality in question—such as "patience" or "tolerance"—and use the image to focus our energy toward the chosen goal through meditation and ritual.

But by far the most common way we use image magic is for the purpose of creating a specific short-term effect in our lives. In this case, the image represents us, and it is treated in a way designed to create the desired effect.

For this kind of image magic, the image is usually quite simple. Most commonly it is a simple doll made or dressed in a color that represents what we desire to do: green for healing, as an example. This kind of image can also be a drawing, or even a photograph.

Once the image is created, there are a number of symbolic ways to stimulate the desired effect. The most famous is by use of pins. Most people think that you stick pins into the doll to cause pain or harm to someone, as this is what they've seen on TV or in the movies. In fact, what you are doing is placing the pin in an area to which you wish to focus energy. The pin gives you something to concentrate your focus on, and some people feel that it physically helps to conduct the energy as well.

Where you place the pins depends upon what you wish to do. If you are doing healing, you would place the pins in the parts of the doll that correspond to the parts of the body that need healing. If you are working to attract love, pins might be placed in the heart and in the pelvic region. Of course, you should never do a love spell to attract a specific person—this would violate their free will and bring you bad karma. Rather, you should work to draw the best love for you.

If you are seeking to draw prosperity, you might place the pins in the belly. If you are working to draw success in some venture, you might choose to insert the pins in the top of the head and again in the belly. But, as always, you should pay attention to what feels right to you and do that. Let your inner voice guide you. If you feel that a pin should go in a particular place, you should listen to this, because it is a message from your Higher Self.

Ideally, you would use the kind of pins that have colored tops, choosing the color according to the effect you wish to create: red for love, green for healing, yellow or green for prosperity, and blue or black for protection.

Other ways to use the doll include dressing it with appropriate props: for prosperity, for example, you might place coins or bills upon the doll. You can also use yarn: for protection, for example, make a circle of red yarn around the doll, and for healing, wrap the doll in green yarn. However you use the doll, remember that the symbolic act is only to help you focus your energy. It is not the pins or the yarn that work the magic, but you.

When you have created the doll, you must empower it. The best time to do this is during the waxing moon. Begin by clearing and releasing all excess energy. You should always clear and release before and after any magical working. It will help to have several candles lit, and maybe some incense.

Speak to the Goddess, asking her for her help. You might say something like this:

"O Goddess, I pray that you will
help me now to have success in
this work that I am undertaking."

Concentrate on what it is you are trying to do with this doll. Meditate on this for a few moments, and fix it strongly in your mind. Now imagine the doll surrounded with a ball of white light. Concentrate on that ball of light, and imagine it growing stronger and brighter, radiating out in all directions. While you do this, focus on the goal that you wish to bring about. Concentrate strongly on it.

Now speak an incantation. This is an example of what you might say:

"There is one Power
in the universe,
and I am a perfect manifestation
of that Power.
And as such, I will that
[insert your goal here].
By my will, with harm toward none,
I will it, I manifest it,
I draw it to me,
I receive it, I accept it,
and I give thanks for it.
By my will, so mote it be,
and it is so."

Concentrate strongly as you speak these words, and imagine your goal is coming to pass. Be confident, and know that you are creating this even as you speak. Now put the doll in a safe place. Clear and release all excess energy, and you are finished.

Remember that everything gets better with practice. The first time you try this, you may not get as strong an effect as you would like. You may wish to perform the ceremony several times. But if you keep working with it, you will get better and better and stronger and stronger. Remember also that the effect will probably not be instantaneous but gradual. This is normal. Give it time to come about, and trust what you have done.

God for Lesson III
The Maiden

The Triple Goddess has three aspects: Maiden, Mother, and Crone. Though we approach these aspects as individual personal deities, all three are aspects of the same power: the feminine polar force, the Goddess.

Of the Triple Goddess's three aspects, her aspect as Mother probably receives the most attention. But in fact, all three aspects are equally important: they form a cycle, and each naturally flows into the next.

The Maiden is the aspect of the Triple Goddess in her youthful form. Sometimes the Maiden is conceived of as a child, but more often as an independent young woman. The image of the Maiden is strongly affected by the customs of a given culture; there is much more variety in the image of the Maiden than in either the Mother or the Crone. Sometimes the Maiden is shown as an ascetic virgin, like Athena or Vesta. At the other extreme, she may be strongly associated with pleasure and sexuality, like Hathor, Ezili, or Venus. Though this may seem like a contradiction, in fact it is not. Rather, it reflects the variety of activity that falls under the Maiden's IMPERIUM.

The Maiden is the goddess of beginnings, growth, and expansion. She is symbolized by the waxing moon. The Maiden rules over the dawn, the season of spring, and the direction of the east. The Maiden is the goddess of passion and creativity. All arts, crafts, and sciences are sacred to her, and the tutelary goddesses of the various arts and sciences are often forms of the Maiden (as is Sesheta, Egyptian goddess of writing). All forms of inspiration, self-expression, and creativity—all things that stir the soul or incite the mind—belong to the Maiden.

The Maiden Goddess tends to be shown in one of the three following main forms:

The Artist

Goddess of all arts and crafts, skills and sciences. The mind, intellect, and inspiration fall within her purview. She delights in beauty and is often specifically associated with flowers or the rainbow, as well as with both inner and outer fire. Examples of the Maiden Goddess in this guise include Brighid, Flora, Kore, Minerva, and Sesheta.

The Guardian

The Goddess as warrior and protector—patron of quests and causes, champion of heroes and adventurers, defender of those in need. In this form, the Maiden grants courage, guidance, and fortitude. Examples of the Maiden Goddess in this guise include Anat, Artemis, and Durga.

Lesson
III

The Lover

Goddess of love, beauty, and sexuality, she is the patron of lovers and romance. Examples of the Maiden Goddess in this guise include Ezili, Hathor, and Venus.

• • • •

Though these forms may at first seem contradictory, they in fact are not. Rather, they each represent a different focus of the Maiden's energy of creativity and self-expression. Sometimes a form of the Maiden Goddess will express only one of these facets, but many express several or all at once. The Greek Athena is both artist and guardian, as is the Roman Vesta, while the Mesopotamian Ishtar is both guardian and lover.

The following passage was written about the Afro-diasporic goddess Ezili-Oshun, a form of the Maiden, but it may be taken as representative of the qualities of the Maiden Goddess in general:

Goddess of the fulfilled and independent woman, mistress of Her own fate and pursuing Her own dreams. . . .

Goddess of romantic love, and also of sexuality. She is the mistress of everything that delights the senses.

All pleasure and enjoyment in life are Hers—anything that is beautiful and fine.

She governs the arts and crafts, music and dance, poetry and writing. All luxuries and conveniences are Hers.

She is the creative individual, striving to fill Her own needs and expressing Herself in every way. She is competent and dexterous, making Her will manifest all about Her on the material plane with skill and style.

All joy and laughter are Hers.[i]

• • • •

Below are several examples of the Maiden Goddess.

Athena

Tutelary Goddess of the Greek city-state of Athens, Athena is the goddess of the mind and intellect and patron of all arts and crafts, especially weaving. Athena is the goddess of science, books, and learning and is symbolized by the owl of wisdom. A warrior goddess, Athena inspires people to great acts, and she acts as a protector to those in need, especially women.

Brighid

Celtic goddess of fire and inspiration, Brighid rules over the arts and crafts, especially the three great skills of poetry, smithcraft, and medicine. Music is sacred to her, and she was a patron of the sacred bards. Brighid is a goddess of wisdom and learning, as well as cunning, and she can overcome all obstacles. Brighid is often likened

• • • •

i (reprinted from *The Wheel of Hekate*, AD 1988/1588 Pisces to the spirit of the grain in the fields, and corn dollies are made to represent her. Her festival is La Fheila Bride ("Law EYE-luh VREE-ja"), or Candlemas, celebrated on February 1. Brighid is also known as Bride, Brigantia, and Brigantina.

Ezili

Called Ezili or Erzulie in Haiti, Oshun in Cuba and the United States, and Ochum in Brazil, this is the Afro-diasporic goddess of love and beauty. Ezili is the goddess of art and self-expression. Poetry, song, and dance are sacred to her. She is a patron of both romantic and sensual love, and she promotes happiness and joy in life. She is a goddess of independence, fulfillment, and personal strength.

Hathor

Egyptian goddess of love, beauty, and personal fulfillment, Hathor is often depicted as a cow or with the head of a cow, symbolizing fecundity. She is the patron of art, music, dance, and all things beautiful and pleasing. Hathor is often symbolized by a mirror, representing self-knowledge and fulfillment. Identified with the sky, Hathor is the consort of Horus, the sun god; in fact, the name "Hat-Hor" means "home of Horus." Hathor also has aspects as a Mother goddess.

Vesta

Roman goddess of the hearth fire, Vesta is the protector of the home and of the peo-ple in it. The safety of the family is in her hands. Vesta is conceived of as a sober and dignified Maiden, patron of the homely arts: cooking, weaving, and housekeeping. Vesta is also a goddess of honor and justice, protector of the virtuous and guardian of the weak. In former times, Vesta was the protective deity of the Roman state and was served by the famous Vestal Virgins, celibate priestesses who cared for the spiritual heart of Rome.

• • • •

Glossary for Lesson III

Correllian calendar—The Correllian calendar was developed as a Pagan response to the Gregorian calendar. The Gregorian calendar is based on the supposed date of the birth of Jesus and divides all of history in half based on that date. Pre-Christian dates must be calculated backward in this system, which not only makes Jesus appear to be the center of time, but also effectively veils pre-Christian history behind a wall of unwieldy calculations and an artificial sense of separation from modern events. The Correllian calendar is cyclical, never using backward dates as such and having no single "beginning" that might serve to divide time into "us" and "them."

Dark half—The Dark half of a thing is its process of involution, or looking inward. During this process, things narrow and appear to decrease or become constrained—to force a tight focus. The night is the Dark half of the day, the waning moon is the Dark half of the lunar cycle, the winter is the Dark half of the year, and so on.

Esbat—An Esbat is a monthly ceremony or ceremonies, usually tied to the cycle of the moon. Esbats are commonly held at the new or full moon, but they can also be held at the dark moon.

evolution—Involution is a process of going inside, of narrowing one's view to the extremely personal and individual. Evolution is the process of coming out from the separate and personal toward the unified and divine. Evolution increases the vibration and lightens the density of a being, allowing it to become progressively less physical. This is the process of returning to the Goddess and to a perspective of universality. When the involutionary process has achieved its end, the natural result is evolution; as is revealed in the sacred labyrinth, one first winds in, then winds back out. This process is repeated in countless ways in every moment of existence.

great year—The passage of an entire series of twelve zodiacal ages, from one sign all the way back to itself, is said to be a great year. According to Correllian reckoning, this is a period of 19,200 years.

imperium—This term refers to those things that are under one's direct power or that fall in one's natural sphere of influence. Thus the imperium of an astrologer includes subjects related to the stars and their influences, while the imperium of an herbalist would have to do with the medicinal and magical uses of plants. The term is of particular importance to offices one might hold, where it makes reference to one's sphere of authority.

involution—The *Vangelo delle Streghe* says that the God "fell into matter." This means that he "involved." To involve is to focus solely on a part of creation, assuming a spiritual tunnel vision. Involution slows the vibration of energy and increases its density, thus physicalizing it. Involution gives an illusion of separation from the Goddess, affording a singularity of perception that allows a thing to be studied in great detail by blocking out the rest of creation. Since all above is also below, the process of involution is reflected in all things that must first involve before they can evolve—that is to say, they must first adopt a highly personal and focused view, from which deep understanding and integration is possible, before they can widen their view to contemplate the wholeness of existence.

Light half—The Light half of a thing is its process of evolution, or looking outward. During this process, perspective expands and the connection between all things is felt. The day is the Light half of the night, the waxing moon is the Light half of the lunar cycle, the summer is the Light half of the year, and so on.

physiognomy—Physiognomy is the art of interpreting personality characteristics from the features of the face and body. In physiognomy, every part of the body has a meaning; for example, the eyebrows indicate temperament, the shoulders reflect the ability to deal with pressure, and the feet refer to qualities of the life path. Physiognomy can be very useful for personality readings, for discerning the causes of psychic blockages or imbalances, and for a variety of other purposes.

precession of the equinoxes—It was long ago observed that the physical position of the constellations had diverged from the theoretical positions used by astrology. Thus, the spring equinox, which once coincided with the sun's apparent entry into the zodiacal sign of Aries, has not done so for many hundreds of years, and it now more closely corresponds to the sun's apparent entry into Pisces. From this fact, the theory of the zodiacal ages was developed, based on the idea that because "As above, so below," celestial phenomena must reflect earthly conditions.

psychic tide—This term refers to the eternal cycles of energy in the universe, which move in a constant process of involution and evolution, spiraling always inward and then outward. Everything that exists moves in the rhythm of the psychic tide, which has waves and currents and eddies at all levels of being. The galaxy, the planet, the individual—all move to the psychic tide on many different levels.

Sabbat—A Sabbat is a major Wiccan festival. There are four Grand Sabbats, whose energy is primarily feminine. These are Samhain, Imbolc, Bealteinne, and Lughnassadh. There are four Lesser Sabbats as well, whose energy is primarily masculine. These are the spring equinox (Ostara), the summer solstice, the fall equinox, and the winter solstice (Yule). The Lesser Sabbats are keyed to the position of the sun and are reckoned by the solar calendar. In former times, the Grand Sabbats were reckoned by the lunar calendar, but they were long ago tied to the Kalends (or first day) of the months in which they occur and are now usually reckoned by the solar calendar as well.

solar circuit—The solar circuit is the principal energy circuit of the human body, having its origin at the solar plexus chakra (hence the name). From this point, energy enters the body from the Higher Self, and ultimately from the Goddess. This energy is limitless in theory, but in practice it may be restricted or blocked for a variety of reasons. The solar circuit is used primarily for the sustenance of the body and the continuation of physical life.

vortices—Vortices are the energy centers or chakras of the earth. The earth's energy is stronger and more easily interacted with at a vortex, just as our own energy is stronger and more easily interacted with at our chakra points. Vortices are ideal spots to receive energy from the earth and to send healing to the earth. For this reason, vortex points are usually considered sacred spots and are often used as worship centers. Just as the chakras of the body are connected by meridians that transmit energy between them, so too the earth's vortices are connected by ley lines.

Wheel of the Year—The Wheel of the Year refers to the yearly cycle of the seasons and to the sacred festivals that celebrate them. These festivals describe the process of involution and evolution on personal, seasonal, and divine levels.

zodiac—The zodiac is a system of constellations used since ancient times to structure the practice of astrology. Developed in the ancient Near East, astrology uses the theoretical position of stars and planets to address issues of internal character and future events. Though tied to the position of heavenly bodies, it could be argued that astrology really has more to do with the mathematical calculation of repeating cycles of time and their individual character, using the stars and planets as markers.

zodiacal age—A zodiacal age is a period used to mark time by a zodiacal ruler, theoretically reflected in the precession of the equinoxes. Each zodiacal age is ruled by a sign of the zodiac, from which the age is said to take its character. Different schools of thought assign different lengths to the zodiacal age. According to the Correllian calendar, a zodiacal age lasts for 1,600 years, or four sets of four hundred years each. By Correllian reckoning, we are currently at the end of the Piscean Age and the beginning of the Aquarian Age, with the year AD 2000 being an intercalary year that was both 1600 Pisces and 0 Aquarius.

Study Questions for Lesson III

1. What is an energy vortex?

2. What is involution?

3. What is the psychic tide?

4. It is said that everything has a "Dark half." What does that mean?

5. What is the precession of the equinoxes?

6. What is a zodiacal age? According to the Correllian calendar, how long does a zodiacal age last?

7. What zodiacal age are we currently in? When will it end?

8. What is the great year? According to the Correllian calendar, how long does the great year last?

9. What is a Grand Sabbat? How does it differ from a Lesser Sabbat?

10. What is Roodmas? When is it celebrated?

11. What is the Oidche Shamna? When is it celebrated?

12. What is an Esbat?

13. What is the solar circuit? What role does the heart chakra play in it?

Lesson

~ IV ~

The Altar

The main purpose of an altar is to provide focus. It can be used to focus on the divine powers—this is worship. It can be used to focus energy for making changes in our lives—this is magic. It can be used to focus on communication with our Higher Selves and SPIRIT GUIDES—this is meditation. All of these—worship, magic, and meditation—are ways of focusing our psychic energy to accomplish specific ends. The altar can aid in that focus and can be used to augment that energy and enhance the result.

Because so much of this process depends on the energy of *you*, your altar should be so designed as to have meaning for *you* and to provoke an emotional and spiritual reaction from you. This is particularly important, because no matter how beautiful or "correct" your altar is, it won't matter to you if it doesn't help you access your own inner energies.

Altars have many variations. The simplest altar need be no more than a picture on the wall or a clear space on a table. The most elaborate altars are masterpieces of exquisite art. Most altars are somewhere in between. In this lesson, you will learn how to construct a basic altar, which you can then adapt to your personal needs. At this altar, you can do magic, work ritual, and commune with the powers that be.

• • • •

Geomancy

Your first consideration is where to put your altar. Most people put their altar in their bedroom. This makes it a very personal space and assures privacy. This is especially good if you live in a home with non-Pagan roommates or family members who might be intimidated by a holy object such as an altar in the living room.

If, however, your home is wholly Pagan, you may wish to have a more public altar, placed in a living room or a special temple room, at which your whole family can worship. If you do this, you will probably still want a personal altar in your bedroom to use privately, one that is attuned solely to your own energies. In this way, you can enjoy with your family the best aspects of both personal and communal religious devotion.

Once you've decided what room to put your altar in, you must decide where in the room to put it. For many, this is an easy decision: if you have only three feet of

open wall space in your room and no way to rearrange the room otherwise, obviously the altar will go within that three feet. But if you have more than one choice available to you, you will wish to consult the principles of GEOMANCY.

Geomancy is the art of reading the earth's energies and aligning ourselves and our works to them—and through them to the energies of the universe as well. Geomancy is an ancient art in all parts of the world. Different peoples have developed different ideas about it, depending on the needs of their differing cultures. In Asia, it is called FENG SHUI, and this form of geomancy has become quite popular lately.

The idea of geomancy, like so many other things in magic, comes from "As above, so below," the ancient maxim of Hermes Trismegistus. This is the idea that the essential nature of the universe will be reflected in all of its parts, no matter how great or small.

The main principles of Western geomancy are exemplified by the magic circle. Briefly, the direction of east represents creativity and new beginnings. South is action and manifestation. West is emotion and the subconscious. North is wisdom. Everything that is above or that goes to the right (DEOSIL) is connected to the God, to matter, and to physical manifestation. Everything that is below or that goes to the left (TUATHAIL, or less correctly "widdershins") is connected to the Goddess, to spirit, and to cleansing. You will learn more about this in Lesson V.

Your altar may be aligned to any direction whose qualities you desire to draw on, but it is traditional—and generally best for the beginner—to place the altar toward the north. North is the direction of wisdom and understanding, where the qualities of the other directions are integrated and learned from. Placing the altar in the north will help you to align yourself to wisdom and integration and will help you to bring these qualities to your magical and meditative practice.

Your altar itself also has a geomancy to consider. The right side of the altar is warm. It is associated with the God, the sun, day, physical energy, and the elements of air and fire. The left side of the altar is cool. It is associated with the Goddess, the moon and stars, spiritual energy and magic, and the elements of water and earth.

The middle of the altar is associated with Spirit, or Primeval Deity, who is within both the Goddess and the God, as well as all other things. The back part of this middle area is associated with Primeval Deity, that aspect of the Goddess that existed before the creation of the God and might be described as the Higher Self of the universe. Here is the divine plan, the blueprint of the universe that is mirrored in every aspect of creation. This is the soul

of Deity, which is expressed in many different faces. This is often the focal point of the altar, where Deity is honored in whatever form is being invoked at the time. The front part of the middle space represents spiritual energy manifesting in the physical world—the union of Goddess and God in the ongoing process of creation. This is where your magical working will be done. This area is normally left empty when work is not being done.

· · · ·

Creating Your Altar

Before you set up your altar, you will want to purify and bless your altar space. Magic is the focusing of spiritual energy, and spiritual energy is constantly being affected by the actions and emotions of people. Consequently, it needs to be purified or cleansed to have the residues of emotions and actions removed, so that energy can be refocused and redirected. You will remember that this spiritual energy, which comes from the Goddess, suffuses all people and things and is the basis of existence; it is directed and shaped by concentrated thought, emotion, and physical action.

You will find a basic space-cleansing ritual in the spell section of this lesson, which you may use to prepare your altar space to receive your altar. Once you have cleansed the energy, you may proceed to assemble your altar. This is best done immediately after the cleansing, and you should have all the necessary materials nearby beforehand.

• • • •

The Altar Table

The ALTAR TABLE is the surface upon which your altar is set up. It is not necessarily a table as such, but rather can be any of a wide variety of surfaces.

Traditionally, altars have often been erected outdoors, and they still are at ritual gatherings and for certain observances. In this circumstance, the altar is often placed directly on the ground or upon a log or boulder. This is the ideal, as it connects directly with Mother Earth and, through her, the universe. In this same spirit, your indoor altar table is best made of wood or stone (marble, for instance). Metal is not considered desirable—for the horizontal surface, at least, though the altar table may stand on metal legs and often will include metal components.

Most commonly, an ordinary piece of household furniture is used for the altar table, to conserve space. Many people set up their altars on the top of their bedroom dresser or on a nightstand. Some people use the top shelf of a bookcase, showing reverence for knowledge.

Some people, to maintain an even closer link with the earth, will place a bowl or box lined with soil on their altar table and then assemble their altar in this, though this is an unusual practice. More commonly, a jar or bowl of earth will be kept *on* the altar for the same reason, rather than being used *as* the altar.

• • • •

The Altar Cloth

You may want to use an altar cloth. This is an ancient tradition arising from the time when all cloth was hand-woven and precious and any type of embroidery was a luxury.

Today, altar cloths are used because of their beauty and capacity for symbolism. Details of color and decoration can greatly influence the flavor and energy of the altar. If you wish to use an altar cloth, you will want to consider the following details when choosing it.

If you are able, decorate the altar cloth yourself, with embroidery or fabric paint, using symbols that have relevance to your personal philosophy and relationship with Deity. This will bond it to you and fill it with your energy. Concentrate on positive, self-empowering thoughts as you work, so that the cloth will be imbued with these and radiate them back to you during ritual and magical working. If you prefer a less handmade altar cloth for any reason, choose a cloth that resonates strongly with you: an heirloom, a treasured gift, or a cloth that puts you in mind of your hopes and dreams.

To prepare the altar cloth for the altar, you will want to consecrate it. Do this by holding the cloth in your hands. Say, "I send out from this cloth any negativity that may lie within it," or words to that effect, and visualize the cloth flooded with a strong yellow light. Imagine this light passing through the cloth, carrying out all impurities. Then say something like, "I do bless and consecrate this cloth to my altar, that it may aid me in my workings and my growth," and visualize a clear blue-white light coming down from above and filling the cloth until it glows with white light like the moon. Use this same basic technique to consecrate the altar pieces described below as well.

・・・・
Altar Pieces

Of your altar pieces, the most important will be these: candles, incense, water, and salt. These represent the four ELEMENTS, which are considered the building blocks of creation. You will learn more about the elements in Lesson V.

Of course, you will also need matches or a lighter (or, as we call it, the sacred lighting instrument). Strictly speaking, it is preferable to have matches or lighters that are used only for the altar and for no other purpose, but since this is not always practical, a household lighter will do if necessary.

You will also keep your MAGICAL TOOLS on the altar, but you will not learn about these until Lesson V, so we will leave off discussion of them until then.

・・・・
Using Candles

Candles represent fire and are often the most visible element on an altar. Candles have always been used on altars—either actual candles or torches or oil lamps. In earlier times, a bonfire might have been built, and this would serve as the "candle" and also as the actual "altar" itself. Sometimes this is still done in outdoor ritual.

Since the earliest times, the presence of fire in Pagan ritual has been of extreme importance. Fire represents the God (as you should remember from Lesson II), and when you light a flame you are repeating the Goddess's act of first creation. Each ritual then begins with the symbolic reenactment of the first creation when the candles are lit. The candle flame bursts forth from darkness, even as the God burst forth from the Goddess in an explosion of flame and light. Moreover, flame generates energy. Each candle that you light puts out energy of its own, which will add to your working; it will act as a kind of battery, raising the available energy level and increasing your ability. This is why you sometimes see so many candles burning at once on an altar.

You can add to this effect by imagining a ball of white light around the flame when you light your candle; this increases the energy the flame puts out. Imagine the ball of light expanding out from the flame for several inches. When you put out the candle, imagine the ball of light shrinking down and disappearing. You can use the ball of light without the flame too, but if you do, make sure you remember to shrink it down when you are done.

You may also wish to "dress" your candles before you use them. (This does not mean putting little clothes on them.) You dress a candle with anointing oil. The most common reason to dress a candle is to do CANDLE MAGIC, about which you will learn more later. But some people like to dress candles whenever they use them. Dressing a candle gives you a chance to focus on the candle and put energy into it, "programming" it for the purpose it will be used for. By doing this, you imprint your INTENT on it and cause it to focus naturally on what you are trying to do. Then, when the candle burns, the energy it generates will already be programmed for your purpose.

To dress a candle, you take an appropriate anointing oil (say lavender for a purification or sandalwood for general ritual) and put a little in the palm of your left hand. Now rub your two hands together so that they are coated with the oil. As you rub your hands together, visualize white light shining out from between them and see this white light expand and grow into a ball of light around your hands. Now take up your candle, holding it by the middle. Slowly work the oil up toward the top of the candle, a little bit at a time, and then down toward the bottom. As you do this, imagine the candle filling with white light, and concentrate on what it is you wish to do with this candle. The harder you concentrate, the more you will impress your intent on the candle. Coat the whole candle with oil, including the wick. As the candle burns, it will release energy imprinted with your intent, as well as the scent of the oil it has been dressed with.

The number and color of candles you want on your altar is entirely up to you. A chart of colors and their meanings is included to help you choose. You will want to consider this choice carefully, as it will add a great deal to the atmosphere and energy of your altar.

Beeswax candles are considered preferable, and some people go so far as to make their own, infusing the candles strongly with their personal energy by doing so. But in practice, most people buy regular candles at the local store, and they work perfectly well.

Some people use only a single candle on their altar, to represent Spirit, or Primordial Deity. Or they might use a single candle to represent only that aspect of Deity they are invoking at the moment.

COLOR CHART FOR CANDLES

Color	Meaning
black	wisdom, guidance, protection
purple	spirituality and psychism
blue	communication
green	healing, prosperity, fertility
yellow	happiness, success
orange	creativity
red	strong emotion, passion; adds extra energy to any working
pink	romantic love, compassion
white	innocence, manifestation, general purpose

Others use a matched or contrasting pair to represent the Goddess and the God—spirit and matter, death and life, the great duality whose interaction forms the universe as we know it. These candles might show up in any of a number of color combinations used to represent the Goddess and the God, including black and white, silver (white or gray) and gold (yellow), green and red, indigo and yellow, and so on. In such an arrangement, the Goddess candle goes to the left and the God candle to the right, in keeping with the geomancy of the altar as discussed above. Sometimes a Spirit candle is placed between them to symbolize their inner unity.

You might want to use altar candles to symbolize the four elements in elemental colors or the three phases of the Goddess or whatever else conveys the idea of holiness to you and helps you to make the magical shift in consciousness. You may want to include a special candle to honor your ANCESTORS (whether by blood or affinity) or your spirit guides. Candles help to raise energy, so the more the merrier—just be careful not to set yourself on fire! Also, many magical workings require special candles that will only be used for that working. These candles will be on your altar for anywhere from a few minutes to few weeks, depending on the working. So you can see why candles are such an important part of the altar.

When you finish a magical working, do not blow your candles out. Use a candle snuffer, your fingers, or a magical blade. This is to make sure that the candle goes out the first time, as it is a bad omen otherwise.

In general, you may use as many candles on your altar as you wish, in any colors that have significance for you. Even the guidelines we have outlined here are just that: guidelines. If you feel strongly that you should arrange your candles in a way that is not consonant with the geomancy we have discussed, you should listen to your intuition and do as it tells you.

Candles can also be used to represent the fifth element—Spirit. In this aspect, the wax represents Spirit and the flame represents the body or physical existence. Thus the Spirit (wax) feeds the body (flame). And just as the candle can be relit any number of times, so too we see that the soul passes through any number of bodies.

• • • •

Using Incense

INCENSE represents the element of air. Incense may be of any sort: stick, cone, oil, or powder. But remember, in some rituals you may have to pick the incense up, so choose a form of incense or an incense burner that allows for this. (I have vivid memories of impulsively picking up my grandmother's metal tripod burner by the bowl when it was hot, rather than by the legs, as it was meant to be lifted. Don't make the same mistake!)

With stick incense, lifting is no problem, and it is easy to light—hence its popularity. But it lacks the drama of powdered incense burned over charcoal. In recent years, "smudge sticks"—loose bundles of dried aromatic plant material, usually sage, cedar, or lavender—have become popular as a kind of stick incense, but if you choose to use these, be aware that they tend to give off sparks, which can be dangerous. If you are going to use cone or powdered incense, you will want to use either a standing incense burner or a hanging THURIBLE on a chain.

If you're sensitive to smoke, there are also noncombustible forms of incense, notably essential oil. Essential oil comes in all of the same fragrances as combustible incense and in fact is often used in their manufacture. To use essential oil in place of incense, a small quantity can be dropped into a candle flame, just as powdered incense might be dropped on hot charcoal.

If you are truly sensitive to scent, you can also use more symbolic forms of incense, such as a cinnamon stick or a sprig of some aromatic plant, such as sage, which can be waved over the candle instead of added to the flame. Feather fans are often used to fan the smoke of combustible incense, but they can also be used in its place to simply fan the flame of the candle in a symbolic manner.

You will want to place the incense to the right of your altar. Later you will learn how to use it more specifically, but for now just enjoy its scent and let it help you achieve the magical shift in consciousness.

Water and Salt

The elements of water and earth are represented on the altar by water and salt. These are often placed in matching bowls, as they are commonly mixed in ritual. The salt is preferably sea salt, and it can be particularly nice to use a seashell for a salt dish. Rock salt can also be used, but table salt, though acceptable, should be regarded as a last resort. Salt is always useful, as a little placed on the tongue after any magical or psychic work helps to ground the excess energy.

Place your water to the left of your altar. Salt may also be placed to the left of the altar as representative of earth, but it is often placed to the right to facilitate the mixing of salt and water. This is because in certain connotations the water and salt also represent the Goddess and the God, respectively.

• • • •

Other Items

In addition to these items, your magical tools will also have a place on your altar. You will learn about these in Lesson V. There are also several other items that people usually keep on their altars, and these are described below.

Libation Dish

A libation dish is used to make liquid offerings to the Goddess, the God, or spir-

its. Often a cup of juice or wine is shared in ritual, and some of this will be offered to the deities or spirits either before or after the human participants have drunk. To make this offering, or LIBATION, a portion is placed in the libation dish and dedicated to the deities or spirits. This is a gesture of respect and sharing, a means of giving back a portion of what you receive to its source. When the ritual is done, the libation is normally disposed of by being returned to the elements; that is to say, it is emptied outside either onto soil or into running water, or perhaps into a special earth pot. In this way, its physical essence is returned to Mother Earth to nourish her and be reused for the sustenance of new life. However, some people consume the libation themselves after the ritual has ended, feeling that Spirit has taken the part of the offering it desired and left the rest for them. Which of these alternatives is preferable is largely a matter of opinion.

Offering Dish

In this same vein, a dish for food offerings may be used. An OFFERING, such as flour, corn or cornmeal, rice, a cookie, a small piece of fruit, and so on, is placed in the offering dish and dedicated to deities or spirits. Since such offerings are symbolic in nature, only a small quantity need be used. This is a means of building a psychic bond and showing respect, not giving sustenance. Like the libation, a food offering is commonly released to the elements, though it may be eaten by the celebrants in the knowledge that Spirit has taken of its essential nature, leaving the physical behind.

Burning Dish

You may wish to have a burning dish on your altar in which to burn paper in rituals that require this. Burning a paper on which we have written our desires is a common form of SYMPATHETIC MAGIC: as the paper burns, it is believed that our desires are released into manifestation. Obviously, a burning dish must be fire-resistant and big enough to accommodate a sheet of paper that has been folded once or twice.

Images

Frequently, the altar includes images of the Goddess and the God or tokens representing them (for example, an antler or acorns might betoken the God, and a seashell or a moon betoken the Goddess). You might also want images of other spirits you call upon, such as photos of ancestors or drawings of spirit guides. Also useful perhaps is a picture or a doll representing an aspect of yourself with which you commonly work or which you wish to develop further—for example, your Higher Self, or YOUNGER SELF, or key past lives.

Earth Pot

This a bowl filled with earth or rocks to honor Mother Earth and the element of earth. The earth or rocks you keep in it might come from your backyard or your birthplace or some favorite spot—or it might be gathered from various travels, the homes of friends, and so on. This lends a very special stabilizing energy to an altar. A similar effect can be achieved by a number of rocks placed loosely on the altar, especially rocks you've found.

Stones

You may want to keep crystals or gems on your altar to amplify and color the energy. You may select them or let them "select you" by finding them or selecting stones that "call" or resonate to you. A common way to tell if a stone (or any item) is for you is to run your hand over a number of items (as a selection of stones), keeping it about an inch above the items, and see which one or ones feel "different" from the others. The one that is different from the others is "calling" you and is the right one to take. Later, you will learn the meanings and uses of different stones, and this will help you to select them. But for now just take ones you like—or that like you.

Found Objects

Found objects are lucky in general and are always appropriate for your altar. They are symbolic messages from Spirit, and knowing their meanings is an ancient art. This can be an excellent way of receiving spirit messages, or OMENS, and you will learn more about it in Lesson XII. This doesn't mean just anything you find, of course, but rather things you happen across in unusual ways or in unusual places or that "speak to" you. Putting found items on the altar helps to strengthen your bond with the altar.

Seasonal Elements

Lastly, remember that you can make use of seasonal elements on your altar: leaves, flowers, acorns, pinecones, and so on. These can do a lot to help you make the shift in consciousness that is needed for magic. They also add tremendously to the atmosphere of your altar, provide variety, and commemorate the sacred Wheel of the Year.

• • • •

Always remember that your altar is personal to you. It is the visible symbol of your personal connection to Spirit. There are traditions and guidelines as to how to set it up, but ultimately it must be right for *you*; that alone determines its proper form.

• • • •

Exercises

With this lesson, you will be beginning a new series of exercises. You will discontinue doing Exercises 1 through 6 on a daily basis, though we advise you to run through them once or twice a week. The new series of exercises works with the so-called major chakras—the seven most important energy centers of the body. There are many things to learn about the chakras, but we shall only give a brief description of them at this time. They are as follows:

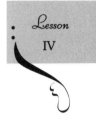

The Root Chakra

The root chakra, or base chakra, is located near the prostate in men and the para-urethral gland (the so-called Graffenberg spot) in women. This is essentially the same location for each, but due to anatomical differences it may be perceived as being different. This difference in perception is the reason why some chakra manuals describe the root chakra as being located at "the base of the spine" and why others locate it in the genitals—the former is more the perception of a male, the latter of a female. One can visualize the root chakra as being roughly centered in the lower hip region. The root chakra has to do with the will to live, vitality, and joy in life. It also has to do with the feeling that one is "in the right place" and doing those things one is meant to be doing in life. The color of the root chakra is red, and its ruler is Saturn.

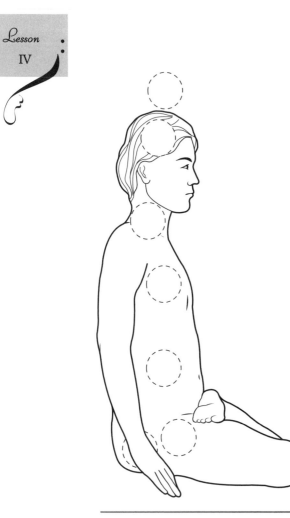

The chakras. From the top: the crown, third eye, throat, heart, solar plexus, second (sacral), and root (base).

The Second Chakra

The second chakra, or sacral chakra, is located in the gonads: for women, the ovaries, for men, the testicles. This gives the second chakra a distinctly different location in the anatomy of the two sexes. As with the root chakra, this difference in location has caused confusion in many chakra manuals. The second chakra has to do with creativity, self-expression, and independence. It also has to do with the ability to stand up for one's self. The color of the second chakra is orange, and its ruler is Mars.

The Solar Plexus Chakra

The solar plexus chakra, as you already know, is located near the navel. The center of the solar circuit, it provides great energy to the body. The solar plexus chakra also has to do with issues of self-esteem, confidence, and acceptance by others. The color of the solar plexus chakra is yellow, and its ruler is the sun.

The Heart Chakra

Located near the heart, the heart chakra has to do with issues of love, self-acceptance, compassion, and balance. The heart chakra also has to do with our ability to understand things on an emotional level. The color of the heart chakra is green, and its ruler is Venus.

The Throat Chakra

Located in the throat, the throat chakra has to do with mentality, willpower, concentration, and communication. It also has to do with our ability to understand concepts mentally and communicate that understanding to others. The color of the throat chakra is pale blue, and its ruler is Mercury.

The Third Eye

Located in the forehead, the third eye has to do with one's ability to receive information psychically and to access and use the psychic powers of the Higher Self. The third eye has to do with our ability to understand spiritual matters and to interact on a spiritual level. The color of the third eye is dark blue, and its ruler is the moon.

The Crown Chakra

The crown chakra is located at the top of the head or just above it. This chakra has to do with our connection to Spirit and our oneness with Spirit. The color of the crown chakra is violet, and its ruler is Jupiter.

• • • •

These, then, are the seven major chakras and a brief description of their qualities. By exercising them, you are working with every aspect of your being as well as preparing your ability to handle major amounts of energy. The exercises that will follow in this and future lessons are more complex than those that have come before, having more steps and more different subjects to visualize at once, but if you've been doing the first six exercises one after the other as instructed, you have had good practice at handling this level of complexity.

Exercise 7

As always, begin by finding a comfortable position and releasing all tension and anxiety. Begin by imagining a ball of red light in the root chakra, at the center of your lower pelvic region. The ball of light should be clear and bright. If the light is muddy, clouded, or dull, take a moment and will it to become clear and bright.

When you have the image of the ball of red light at the root chakra clear in your mind, move to the second chakra. For women, this will be the midabdominal region; for men, it will be at or just above the testicles. Imagine a ball of orange light here, and again, if the light is muddy or dull, take a moment and make it clear and bright.

As you make the ball of orange light in the second chakra, continue to hold the image of the red ball of light in the root chakra too. You may not be able to do this at first, but as you practice, it will become easier. As you move to each successive chakra, try to hold the image of the balls of light in the previous chakras, so that at the end of the exercise you will be visualizing seven balls of light all at once.

Now move on to the solar plexus chakra. Imagine a ball of clear yellow light in the solar plexus chakra—in the center of your trunk, behind your navel. Again, make sure the light is as clear and bright as possible. Try to hold the image of the orange and red balls of light you have already opened in the previous chakras as you create this ball of yellow light.

When the image of the ball of yellow light is clear in your solar plexus chakra, move up to the heart chakra. Create a ball of clear green light in the heart chakra—at the center of your chest, behind your sternum. Make sure the light is clear and bright. Try to hold the image of the previous three balls of colored light as you do this.

Hold the image of this ball of green light and the three that preceded it as you move on to the throat chakra. Imagine a ball of pale blue light in the center of your throat. Make the light as clear and bright as possible.

Now move on to the third eye. Behind the center of your forehead, imagine a ball of deep blue light. Make that deep blue light as clear and bright as you can, forcing out any muddiness or occlusion. Try to hold the image of all of the balls of light you have already opened as you create the ball of deep blue light at the third eye.

When the ball of deep blue light is clear in your mind, move on to the crown chakra. Just above the top of your head, imagine a ball of violet light—beautiful, clear, and bright. Try to hold the image of all seven balls of light at once. Hold this image for a few moments.

You have now "opened" each of the seven major chakras. Now you are ready to go back down. It is extremely important to close the chakras back down after you have finished working with them, and you must make sure you always do this. If you do not, you may find yourself extremely ungrounded. If that should happen, you only need to close the chakra and clear and release the energy, but it is much better to avoid the problem in the first place.

Begin with the crown chakra. Imagine the ball of violet light you have made beginning to shrink. See the ball of light grow smaller and smaller until it disappears. Now imagine a tiny open door, and then close it. Now do the same with the ball of deep blue light you created at the third eye. See it grow smaller and smaller until it disappears. Then see a small open door where the ball of light was, and close it. Repeat this for each of the chakras as you go down: throat, heart, solar plexus, second, root. Finally, clear and release all excess energy as you already know how to do.

When you first try to do this exercise, you may find it difficult to hold the image of all seven balls of light at once. Do your best. It doesn't matter if you can't do it at first—just go from one to the next. As you keep trying, you will find it easier.

By repeatedly opening, expanding, and closing the chakras in this manner, you are making them stronger, just as you would strengthen a physical muscle by exercising it. This will increase your psychic and magical abilities.

• • • •

Spell for Lesson IV
Space Cleansing

As discussed in the body of the lesson, this month's spell is a space-cleansing spell. Space cleansing is very important. Residue accumulates from the energy of the people who have been and events that have occurred in a given space. This is rather like invisible scum that adheres to the area, changing the vibration of its energy for the worse. This is especially true of places where traumatic events have occurred, but even everyday events build up a residue as well. Therefore, this kind of cleansing is very important.

Space cleansing can also be described as "purification" or "blessing" of the area. Any space can benefit from being cleansed, but it is especially important in places where people live—in particular, homes and bedrooms. Space cleansing is also very important for areas where you plan to do magical working or rituals, as energetic residue may

tend to make it harder to raise and direct energy.

The simplest form of space cleansing requires no tools or props, only your own ability to visualize. In order for it to work fully, however, you must concentrate strongly. You may wish to ask your spirit guides to help you—you do not need to know *who* they are to ask their aid, you only need to know *that* they are.

Begin by clearing and releasing all excess energy from yourself, as you have learned how to do. Enter the space you plan to cleanse, or at least stand on its periphery. Set your intent, and speak it with words like these:

> *"Behold, I do cleanse and purify this space. Nothing that is negative or harmful may remain here! I cast out all negativity, returning it to Mother Earth, that she may reuse and recycle it to better purposes."*

Now visualize a clear white or yellow light entering the room and filling it. See the room fill with the white or yellow energy until it is full, and visualize it pushing out the negativity (which you might see as bits of darkness, kind of like psychic dust). As you do this, concentrate strongly on the idea of eliminating all negativity from the place. Now say something like:

*"I do bless this space, and will
that nothing that is negative or
harmful may return here!"*

Visualize the room filling now with a pure blue-white light that goes into every part of the space, and concentrate on the idea that this light will form a barrier against all negativity. When the space is filled with blue-white light, visualize that light changing to a vivid purple in color. This raises the vibration of the energy greatly, making it impossible for negativity to remain.

Now set a seal on it by speaking words of power such as:

*"By my will, with harm to none,
as I do will, so mote it be!"*

Now clear and release all excess energy from yourself.

This is the simplest form of space cleansing. If you wish, you may augment it with certain tools: incense, for example, or holy water. To use incense, choose the form of incense you prefer: cone, stick, smudge stick, powdered, or noncombustible. Then acquire an appropriate kind of incense in that form. Incenses that are especially good for cleansing include sage, lavender, and frankincense, among others. After you fill the space with yellow-white light, take the incense and go through every part of the area, filling it with the smoke while con-tinuing to concentrate on clearing out all negativity. Then proceed as above. If you prefer a noncombustible incense, your best bet at this point in your studies would be a sprig of fresh sage, which would be waved through the area rather than burned.

Along with or instead of incense, you could use holy water. In Wiccan usage, holy water refers to any of several forms of consecrated water. One form of holy water is charged by the light of the full moon or of the sun; this is also called lustral water. Lustral water is fairly rare and is used for specific purposes. The more common form of holy water is consecrated water and salt, which is used in most rituals.

To consecrate holy water, you will need water and salt (preferably sea salt, as discussed in the body of the lesson above). Start by clearing and releasing all excess energy. Place your hand over the water. Make three tuathail or counterclockwise circles over it, concentrating on removing any negativity from it. Say something to the effect of:

*"Behold, I exorcise you, O creature
of water, casting out from you any
impurities that may lie within!"*

Imagine yellow-white light pouring down from your hand into the water and forcing out all negativity. Now make three deosil or clockwise circles with your hand over the water and say something like:

"And I do bless and consecrate
you to this work!"

Visualize the water being filled with a clear, bluish-white light. Imagine the water filling with this light until it shines as brightly as if there were a blue-white sun within it.

Now repeat this process in the same way for the salt. As water is (obviously enough) the "creature of water," so salt is the "creature of earth." When the salt is blessed, say:

"Behold, the salt is pure! Behold,
the water is pure! Purity into purity
then, and purity be blessed!"

Add three pinches of salt to the water and stir. You have now made the simpler form of holy water.

· · · ·

God for Lesson IV
The Mother

The preeminent expression of the Triple Goddess is as the Great Mother. Though the three aspects of the Goddess—Maiden, Mother, and Crone—are all equally important and form an eternal cycle of creation and re-creation, nonetheless it is her aspect as Mother that is most commonly invoked.

In her simplest form, the Great Mother represents Deity as mother of creation,

eternally loving and eternally nurturing. The Mother created the universe from herself and sustains it with her divine love and providence. In this sense, the Mother is a goddess of unconditional love, compassion, and nurturing. She is the goddess of the deep fertility and creativity necessary to create and sustain life, and she has endless reserves of strength and will.

As well as the creator of the universe, the Mother is also the ruler of the universe, but she governs the universe as a mother governs her children: with love and a desire for their growth and security.

In a more abstract sense, the Mother Goddess is "Spirit." In the *Vangelo delle Streghe*, we are told that the Primordial Goddess divided herself between the energies of the God (material world) and the Goddess (spiritual world). The Mother is that spiritual essence that infuses all things and without which our world would be nothing but lifeless matter. When we speak of the Mother Goddess in this sense, the concept of her nurturing and sustaining the universe takes on a fuller meaning.

The Mother Goddess produces all life from herself—all things are her children. She loves all of creation deeply and equally, and her only motivation is love. All things that exist are produced by her love and sustained by it—and though it may not seem so in the moment, all things ultimately move in accordance with her love.

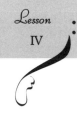

The Mother Goddess is symbolized by the full moon, representing Spirit at the height of its powers. She rules over the season of summer and the direction of the south. She rules the night as opposed to the day (the God), but from another viewpoint she is the day that follows the Maiden's dawn and precedes the Crone's dusk.

As the source of all life, the Mother is likened to the earth in some places and the sea in others. This is because each is viewed as a source of bounty and sustenance by different peoples. Sometimes she is also likened to the stars of the heavens.

The earth is often spoken of as her body, though in a wider sense the whole of the universe is her body. Every creature of the earth, from amoebas to elephants to people, is a part of the complex and interdependent ecostructure of the earth. Though they appear independent, they are no more separate than the cells that make up your body, even though each is a system unto itself. Similarly, the earth itself is an interdependent part of the universe, and it can no more be separated from the universe than your cells can be separated from you. The Universe and everything in it—All That Is—is the body of the Mother Goddess.

Thus, when we invoke the Mother Goddess, we can invoke her in a personal sense as the loving divine parent, or in a cosmological sense as the spirit of All Things.

Below follow several examples of the Goddess as Mother:

Demeter

Greek goddess of the earth and of growing things, Demeter created agriculture as a gift to humankind. The name "De Meter" means simply "the Mother." When her daughter Kore was kidnapped by the king of the dead and became Persephone, queen of the Otherworld, Demeter fell into mourning and winter came to the earth. The plants that people and animals lived on withered and died, and there was great suffering upon the earth. At length, Demeter found her daughter, and it was agreed that Persephone should spend part of the year with her mother and part of the year as queen of the Otherworld. Each year, when Persephone was in the Otherworld, winter would return to the earth, but so that people would not suffer from starvation, Demeter created grain and gave the secret of its cultivation to Triptolemus, prince of Eleusis, who then taught it to the world. In early times, Demeter was sometimes depicted as being a horse or as being horse-headed, linking her to Celtic Mother goddesses like Danu, Epona, and Rhiannon. The principal center of Demeter's worship was at Eleusis, near Athens, where the great Eleusinian Mysteries were held in her honor each year.

Gaia

Gaia, or Ge, is the Greek goddess of the earth. In Greek myth, Gaia was the Primeval Mother. Gaia's first child was Uranos, the sky god, who had no father. Thereafter, Gaia took Uranos as her consort. She became the mother of the Titans, the elder gods of Greek mythology, and of all living creatures. In time, Gaia and Uranos, earth and sky, were separated by their son, the Titan Chronos (time), who castrated his father and gave the world its current form. In modern belief, Gaia is the *Nouos*, or "World Soul"—the soul and consciousness both of the earth (as she is most commonly perceived) and, in a larger sense, of the universe, which is a single, integrated living being having both a spiritual (Goddess) and physical (God) aspect.

Laksmi

Laksmi is one of the most popular Hindu manifestations of the Great Mother Goddess. Symbolized by the "sacred cow," Laksmi is viewed as the source of material sustenance, wealth, and good fortune and as the origin of all material blessings. Laksmi is said to have arisen from a primordial sea of milk while mounted upon a lotus—a legend that links her with Padme, a creator goddess also symbolized by the lotus. Laksmi's consort is Visnu, the pre-server, and they figure together in many myths. The most famous avatars, or incarnations, of Laksmi and Visnu are Sita and Rama, and Radha and Krisna.

Mati Suira Zemlya

Mati Suira Zemlya means "Mother Moist Earth." She is the Mother Goddess of ancient Russia, and she represents the fertility of the earth itself. Mati Suira Zemlya's consort is Svarog, the sky god, and together they became the parents of the gods and of all living things. Spirit of the earth, Mati Suira Zemlya is greatly revered. She is held to be the origin of all stability, strength, and good things. When Russians speak of the "Mother Country" or "Mother Russia," it is ultimately to Mati Suira Zemlya that they are referring, though they may not always be conscious of the fact.

Yemaya

Also called Iemonja, Yemaya is the Afro-diasporic Mother Goddess. Goddess of the life-giving sea, Yemaya represents the bounty of the ocean and the waters that give fertility to the earth and sustenance to living creatures. A goddess of compassion, strength, and nurturing, Yemaya is the special patron of mothers and children and of the family.

Glossary for Lesson IV

Lesson IV

altar cloth—A cloth placed upon an altar table to enrich or decorate it. Altar cloths originated in a time when all cloth was woven by hand and embroidered cloth was a status symbol and its use a sign of an important occasion. Altar cloths are often very beautiful, and altar setups sometimes include a wall hanging behind the altar as well.

altar table—The surface on which an altar is set up, an altar table can be most anything, from a patch of ground to a marble pedestal—and anything in between. It is generally considered preferable that an altar table be made of wood or stone (or such materials as plaster or terra cotta, for that matter). Metal is usually not used because of the conductivity of its nature. However, altar pieces are often made of metal, and it is not unusual for an altar table to be decorated with metal ornaments or inlay or to have a metal frame.

ancestors—Ancestors are spirits of people who have helped to shape us into who we are. Commonly these are deceased family members, and it is in this way that the term is primarily used. But ancestors need not necessarily be people to whom we are related by blood. A deceased person who helped us in some important way or whom we particularly admire may also be considered an ancestor. Sometimes a historical personage to whom we are drawn (perhaps because of a past-life connection, of which we may or may not be conscious) will be considered an ancestor. Ancestors are the spirits we honor as being fundamental to the development of our character and to whom we have a strong psychic bond. Often they will act as spirit guides to us, advising and aiding us as we go through life. Ancestors should be acknowledged and honored regularly to strengthen the bond between us and them.

candle magic—Candle magic is the art of using a candle to focus your energy and intent to bring about a desired result. Usually, the candle is lit and focused on for a period of meditation. The candle may then be allowed to burn until it is consumed, in the belief that its burning is bringing the desired result into manifestation. Alternatively, the candle may be extinguished and the ritual repeated at intervals, such as every day for a set number of days. In addition, there are many other ways to use candles in the practice of magic. Always remember that magic is a tool of self-improvement and transformation and should be used with care and for the good of all.

deosil—This term is used to indicate clockwise movement. It literally means "southward," from the Gaelic *Deas*, or "south." Deosil movement represents the movement of spiritual energy into physical manifestation.

elements—Elements are thought of as the basic building blocks of creation. Different cultures have used different substances to symbolize the elements, and there are sometimes different numbers of them. Their correspondences also vary widely according to location. In the Wiccan religion, they are normally said to be air, fire, water, and earth. All things are said to be made up of these elements in differing proportions. It must be understood that it is not the physical substance that is meant here, but rather the spiritual qualities they represent. Air represents inspiration; fire, action; water, reaction; and earth, integration. In addition, Spirit is said to be the fifth element, of which all of the others are manifestations.

feng shui—Ancient Chinese art of geomancy based on the directions and the Asian system of five elements. Feng shui is used to align the position of buildings, to decorate rooms, and in general to divine the most auspicious place to put things to allow for a free flow of chi (spiritual energy).

geomancy—Geomancy is the art of reading the earth's energy and aligning ourselves and our works to take best advantage of it. By aligning to the natural orientation and flow of energy in this manner, we add to the effectiveness of our workings. Geomancy is a very ancient art and has a number of local variations that are still in use. On one level, geomancy deals with the earth's vortices and ley lines, delineating the energetic character of differing physical locations and the nature of their connection to each other. More commonly, however, the term *geomancy* refers to interpretation by direction. Geomancy has many uses, including selecting auspicious locations for structures or events and determining the proper directional alignment of buildings or objects.

incense—Incense is an aromatic substance used to scent the air. Incense has many forms, both combustible and noncombustible, but people generally use the term to refer to any of several varieties of combustible incense that are commonly available. These include incense cones, incense sticks, and smudge sticks—all of which are directly lit with an open flame, as from a match or lighter—as well as powdered incense, which is burned over hot charcoal rather than being directly lit itself. The use of incense is very ancient, and in its earliest form it was probably thrown directly on the fire or used to fuel the fire. Incense is used to raise the vibration of a place and to lend its own qualities to the energies being raised there. Some of the many different incenses that are commonly used include sage (cleansing and purification), cinnamon (protection and prosperity), rose (love), and sandalwood (psychic opening).

intent—We do magic by consciously focusing energy. We shape that energy through thought and emotion. The energy takes its direction from the "intent" we set into that thought and emotion. Intent is your goal or purpose—what you wish to achieve. And it is very important to be clear in intent. When you concentrate on your intent during a magical working, you are imprinting the energy with your intent so that it will shape itself to bring your intent to pass.

libation—A libation is a drink offering made to a deity or spirit. The most universal example is the pouring of a small amount of liquid directly on the earth. Another famous example is the breaking of a champagne bottle on the bow of a ship for "her" maiden voyage—this is an offering to the spirit of the ship, personified as female, in the hopes of safe and successful future voyages. Libations were one of the most popular forms of offering in the ancient world, and their use is richly attested to in classical literature. Libations are made as a sign of respect to Spirit and out of a desire to share and give back to Source, rather than as an offering of sustenance to Spirit.

magical tools—In the wider sense, magical tools are any items dedicated to use in magic. They are usually highly personal and important to the user. In a narrower sense, a Wiccan's magical tools are four: the athame or magical blade, the wand, the chalice, and the pentacle. These are the same tools around which the tarot is based, and they have roots in very ancient practice.

offering—An offering is a gift dedicated to a deity or spirit. Many different terms exist to qualify the type of offering meant: a votive offering, for example, given in fulfillment of a vow. The practice of making offerings is very ancient, and the offering must be understood to be symbolic in nature—an act of respect and honor that strengthens the bond between the deity or spirit and the offerer, rather than as giving sustenance to the spirit.

omens—Omens are messages from Spirit delivered in symbolic terms. Omens have been believed in all around the world, in every time and place. They are symbolic and are personal rather than universal in nature. That is, an individual or culture creates a language of symbols that Spirit then uses to communicate with them, so that different symbols will be used in different places. An example of an omen is the famous black cat crossing in front of someone, warning of a need to seek and heed inner guidance. Omens are based on the idea that there is no such thing as a "chance" happening and that everything that happens reflects the will of Spirit.

spirit guides—Every person has a number of spirit guides, or familiar spirits, around them. These spirits are there to help us in our lives, especially in dealing with major life lessons. They are also there to advise us, if we know how to listen to them. Spirit guides are drawn from among the spirits of people we have known and with whom we still have a strong connection. Sometimes these are people we have known in this life, and sometimes they are people we have known in other lifetimes, of which we may or may not have conscious memory. A person may have many spirit guides, but usually one special spirit

will be the main guide. This spirit is a companion and guardian throughout life, even if the person has no conscious knowledge of their presence. There are many different kinds of spirit guides, some of whom specialize in healing or the development of particular qualities or talents. But it is not necessary to know what a spirit guide specializes in to receive their help. Indeed, it is not even necessary to know they are there to be helped by them. In medieval times, spirit guides were called fairies before that term came to be attached to nature spirits instead. They are also sometimes called "guardian angels." But whatever they are called, the concept is always the same: a spiritual guide and helper who eases our journey through life.

sympathetic magic—Sympathetic magic is based on the idea of "sympathy": that items that have similar qualities can be used to represent each other and can be used to affect each other magically. Thus, because growing plants are green, green is the color of growth and increase; therefore, burn a green candle to bring prosperity. Because fire brings transformation—changing raw food to cooked, wood and other materials to ash—burning a magical charm on a piece of paper can bring transformation to a situation. In reality, these are keys or symbolic tools that we use to focus our energy and intent, which is what really makes the change.

thurible—A thurible is an incense holder suspended from a chain, and it can be hung or swung to disseminate the smoke through a given area. Sometimes extremely richly decorated, they are considered the most formal type of incense burner. They are normally used with powdered incense and charcoal, but other methods do exist. The use of the thurible is very ancient, and magnificent historical examples of them exist.

tuathail—This term is used to indicate counterclockwise movement. It literally means "northward," from the Gaelic *tuath*, or "north." The term is commonly replaced with the colloquial "widdershins," which is preferred in the Gardnerian Tradition. (Again, you will learn more about deosil and tuathail in the next lesson.)

Younger Self—"Younger Self" is a term used to describe the part of the self that is creative, spontaneous, and nonjudgmental. Commonly, this part of the self is visualized as a child version of the adult. Younger Self is sometimes described as being the place of innocence, from which all things are possible. Many people have cut themselves off from this aspect of their persona and have neglected it—sometimes as a result of trauma. Such people must make an effort to reconnect with their Younger Self and give it love and nurturing until it is fully active within them. There are many techniques for doing this, most of which involve symbolically externalizing Younger Self to show it love. But even if we have not cut ourselves off from Younger Self, we should still make a strong effort to stay connected to it and to keep it healthy and active.

Study Questions for Lesson IV

1. What is the purpose of an altar?

2. What is geomancy?

3. Which side of the altar is cool?

4. What part of the altar represents the elements of air and fire? Can you say why this is so?

5. What is an altar table commonly made of? Why?

6. Name three ways that we can use our altars.

7. How many candles should you have on your altar?

8. What does it mean to dress a candle? Why would you dress a candle?

9. Where on your altar might you put a candle to represent the Goddess?

10. What is a libation? What do you do with it after ritual?

11. What is sympathetic magic?

12. What is Younger Self?

13. What is an omen?

Lesson

IV

Lesson
V

The Airts

One of the most fundamental aspects of Wiccan thought is the importance of the four AIRTS (pronounced "eights"). The four airts, or quarters, are the guardians of the MAGIC CIRCLE. The airts are sometimes visualized in abstract form and are sometimes personified as GUARDIANS, or personal deities for the quarters.

The four airts are invoked at the beginning of almost every major Wiccan ceremony. The airts represent the totality of all existence and the furthest extent of being. They correspond to the four DIRECTIONS and the four ELEMENTS. From ancient times, all of existence was defined by these: the universe was believed to stretch outwardly toward the four directions and to be composed inwardly of the four elements. By invoking the four airts, then, we symbolize our connection to all things that exist.

Airt is a Scottish word meaning something to the effect of "wind." Throughout history, the four directions have often been

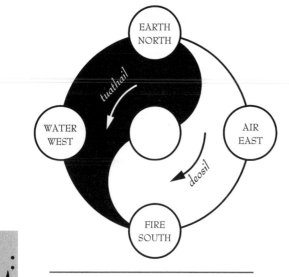

The four airts, or quarters, are
the guardians of the magic circle

represented by the four winds, especially in
classical times. The airts take their elemental correspondence from the character of the prevailing winds of the region,
and so the relationship between direction
and element varies according to different
systems.

The Scottish names for the airts are as
follows: east is Aiet, south is Deas, west
is Iar, and north is Tuath. These were the
guardians of the directions, who marked
the extent and nature of existence and
who defined the limits of the magic circle.
Clockwise movement in the circle is called
DEOSIL, or southward, and is used to raise
or charge energy. Counterclockwise movement is called TUATHAIL, or northward.
Counterclockwise movement in the circle
is used to cleanse or release energy.

The normal Wiccan correspondences of
airts to elements are as follows: east—air,
south—fire, west—water, north—earth.
The origin of these is based on the prevailing winds of Britain, but they are commonly used by Wiccans the world over today.

The four elements were believed to be
the building blocks of creation, and all
things that exist were believed to have
these four elements within them. The gull-
ible might take this literally, but in fact it
has always been understood that the names
of the elements refer not to the physical
substances of air, fire, water, and earth, but
rather to qualities represented by them.

Simply put, air represents thought,
ideas, and conceptions. It also represents
beginnings and new things. Fire represents
action and physical manifestation—creating and doing. Water represents emotion and reaction—the natural effect of
responding to what has been manifested.
Earth represents integration, wisdom, and
understanding.

This will be seen to be a microcosmic
version of the process of creation. If you
remember the creation story from the *Vangelo delle Streghe*, this idea will become even
more obvious. Air represents the period of
Diana's preexistence and her thoughts and
dreams. Fire represents Diana's creation
of the God—that is, the manifestation of
physical existence. Water shows the Goddess's reaction to her own creation: how

she was filled with emotion and desire by the beauty of the Light—that is, the God. And earth is integration: how the Goddess reunited with the God by sending souls into matter. Every time we invoke the four airts, we are symbolically reenacting this process.

Other systems of thought have had other correspondences between the elements and directions. In the Ceremonial Tradition, east is usually thought of as being fire, while south is air. Many ancient peoples, notably the Egyptians (at least in some periods), considered west to be the direction of earth and north to be water. But these variations are only different ways of understanding the same process.

The four airts are at the center of a vast system of CORRESPONDENCES that are integral to the transmission of Wiccan thought. In earlier times, wisdom was transmitted orally rather than being written. People then used the airts and their correspondences as a system of memory and patterned thought.

Some of the correspondences of the airts are as follows:

East: air, dawn, spring, youth, the Maiden Goddess, the Young God, thought, and beginnings of all sorts

South: fire, noon, summer, adulthood, the Mother, the sun king, manifestation, and action

West: water, dusk, fall/harvest, parenthood, the queen, the judge, emotion, and reaction

North: earth, night, winter, old age, the Crone, the Sorcerer, wisdom, and integration

The airts are further associated with several systems of color. Some common ones you may encounter are:

Gardnerian Wicca: air—yellow, fire—red, water—blue, earth—green

Traditional Wicca: air—red, fire—white, water—gray, earth—black

Hindu Tattwa: air—blue, fire—red, water—white, earth—yellow

The Correllian Tradition favors using the Gardnerian colors for the quarters but the traditional colors for the guardians of the quarters.

In recent years, many people have suggested that the four quarters are a newer development in the so-called Western Tradition. This is not true. The presence of the four quarters can be demonstrated over the course of thousands of years of history, particularly as guardians of the physical world. It is harder to document their use in the magic circle, yet if the magic circle is considered a microcosm of the universe, the presence of the four quarters is clearly inferred at least.

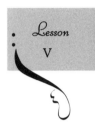

Most civilizations in the Western Tradition have included the concept of the four quarters, usually personified as their guardians. Some of these are as follows:

Egypt

The four sons of Horus: east—Qebesenuf, south—Tuamutef, west—Amset, north—Hapi

The four goddesses: east—Nephthys, south—Neith, west—Isis, north—Selket

Rome

The four winds: east—Eurus, south—Notus, west—Zephyrus, north—Boreus

Ceremonial

The four archangels: east—Raphael, south—Michael, west—Gabriel, north—Auriel

The four kingdoms: air—Sylph, fire—Salamander, water—Undine, earth—Gnome

· · · ·
Tools

The Wiccan traditions have four sacred tools. These are the ATHAME (blade), the WAND, the CHALICE, and the PENTAGRAM. Each of these corresponds to one of the airts and to all of the things associated with that particular airt. Thus, just as each airt has many correspondences, so too the Wiccan tools have many correspondences and meanings on many levels.

The Athame

Pronounced "Uh-THAH-meh" or "AH-thuh-meh," the athame, or ceremonial knife, is the first of the four major working tools. The athame is considered very sacred and is symbolic of the Wiccan religion.

The athame represents the element of air in its connotation of thought or decision. It represents the moment of first creation and symbolizes the God as son and brother of the Goddess, lord of manifestation. It is also called the Sword of Art, and it represents the phallus of the God.

More properly termed *arthame*, the athame is used in modern Wicca for a variety of purposes, most notably to cast the magic circle. The magic circle, or circle of art, is used to contain and focus the energy raised during a ritual. This is one of the central acts of Wiccan religious practice. You will learn more about the circle of art in Lesson VI.

At one time, several different sorts of ritual knives were in use, and these were differentiated by the color of their hilts. Most common were the athame, which had a black hilt, and the BOLEEN, or burin, which had a white hilt. The athame was used to cast the circle, cut herbs, and so on. The boleen was used in the creation of magical artifacts. The athame was sacred to the Goddess, while the boleen was sacred to the God. This custom, however, is not in general use today. Today, the term *athame* is used to describe any ceremonial knife, and a single blade can serve all purposes. The color of the hilt is no longer necessarily black, but rather may be and often is of any color. Contemporary athames often have hilts of wood or horn, while others have hilts of metal set with gemstones. In choosing an athame, select one that appeals to *you* and makes you feel "magical" to use. Once you have selected your athame, you will need to consecrate it. You will find simple instructions for the consecration of each of the four sacred tools in the spell section of this lesson.

You will mainly use your athame to create the magic circle. The magic circle can be used in personal workings as well as group workings. It is not necessary for everything you will do, but it can be helpful. You will learn how to cast the magic circle, or circle of art, in Lesson VI.

The Wand

The wand is the second of the four sacred tools. The wand represents the element of fire and the power of the God as consort of the Goddess, lord of cycles. In the Correllian Tradition, the wand is primarily used in invoking the quarters, for cleansings, and as part of certain specific rituals.

The purpose of the wand is to facilitate the directing of energy. One holds the wand and focuses energy through it, visualizing the energy emerging as a beam from its tip.

Wands are available in a great variety of types. You can get them made of wood, crystal, copper, or silver, or you can make your own. They can be very complex, but they can also be quite simple. The simplest form of wand, and also the oldest, is just a stick decorated in a way that has meaning for you. Feathers, stones, shells, ribbon— these and many other things can be used to decorate a wand. Many people believe a wand must be complicated, but the ancient Egyptians used wands that were simply carved in symbolic shapes, and their magic was unparalleled.

As with the athame, when you've made or selected your wand, you will want to consecrate it before use.

The Chalice

The chalice is the third sacred tool, and it represents the element of water and the power of the Goddess as mother of all creation.

A chalice can be any kind of glass or cup, and every kind imaginable is used. The chalice is used mainly to make libations, or drink offerings, and to confer blessing. To make a libation, a little bit of water, wine, or juice is placed in the chalice and then cleansed and consecrated. Blessed in ritual, the libation is offered to the Goddess, the God, ancestors, spirit guides, one's Higher Self, and so on. The libation is then left on the altar for the rest of the ritual, and perhaps a while afterward; it is then disposed of outdoors.

To confer blessing, the cup is filled with water, wine, juice, or other beverage, which is then cleansed and consecrated. The cup is blessed in the name of the Goddess and God and then drunk. As the liquid is drunk, the blessing symbolically enters the drinker. This can be done in individual or group worship.

The same technique can be used as an act of magic. In this case, the chalice is blessed for a certain effect, such as improved health. It may be drunk at once, or it can be further charged by being placed in direct sunlight or moonlight for several hours.

When you fill the chalice, bless the liquid in the following manner. Make three tuathail circles over the liquid and say, "I exorcise you, casting out from you any negativity that may lie within," while visualizing the chalice filled with yellow light. Then make three deosil circles, saying, "And I do bless and consecrate you to this work," while visualizing the chalice filled with blue-white light. Like your other tools, you will need to consecrate your chalice before you begin to use it.

The Pentagram

The pentagram is the fourth sacred tool. It represents the element of earth and the Goddess as Union of All Things. The pentagram is a five-pointed star in a circle. As a tool, it is usually worn as a medallion. The pentagram medallion can be used to focus energy and also to ground it.

To focus energy through the medallion, you visualize a ball of light in your heart chakra or your throat chakra, and then focus a beam of that light through the medallion. You can also hold the medallion in your hand and focus energy through it. In this case, you would focus through your palm chakra. You can also pull the energy down through your crown chakra and focus it through the medallion. To ground energy, you place both hands over the medallion and release into it, visualizing all excess energy going into the medallion. Then you must cleanse the medallion under running water.

You will learn more about how to do these things in future lessons. As with the other sacred tools, you will need to consecrate your pentagram medallion before use.

This image is a representation of the cosmological significance of the pentagram. The pentagram represents the four elements (air, fire, water, earth) plus the fifth element, Spirit, which gives life to all. It is also likened to a human body with arms and legs outstretched, indicating openness. In this sense, the pentagram illustrates the idea that the microcosm is one with the macrocosm, or "As above, so below." This idea is further emphasized by the division of the circle into quarters, which represent the four directions and four elements as well as the four seasons, whose sigils appear in their repective quarters. The symbols on the body of the microcosmic man illustrate the energetic circuits of the body (of which we will discuss more in future lessons). The pentagram is the sigil of the Second Degree of priesthood, and when shown with a triangle above it, as here, it is the sigil of the Third Degree's high priesthood.

The pentagram has a very ancient history. In Egypt, the five-pointed star was called Tuwa and represented the divine power, and magic in general. The pentagram, the five-pointed Tuwa star in a circle, was called Tuwat and represented the spirit realm. In Greece, the five-pointed star was the symbol of PYTHAGOREAN thought. The Pythagoreans called it the PENTALPHA, or "five As," because it could be broken down into five letter As. The Pythagoreans considered it very sacred that the pentalpha could be drawn with a single line, and they extrapolated all manner of mathematical and metaphysical theories from it. The Pythagoreans also marked the pentalpha on their palms as a sign of identification. To this day, to have a natural pentagram marked in the lines of the palm of the hand is considered in palmistry to be a sign of extreme magical potency.

The pentagram is said to represent the four elements together with the fifth element, which is Spirit. It is also said to represent the human form with arms and legs outspread.

• • • •

Exercises

You are now ready for Exercise 8. If you have not yet perfected Exercise 7, do not let that hold you back; begin practicing Exercise 8 anyway.

Exercise 8

It may be no surprise to you to find that Exercise 8 begins just like Exercise 7 did. You may have noticed something of a pattern in this by now.

Begin as usual by finding a comfortable position and releasing all tension and anxiety. Proceed through Exercise 7 just as you normally would, opening a ball of colored light at each chakra. Continue until you have all seven balls of colored light open. Instead of closing the seven balls down, however, we're going to change them.

Go back to the red ball of light at the root chakra. Imagine it changing from red to white. Make it as clear and bright a white as possible. Move up to the ball of orange light at your second chakra. See it turn from orange to white. Again, make the light as strong and clear as you can. Do the same thing for the ball of yellow light at the solar plexus chakra, then the ball of green light at the heart chakra. Go through all of the remaining chakras, changing them from the balls of colored light you have already opened to balls of clear, bright white light. At the end, you will have seven balls of white light, one in each chakra.

Hold this image for a few moments, and then shut the balls of white light down, just as you shut down the balls of colored light in Exercise 7. See each ball shrink down and disappear, and then imagine a tiny open door and close it. When you finish, clear and release.

When you can do this exercise easily, you will be ready to progress to Exercise 9.

Exercise 9

Begin by doing Exercise 8, opening the seven balls of colored light and then transforming them into seven balls of white light. When you have all seven balls open and white, return to the root chakra.

See the ball of clear white light in the root chakra. Imagine that ball of white light turn into a ball of violet light. Make the violet light as clear and bright as possible. Now do the same at the second chakra: see the ball of white light transform into a ball of violet light. Continue this through each of the chakras, transforming the balls of white light into balls of violet light. Proceed until you have a ball of violet light in each of the seven chakras.

When you have a ball of violet light in each chakra, hold that image for a few moments. Then close the balls back down as you have done in the previous exercises: see each ball of violet light shrink away, imagine a tiny open door, and close it. When you have closed the seven chakras back down, clear and release.

At this point, you should have the following daily sequence: Open seven balls of colored light, one in each chakra. Transform each ball of colored light into a ball of white light. Change each ball of white light into a ball of violet light. Then close the chakras down. Finally, clear and

Lesson

V

release. Do this on a daily basis, preferably at the same time each day, just as you have done the previous exercises. You will find this greatly beneficial to your magical and psychic growth.

. . . .

Spell for Lesson V

Consecration

This lesson's spell is a simple form of consecration that has been adapted for each of the four sacred tools. To consecrate something is to bless it for sacred use. Consecration normally involves cleansing the object of past influences and then charging it with new energy to confer the blessing and help increase the object's effectiveness. You have already seen this process in earlier lessons. In Lesson IV, you learned a simple way to make holy water, which is consecrated water.

Consecration is really quite easy. However, this has not prevented people from making it seem very complicated. It is a truth of life—and rarely more so than in the field of magic—that the simplest task can be made into quite a production number. People have devised rituals for consecration that take days—sometimes even months—to finish. But this sort of extravaganza, while it can act as a key to help us connect to our Higher Self, is certainly not a necessity.

You will find the methods outlined below quite effective—and quite easy if you've been doing the exercises provided in the Exercises section for each lesson. Use these methods as a guide, but do not feel bound by them. Remember that intent and focused concentration always matter more than outer form.

The Athame

Begin as always by clearing and releasing. Hold the athame firmly in both hands, so that the blade points toward the earth. Imagine a ball of white light in your heart chakra. Focus for a moment on the idea of cleansing and purification—in this way, you charge the light with cleansing power.

Now imagine white light flowing from your heart chakra down through your arms. See this light flowing through your hands and into the athame. Concentrate on removing all extraneous energies from the athame, and visualize the light shooting out through the blade of the athame in the form of golden-yellow flame.

As the light flows through the athame, affirm:

> *"Behold, I do cleanse and*
> *purify this sacred athame,*
> *removing from it any negativities*
> *that may lie within!"*

Continue to visualize the flame shooting out through the blade until the athame "feels" clean. Then raise the blade and point it away from you.

Again, focus on the ball of white light in your heart chakra. Allow the light to flow down through your arms and through your hands into the athame. Visualize the energy flowing through the athame and shooting out through the blade in the form of blue-white light. Affirm:

"Behold, I do bless and consecrate this athame to my use!"

Continue to focus blue-white energy through the blade for several moments. When you feel that you have done enough, stop, lower the blade, and clear and release as always. You have now cleansed and consecrated your athame. You may use this same technique whenever you feel that it needs cleaning.

The Wand

Begin as always by clearing and releasing. Hold the wand straight up and down before you, pointing it upward. Imagine the wand surrounded by a ball of yellow-white light. Focus on this light, and see it grow and expand. Concentrate on the idea of purifying the wand and cleansing it of all impurities. Say something to the effect of:

"Behold, I do cleanse and purify this sacred wand, casting out from it all negativity."

Now imagine a beam of light coming from the wand and going down to the ground. Imagine that beam of light descending into the earth, going deeper and deeper. As the beam of light goes down into the earth, it takes the impurities you have banished with it.

Now imagine a stream of blue-white light coming up from the earth and going through the beam of light and into the wand. See the wand fill with this blue-white light. Say something like:

"And behold, I do bless and consecrate this wand to my use."

Now imagine the blue-white light shooting out through the top of the wand like a geyser or a fountain of fireworks—light shooting up and arching all around you like an umbrella. Allow this to continue until you feel that there has been enough.

You have now consecrated your wand. Clear and release as always. Whenever you feel that the wand needs to have its energy cleansed or strengthened, repeat this process.

The Chalice

Begin as always by clearing and releasing. Now hold the chalice before you and imagine a stream of clear yellow-white light pouring down into the chalice from above. Concentrate on the idea of cleansing and purifying. As the light enters the chalice, imagine this light removing all negative vibrations. Continue this until the chalice is completely filled with light. See the light shining forth from the cup in all directions, like a sun. Say words to the effect of:

"Behold, I cast out all negativity
from this sacred vessel."

Now hold up the chalice and visualize it filled with blue-white light shining out in all directions. Say:

"And behold, I do bless and
consecrate this chalice to my use."

You have now consecrated your chalice. Now clear and release as always. Every time you use the chalice, bless and consecrate it again in this same way.

The Pentagram

Begin as always by clearing and releasing. Now hold your pentagram in your hands or place your hands directly over it. Imagine a ball of yellow-white light around your hands, encircling the pentagram. Concentrate on the idea of cleansing all negative energies from the pentagram. Imagine the light forcing out all impurities. Say something to the effect of:

"Behold, I do cleanse and purify
this sacred pentagram, casting
out from it any impurities
that may lie within."

Now lift up the pentagram. Imagine it glowing with blue-white light. Visualize that blue-white light growing stronger, expanding to form a ball of light around the pentagram. Now say something like:

"And behold, I do bless
and consecrate this
pentagram to my use."

You have now consecrated your pentagram. Remember to cleanse and release as always. Repeat this process anytime you feel that the pentagram needs to have its energy cleansed.

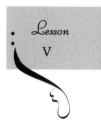

• • • •

God for Lesson V
The Crone

The third expression of the energy of the Triple Goddess is the Crone. The Crone is commonly conceived of as an elderly grandmother, and she represents the last stage of life, when the body is at its weakest but psychic and magical power are at their strongest. The Crone represents the height of feminine power and the wisdom and experience that come with age. She is the goddess of wisdom, magic, and spirituality and is traditionally thought of as the patron of Witches and Witchcraft.

The Crone is the goddess of death and endings. She is associated with the waning moon, just as the Maiden is associated with the waxing moon and the Mother with the full moon. As such, the Crone represents the ending of one cycle and the beginning of the next. In this way, she is a goddess of transformation and regeneration—the night without which there could be no dawn, the alchemical NIGREDO, or period of decay, that creates the fertile conditions for new life to grow.

As the goddess of death, the Crone breaks down our old forms to make change and rebirth possible. Since the soul can never be destroyed but can only change its outer shape, death must be understood not as an ending but as a process of growth and continual regeneration. Thus, the Crone is not so much the Destroyer as the Transformer, and her work is a benefit to the soul, which would otherwise grow stagnant and be unable to complete its purposes in the material world. Without the "destruction" brought by the Crone, physical form would be immutable and thus limiting rather than empowering to the soul. In this sense, the Crone might be compared to science's BLACK HOLE: constantly swallowing up matter in one place only to spit it back out in a new form elsewhere.

This aspect of "destruction" is one reason why the Crone is often regarded with fear. Because we readily perceive the destruction of the old form but rarely see the emergence of the new one, we are afraid of change. We do not realize that only through change can growth come. And so for many, the Crone Goddess is a fearsome and terrifying deity. But this should not

be so to the Wiccan, who should strive to understand the Crone's inner mystery of rebirth and regeneration.

As well as a goddess of death, the Crone is also a goddess of wisdom and of secrets revealed. The Crone rules all of the arcane arts and, as goddess of the Otherworld, is patron of the higher powers of the soul. It is in this sense that she is patron of Witchcraft. But here too the Crone is sometimes perceived as a terrifying figure—for the path to wisdom is not an easy one, and the seeker is confronted with many challenges along the way, chief among which is the need for self-knowledge. Nothing does more to empower us and further our psychic and spiritual growth than knowledge of self, yet it is often the case that few things terrify us more, because in knowing ourselves we must in time confront and heal every weakness, every regret, and every psychic wound we have suffered—and most of us would rather just bury these. This path of self-knowledge is the very heart of true Wicca and is the demesne of the Crone.

It is as the patron of the quest for self-knowledge that the Crone most often figures in mythology. Whether as Baba Yaga in contemporary Russian folklore or as Venus in the story of Cupid and Psyche, a central myth of the Crone has a youthful protagonist seek her out in search of some boon, great or small. The Crone—who is usually portrayed as living far from the mundane world, as true wisdom often does—always agrees to grant the boon that is sought, but only if the protagonist can fulfill a series of seemingly impossible feats. Many others have failed before, the frightened protagonist is told. Yet—usually with supernatural help, commonly in the form of "the animals"—this protagonist succeeds against all odds and gains the desired boon.

From this myth, it can be seen that while the uninitiated may view the Crone as a fearsome and terrible goddess, those who confront her mysteries without fear will invariably find her their benefactor.

Below follow several examples of the Goddess as Crone:

Baba Yaga

Baba ("Grandmother") Yaga is the Russian form of the Crone Goddess. Yaga figures in many contemporary folktales in which a young protagonist seeks out or stumbles upon her enchanted cottage and asks a boon from her—receiving it only after fulfilling many near-impossible tasks. Baba Yaga is portrayed as an ancient and wizened Witch who flies through the air in a magical MORTAR AND PESTLE, or sometimes a flying horse, and has power over the elements. Yaga lives in a remote forest in a magical cottage that walks around of its own accord on giant chicken's legs, and her home is guarded by a fence of stakes on which are mounted the skulls of unsuccessful seekers (the protagonist's own previous lives).

Hekate

Hekate is the ancient Greek form of the Crone Goddess. Associated with the moon, Hekate was often shown with three heads or faces or as three women standing together. This was to represent the moon's three phases, and in this sense Hekate has aspects of Maiden and Mother as well as Crone, though it is primarily as Crone that she is worshipped. Goddess of prophecy, magic, and Witchcraft, Hekate was worshipped at the crossroads and was considered a queen of the Otherworld. Her principal symbols included the key and the torch, as her wisdom could unlock and illuminate all mysteries. Hekate's totem animal was a black dog. In medieval Europe, Hekate was called Dame Hecat.

Kali

Kali is the most famous Hindu example of the Crone form of the Goddess. Kali is usually shown as a jet-black goddess with many arms, wearing a necklace of skulls that represent the cycle of death and rebirth. Sometimes also she wears various other human body parts or serpents as part of her costume. Her blood-red tongue is shown extended, like that of the Greek Gorgon; this shows her regenerative aspect. Kali's consort is Shiva the Destroyer, and she is often shown standing or dancing upon his recumbent body, as goddess of death and transformation.

Morrighan

Morrighan, the Irish name of this Celtic form of the Crone Goddess, means "Queen of Ghosts," emphasizing her role as a goddess of the dead. Other versions of her name, such as Morgana and Morgaine, make reference to the sea, which in insular Celtic religion is associated with the Otherworld. Morrighan is a goddess of magic and sorcery and is sometimes shown as ancient and withered, or conversely as preternaturally beautiful. Morrighan is also the goddess of sovereignty, and in many myths she approaches a would-be King or Hero in her aged form, demanding sexual favors. When the Hero makes love to the aged woman, she transforms into a beauty in his arms and prophesies his rise to kingship. Morrighan has different consorts in different areas, including both the Dagda and Mannanan Mac Llyr, both gods of the Otherworld. Morrighan figures in the myth of King Arthur as Arthur's magical half-sister, who is sometimes a friend and sometimes an antagonist but who in many versions ultimately conveys Arthur to the magical realm of Avallon (the Otherworld).

Tlacolteutl

The name Tlacolteutl means "Refuse Eater," because this Aztec Crone had as one of her chief characteristics the quality of consuming outmoded forms and transmuting them. At the end of their lives, Aztecs could make a confession to Tlacolteutl, who would cleanse their soul of any wrongdoing they related, allowing them to enter the Otherworld without regret. Goddess of magic and sorcery, Tlacolteutl was sometimes portrayed riding naked on a broomstick and wearing a horned headdress, revealing a similarity of archetypes with European Witchcraft. As a goddess of death, Tlacolteutl is sometimes portrayed as an old woman, but she also has aspects as a Maiden and Mother goddess and so is sometimes portrayed as a seductive beauty. The most famous image of Tlacolteutl shows her in the act of giving birth.

. . . .

Glossary for Lesson V

airts—*Airt* is a Scottish Gaelic term meaning something to the effect of "wind." In Scottish Traditional Wicca, when the magic circle was cast, the four winds, or airts, would be summoned to stand guard over it and to aid the ritual being performed. The airts are identified with the four directions, the four elements, and a host of other correspondences. In Gaelic, east was ruled by Aiet, whose color was red and whose time was dawn. South was ruled by Deas (from which the word *deosil* comes), whose color was white and whose time was noon. West was ruled by Iar, whose color was gray and whose time was dusk. And north was ruled by Tuath, whose color was black and whose provenance was the night. This system is illustrated by the ancient song "Black Spirits," used by Shakespeare in *MacBeth*. The first line of the song runs, "Black Spirits and Red, White Spirits and Gray, mingle, mingle, mingle, as ye mingle may!"

athame—The magical knife, or athame (or arthame), is an ancient tool of magic. It is used for many purposes, including casting the magic circle and preparing various magical items or ingredients. In certain traditions, the athame must be of a particular color and be made in a particular way, but in general use today, an athame can be any sort of knife.

black hole—In science, a black hole is a void in space that sucks up and destroys matter. The opposite side of a black hole is a white hole, which spews forth matter. Thus the two, which are opposite sides of the same, simultaneously destroy old matter and use it to create new. In this way, they reflect the nature of the Crone and Mother aspects of the Goddess, which respectively destroy old forms and give birth to new.

boleen—At one time, there were a number of variations on the idea of the magical knife, most of which are no longer in general use. One of these divided the

magical knife into two instruments: the black-handled athame, used for various magical operations, notably casting the magic circle, and the white-handled boleen, used to create magical artifacts such as the wand and various engraved symbols. The athame was considered sacred to the Goddess, while the boleen, or burin, was considered sacred to the God, since it was used in physical operations.

chalice—The cup used in Wiccan ritual, said to be cognate to the Holy Grail and magical cauldron of ancient mythology. The chalice represents the womb of the Goddess, from which all creation proceeds.

correspondences—Correspondence is a teaching system that uses the idea of sympathy to say that items that have similar qualities may be represented by each other. Thus, the direction of east is said to correspond to the element of air, the quality of thought, the dawn of the day, the spring of the year, the beginning of any project, the Maiden Goddess (such as Aradia or the Greek Kore), the Young God (such as Horus or the Green Man at spring), and many other things. Used in part as an aid to memory, the system of correspondence illustrates the idea that "As above, so below" and is used at the heart of the system of allegory

through which many Pagan and Wiccan ideas are portrayed and transmitted.

deosil—The term *deosil* refers to clockwise motions—that is, movement that goes in the same direction as the apparent motion of the sun. For this reason, it is also sometimes called sunward motion. In magic, deosil movement is used for raising energy, while counterclockwise or tuathail motion is used to disperse energy. We raise energy to aid in the working of magic and the manifestation of those things we wish to bring about. For this reason, most motion in the magic circle will be deosil. The word *deosil* means "southward" and takes its name from the Scottish term for the airt of the south, Deas. In correspondence, Deas is also identified with the noonday and the sun. Almost all peoples have considered sunward motion to be indicative of manifestation. You will hear some people claim that such and such a people used counterclockwise motion to indicate manifestation and work magic, but this is not so. The confusion arises from the use of the terms *right* and *left* to describe movement in the circle. Clockwise movement always goes to the right, yet if you stand in a circle with others holding hands and pass energy around the circle clockwise, you will notice that you receive it through your right hand

and pass it on to the left; it is from this that the confusion arises.

directions—The idea of representing the earth as defined by four directions is ancient. Four is said to be the number of manifestation because there are four directions that define the earth and four elements that compose it. Historically, the four directions have been personified in many ways: in Egypt as the four sons of Horus who held up the sky at the four corners of the earth, and in the Greco-Roman world as the four winds, for example. Ceremonials associate the directions with the four archangels, or lesser gods of their tradition. The four directions are represented by the equal-armed cross, often placed in a circle to represent the world of physical manifestation.

elements—Just as there are four directions, so too are there four elements. The four elements are said to be the building blocks of all creation, contained in varying degrees in all things. The elements are usually defined as air, fire, water, and earth, though it should be understood that it is not the physical substances named, but rather the qualities associated with them that are being referred to. It is also allowed that there is a fifth element, Spirit, but it is often listed separately from the four. In different times and cultures, there have been many variations in the theory of the elements, but the basic concept—that all living things contain a mixture of the same qualities—remains the same.

guardians—The "guardians" are the personified powers of the four airts and all they represent. The guardians are represented in many different ways, and have been throughout history. In Egypt, the guardians were particularly represented by the four sons of Horus and also by the four goddesses who guarded the tomb. To the Greco-Romans, the guardians were most often represented as the four winds, while to Ceremonials they are commonly portrayed as the four archangels of Judeo-Christian tradition. In many traditions, the guardians are represented as animals, and this symbolism is evident in many tarot decks. In Wicca, the guardians may be represented in many different ways, both as personifications of the powers of the airts and as abstract forms. A particularly popular form is as a column of white light drawn up from the earth.

magic circle—The magic circle, or circle of art, is used to create sacred space in which to perform ritual, commune with our Higher Selves, or work magic. The magic circle is a microcosmic reenactment of the process of creation and represents our ties to all of existence. Many people think of the magic circle as being primarily for protection, but in fact it serves to heighten and help focus magical power, and this is the principal reason for its use. You will learn more about the magic circle, or circle of art, in Lesson VI.

mortar and pestle—The mortar and pestle are implements used to grind plant or mineral materials into powder. Material to be ground is placed into the cup-like mortar and then ground by rotation of the hand-held pestle. The mortar and pestle were once widely used in household cooking, before packaged spices became readily available. They are still sometimes used as symbols of the apothecary's art. But today, the primary use of the mortar and pestle is for the magical preparation of herbs for incenses, essential oils, and so on. In Spanish, the mortar and pestle are termed *mano y metate* and are still commonly used in cooking; thus, they are available at many Hispanic stores.

nigredo—In alchemical thought, the polar opposites are combined and dissolved through the application of spiritual heat in the athanor, or alchemical furnace. The opposites decay, becoming a thick black residue called the nigredo. Only from this putrefied state can new

growth arise. Out of the nigredo comes the peacock's tail, a series of glorious colors that occur as new life is fertilized and begins to grow. What this means, among other things, is that preconceived forms must first be broken down before true growth can occur. Only then can we ascend the rainbow bridge to the Divine.

pentagram—The pentagram, a five-pointed star in a circle, is the principal symbol of the Wiccan religion. The symbol was used in ancient Egypt to represent the concept of magic (without the circle) and the spirit world (with the circle). In classical times, the pentagram, also called pentalpha, was used by the Pythagoreans, a Greek philosophical school with a reputation for deep metaphysical knowledge. In the medieval period, the symbol continued to flourish, being used by a number of groups, including some Christians. The pentagram has many meanings, notably the union of the five elements (air, fire, water, earth, and the element that underlies them all, Spirit), which in turn corresponds to the union of spirit and matter and the attainment of spiritual illumination, as well as the ancient maxim "As above, so below" (because the five-pointed star can be taken to repre-

sent the human body, illustrating our oneness with all creation).

pentalpha—The pentalpha, or "five As," was the sacred symbol of the Pythagoreans and is more familiarly known today as the pentagram. The Pythagoreans used the pentalpha and the five Tetraktys triangles of which it was composed to convey many metaphysical truths. Extremely popular in Hellenistic and Roman times, Pythagoreanism passed into the medieval period through scholarly sources and continues to be a major building block in most all metaphysical systems of thought today.

Pythagorean—The Pythagorean philosophy was founded by Pythagoras, a native of the Greek island of Samos who lived in the fifth century BC (seventh century of the Age of Aries). To the Greeks, *philosophy* was a term that indicated a private belief system, as opposed to *religion*, which was a system of public rituals centered on family or community. The Greeks had many differing philosophical schools, and the Pythagorean was among the most mystical and profound. Pythagorean ideas have never ceased to be current, and they are a crucial building block of modern Wiccan thought. You will find Pythagoras's teachings reflected throughout this series of lessons. Fascinated by mathematics and the musical scale, Pythagoras was a pioneer of the metaphysical science of numerology: the idea that numbers have individual characteristics that can be used to describe universal truth as well as to divine individual truths. Pythagoras used numerology to illustrate his ideas about the universe, the soul, cosmic laws, and the nature of spiritual evolution. The central symbol of Pythagoras's philosophy was the Tetraktys, the "golden triangle." This sacred symbol, triangular or pyramidic in shape, described the way in which Deity began as one, became two, and added the magic of three to bring about manifestation as four—the whole of which equals ten (10), which numerologically reduces back to one (1), meaning that Deity and the created world are cognate, or in other words, "As above, so below." When five of these Tetraktys triangles were put together, they formed a symbol called a pentalpha ("five As"), from which many other universal truths were enumerated. The pentalpha was the symbol by which the Pythagoreans became known, and today it is more commonly called the pentagram ("mark of five"). When the *Sepher Yetzirah* delineated the ideas of Hebrew

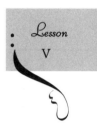

Kabbalah eight centuries later, it drew heavily upon the ideas of Pythagoras. Pythagoreans also taught the concept of reincarnation and the idea of transmigration of souls, and his followers regularly practiced what is today called "past-life regression."

tuathail—The term *tuathail* refers to counterclockwise motions—that is, movement that goes opposite from the apparent motion of the sun. In magic, tuathail movement is used for cleansing, purifying, or removing things. For example, tuathail movement is used when the magic circle is being taken down. The word *tuathail* means "northward," taking its name from the Scottish word for the airt of the north, Tuath. Gardnerians and many Wiccan traditions influenced by them often call tuathail by the colloquial term *widdershins*.

wand—Everybody knows about the Witches' magic wand, right? The wand, or staff, is used in Wiccan ritual for a variety of purposes related to the focusing of energy. In Correllian Wicca, the wand is most commonly used as an instrument to aid in the calling of the airts, or quarters.

Study Questions for Lesson V

1. What does the word *airt* mean? From what language does it come?

2. What is deosil? Why is it called that? What is its opposite?

3. What is widdershins? What is the Gaelic term for this?

4. What are the four elements? Are they thought of the same way in all cultures?

5. With what direction do we identify the element of fire?

6. What do we mean by guardian of the quarter?

7. What are some qualities that correspond with the north?

8. What are the traditional Wiccan quarter colors?

9. What is a boleen?

10. What is an athame? What is the color associated with it?

11. Which of the four sacred tools is associated with the west?

12. Who was Pythagoras?

13. What is the pentalpha? Why did the Pythagoreans use that name?

Lesson VI

The Circle of Art

The circle of art, or MAGIC CIRCLE, is a fundamental part of modern Wiccan practice. The magic circle is cast at the beginning of most Wiccan ceremonies to establish SACRED SPACE and to aid in the raising and focusing of energy. At the end of the ceremony, the circle is opened, releasing the energy of the ritual so that it can become manifest in the physical world.

We use the term *sacred space* to indicate an area used for ritual or magic. An area becomes sacred space when it is specially prepared to aid in the shift of consciousness needed to connect with the Higher Self in magic or worship. It is from the level of our Higher Self that we are able to work magic. There are many ways to create sacred space, but all revolve around the cleansing of the area of NEGATIVE ENERGY, which might hamper the working, and the erection of various ENERGY CONSTRUCTS, whose purpose is to intensify the energy being worked with.

The magic circle is such an energy construct. It is created from energy, shaped by thought and emotion. Though the magic circle has a strong symbolic aspect, it also has an objective reality, which has a definite effect on the people inside the circle. Because it is composed of concentrated energy, the circle acts as a "BATTERY," giving extra energy to whatever is done inside it. And because it acts to focus the energy raised within it, the circle also tends to intensify that energy. In these ways, the circle magnifies the power of the people within it. It is this effect that is the principal reason for its use.

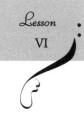

• • • •

History of the Circle

The idea of holding ritual in a circle is very ancient, in all likelihood deriving from nothing more august than the fact that when people "gather 'round" they tend to do exactly that: gather in a roughly round, or circular, form. The circle allowed everyone to hold hands with everyone else and to have the same general view of the proceedings. It was practical. A circle was a sensible way to gather around a central fire, or a sacred tree, or an altar.

The circle was also an excellent form for dancing, which has figured in Pagan rituals since the dawn of time. Many ancient illustrations in art and literature attest to the popularity of the CIRCLE DANCE in ancient times. Though frowned upon by the book religions, circle dancing remained a festival custom of European peasants into modern times, and the practice is nicely illustrated in the works of Bruegels, among other artists. In De Lancre's famous illustration of "The Witches' Sabbat," several circle dances of this kind are shown.

In CEREMONIAL MAGIC, the circle was used for protection, since the Ceremonials often believed that the powers they were dealing with could harm them. But in Wicca, the circle is not used for protection but rather to intensify the powers being worked with.

• • • •

How to Cast a Circle

Casting a magic circle is a basic technique that every Wiccan learns. The more you do it, the better you will get at it and the easier it will become. You will use this technique for casting ritual circles in which to worship and to cast circles to strengthen your magical workings.

Not everything requires the use of a magic circle. The circle is used for worship ceremonies, but it is not necessary for private devotions. Most spellwork does not require casting a circle either, but if a spell is really important, casting a circle will generate much more energy for the spell. Generally, only the individual can determine if they need a circle for a given spell, and once you have sufficient experience, you will find it an easy thing to judge. Casting a circle makes for a longer and more complicated working, but it creates a much stronger effect.

• • • •

Reasons for Cleansing

Before you set up your magic circle, you will first want to cleanse and consecrate the area. By cleansing the area, you remove any negative energies that might be there, and by consecrating it, you prevent those negative energies from returning.

What are negative energies? The term *negative energy* refers to energy that in any way detracts from the effectiveness of a working or the quality of life in general. It should not be thought that "negative" means "evil," but rather "unfocused." Negative energy is energy that is undirected or polluted with various emotional charges that will tend to hamper the free flow of consciously directed energy.

Because energy responds to emotion, it can become charged with all sorts of feelings. A psychically sensitive person can pick up on these feelings, and they can be magnified by magical working. Anger, fear, sadness—these and many other emotions can color energy, shaping that energy without conscious intent. The energy then holds these emotions and can tend to pass them on to sensitive people.

The stronger the initial emotion, the longer negative energy will tend to hold it. Sometimes energy will hold such a charge for a very long time. This is why certain places that have witnessed traumatic events can give us "bad vibes": the energy of the place has been imprinted with the negative emotions experienced there.

Most negative energy is not that focused, however. Usually, the emotional charge is not so strong, and it diffuses over time. Most negative energy contains little bits of many conflicting emotions culled from many sources, which tends to give it a "muddy" feeling. This energy is unfocused and undirected and can tend to make concentration difficult. By removing it, you will find that you can work much more effectively.

• • • •

How to Cleanse

There are many ways to cleanse your ritual space of negative energy. Techniques range from simple to complex and can make use of many different tools. Some use water, some use smoke, others use visualization, and still others use sound or ritual movement. With experience, you will find the one that works best for you. But in this lesson, we are simply going to give you a good technique that we think will work well for you: cleansing with salt and water.

To do this, you will first clear and release all excess energy, as you should before every magical working. Now place your hand over the water. Make three tuathail (counterclockwise) circles over the water, concentrating on removing any negativity from it. Say something to the effect of:

"Behold, I exorcise you, O creature of water, casting out from you any impurities that may lie within!"

Imagine yellow-white light pouring down from your hand into the water and forcing out all negativity.

Now make three deosil (clockwise) circles with your hand over the water. Say something like:

"And I do bless and consecrate you to this work!"

Visualize the water being filled with a clear bluish-white light. Imagine the water filling with this light until it shines as brightly as if there were a blue-white sun within it.

Now turn to the salt. Place your hand over the salt and make three tuathail circles over it, concentrating on removing from it any negativity. Say something to the effect of:

"Behold, I exorcise you, O creature of earth, casting out from you any impurities that may lie within!"

Imagine yellow-white light pouring down from your hand into the salt and forcing out all negativity.

Now make three deosil circles with your hand over the salt. Say something like:

"And I do bless and consecrate you to this work!"

Visualize the salt being filled with a clear bluish-white light. Imagine the salt filling with this light until it shines as brightly as if there were a blue-white sun within it.

Now say something to the effect of:

"Behold, the salt is pure! Behold, the water is pure! Purity into purity then, and purity be blessed!"

Add three pinches of salt to the water and stir. You have now made holy water. Take the holy water and go deosil around the area in which you are going to erect your circle.

As you go around the area, ASPERSE it—that is, sprinkle it with holy water. As you do this, imagine the area being flooded with yellow light. Let the yellow light fill the area, going out in all directions for a good distance. This is the act that actually sends out the negativity, so focus on it as strongly as possible.

As you asperse the area, you may wish to say something to the effect of:

*"Behold, I cleanse and
purify this space."*

When you have made a full circle, replace the holy water on the altar. Turn to face the inside of the circle and say something to the effect of:

"I bless and consecrate this space!"

Now visualize the area being filled with a clear blue-white light, so that it is wholly filled in all directions. You have now cleansed and blessed your ritual space, and you are ready to cast the circle itself.

• • • •

Casting the Circle

Traditionally, the magic circle is cast with the athame, or ritual knife. If you do not yet have an athame, you can use your FIN-GER instead. Just point it as you would the blade of the knife.

Beginning in the east, point your athame outward. The boundaries of the magic circle do not have to conform to the room you are in. Since the circle is an energy structure, it is not hampered by walls, and it can be much larger than the room—so make it a comfortable size. Just be sure that you have cleansed whatever area you include in the circle and that there are not other people wandering through it.

Imagine a beam of light shooting out from the tip of the athame toward the east.

It is best if the light is white or red. (Red will add extra strength to it.) Imagine this beam as being like a bolt of lightning, and focus on the strength of this energy. Send the beam of light out to what will be the farthest edge of your magic circle.

Now begin to walk deosil around the circle, keeping the athame pointed outward with the beam of light coming out from it. As you walk, imagine that you are using the athame and the beam of light to "draw" a boundary line out in the distance. Imagine this boundary as a thick line of bright white light. Concentrate on this boundary being strong and full of energy.

The most important thing is to focus on the boundary being strong, but if you wish to speak, there are a number of incantations you can say during this process. A good example is as follows:

*"Behold, I do cut apart a space
between the realms of humankind
and of the Mighty Ones—a
circle of art, to focus and contain
the power raised herein!"*

Continue on around the circle until you return to the east. Imagine the end of your boundary linking up to its beginning, becoming a solid ring.

Make sure that you and anyone you may be working with have done everything they need to do before the circle is cast, because

once cast, it is best not to "break" the circle. That is, you should not walk through the barrier you have erected. This is because the magic circle acts as a containment, focusing the energy within it and making it stronger. Every time the circle is broken, this effect is weakened and a certain amount of energy "leaks out."

If the circle must be broken, use the athame to "cut a door"—that is, to make an opening in the circle of white light you have drawn. You do this by pointing the athame at the edge of the circle and imagining again the beam of light coming from its tip. Now imagine the barrier of white light broken at the point where the beam of light from the athame touches it, and move the athame tuathail (to the left), imagining the barrier of white light disappearing from that space as you do so. Open only enough space in the barrier for the person to exit, and then immediately reseal the circle by moving the athame back to the right (deosil) and visualizing the barrier of white light filling back in to become whole again.

• • • •

Calling the Airts

Now that you have cast the magic circle itself, you are ready to call the quarters. You learned about the airts, or quarters, in Lesson V. Now you will learn how to call them. As with everything else in Wicca,

there are many ways to do this. For the purposes of this lesson, it is only our intention to give you one simple form to use. Once you become proficient with this form, you can learn others.

The airts are the four cardinal points in the circle: east, south, west, and north. It is normal to invoke them at the beginning of a ritual to guide and aid you in what you are doing. Often, the airts are personified as guardians or identified with deities. Then again, sometimes they will be visualized as animals or as pure elemental forms.

In the Correllian Tradition, we normally begin in the east, the direction of new beginnings, as do many other traditions. Some traditions start in the north, however. This is just one of many variations between traditions: in Wicca, each different tradition, and often each different temple, is free to make what variations it needs for the growth of its members. Thus, we will begin here in the east.

Stand facing in the direction of the east. Imagine a column of white light rising up before you. Invoke the quarter with words to this effect:

"Hail unto you, O guardian of the Watchtower of the East, power of air and intellect. We pray that you will be with us this night in our circle, and that you will give your blessing and your

aid to this our undertaking! We
bid you hail, and welcome!"

Now go to the south. Again imagine a column of white light rising up before you. Invoke the quarter with words to this effect:

"Hail unto you, O guardian of
the Watchtower of the South,
power of fire and manifestation.
We pray that you will be with us
this night in our circle, and that
you will give your blessing and
your aid to this our undertaking!
We bid you hail, and welcome!"

Now go to the west. Imagine a column of white light rising up before you. Invoke the quarter with words to this effect:

"Hail unto you, O guardian of
the Watchtower of the West,
power of water and emotion. We
pray that you will be with us this
night in our circle, and that you
will give your blessing and your
aid to this our undertaking! We
bid you hail, and welcome!"

Finally, come to the north of the circle. Again, imagine a column of white light rising up before you. Invoke the quarter using words like these:

"Hail unto you, O guardian of
the Watchtower of the North,
power of earth and integration.
We pray that you will be with us
this night in our circle, and that
you will give your blessing and
your aid to this our undertaking!
We bid you hail, and welcome!"

You have now successfully invoked the four airts to guard and aid your magic circle. They too will add power to the work you are doing, as does the magic circle itself.

Your magic circle is now cast. You would then commonly follow with invocations to Deity and the body of your ritual or spell.

Lesson
VI

• • • •

Devoking

When you have finished your working, you will have to take down the circle. This is usually easier than erecting it, and it is done in exact reverse order.

You will begin by thanking Deity, but we will talk more about invocations and thanks to Deity in Lesson VII. Next, you must DEVOKE the quarters. Just as you build your circle with deosil movements, you take it down with tuathail movements. Tuathail motions are used for the cleansing and releasing of energy. Thus, you will begin devoking the quarters from the north and then move around the circle in a counterclockwise manner.

Face the north, and again see the column of white light you raised when you invoked the quarter. Speak words to this effect:

> *"Guardian of the Watchtower of the North, power of earth and manifestation, we thank you for your presence here tonight—we thank you for your aid, and your guidance. May there be peace between us now and always. Go if you must—stay if you will. We bid you hail, and farewell!"*

As you say this, imagine the column of white light sinking back down into the earth.

Now move to the west. Again, see the column of white light you raised before. Speak words to this effect:

> *"Guardian of the Watchtower of the West, power of water and emotion, we thank you for your presence here tonight—we thank you for your aid, and your guidance. May there be peace between us now and always. Go if you must—stay if you will. We bid you hail, and farewell!"*

Now see the column of light sink down into the ground.

Move now to the direction of the south. As before, see the column of white light you raised when you invoked the quarter. Speak words to this effect:

> *"Guardian of the Watchtower of the South, power of fire and manifestation, we thank you for your presence here tonight—we thank you for your aid, and your guidance. May there be peace between us now and always. Go if you must—stay if you will. We bid you hail, and farewell!"*

See the column of light sink back into the earth.

Finally, return to the east. See the column of white light you raised when you invoked the guardian of the east. Speak words to this effect:

> *"Guardian of the Watchtower of the East, power of air and intellect, we thank you for your presence here tonight—we thank you for your aid, and your guidance. May there be peace between us now and always. Go if you must—stay if you will. We bid you hail, and farewell!"*

See the column sink back down into the earth.

You are now ready to uncast the circle. Take up your athame and return to the east. Once again point your athame toward the east and imagine a beam of light shooting out from the tip of the knife to the very edge of the circle, connecting with the barrier of white light you created earlier. This time you will walk tuathail, imagining the circle of light disappearing back through the beam of light into the athame. Continue around the circle until you return to the east and the whole of the barrier of white light is gone. The circle is now open.

During the process of opening the circle, you may or may not wish to say something. If you do, the following is a common incantation to use:

"As above, so below. As
the universe, so the Soul.
As without, so within."

And, having finished opening the circle, it is customary to declare:

"The circle is open but unbroken!"

If more than one person is in the circle, it is customary in many groups to end with the following ritual salute:

"Merry meet, merry part,
and merry meet again!"

The salute indicates the desire to continue working together in a spirit of joy and love.

These, then, are the basic instructions for casting the magic circle. There are many possible variations, including different ways to visualize the process, and you may wish to adopt these with time and experience. But this is a good technique to start with.

• • • •

Exercises

You should now regularly be doing Exercises 7, 8, and 9. From here forward, you will use these exercises as the opening sequence for a variety of other exercises, which will be introduced gradually.

Open your chakras as usual with Exercises 7, 8, and 9. But once you have all seven balls of light open and have transformed them from colored balls to white and then to violet, allow that image to simply dissipate or dissolve. You now have all seven chakras open, which will afford you increased energies for the exercises that follow—in this case, Exercise 10. After you have finished Exercise 10, imagine again your seven balls of energy, and then go back down through the chakras and close them just as you normally would.

Lesson
VI

Exercise 10: The Lemon

Do this exercise every day for one week. After that, do it once a week, or more often if you desire. This exercise is designed to help cleanse and purify your energy. It will also help you to access more and clearer energy. In addition, this exercise can be helpful anytime you feel energetically blocked or physically ill.

As has been said, begin by opening your chakras as usual with Exercises 7, 8, and 9. Begin by visualizing a ball of white light in front of you, between your two hands. As always, concentrate on making that ball of white light as clear and bright as possible.

Now, within the ball of white light, imagine a large yellow lemon. Make the image of the lemon as clear and real as you can. See its bright yellow color, feel the texture of its rind, and imagine its fresh citrus scent.

From within the lemon, imagine still more white light radiating, as if there were a tiny sun within the fruit. Lift the ball of light with the lemon inside up and over your head. You can make this gesture with your physical hands, or you can visualize doing it. Now bring the ball of light down into your head so that the lemon is about at the center of your head.

Visualize the lemon contracting, as if squeezed by an invisible hand. Clear yellow lemon juice flows out of the lemon.

The juice is shining with light. Imagine that lemon juice flowing to every part of your body. The juice absorbs all negativity it encounters, turning dull, even brownish, as it does so. Let the juice absorb for a few moments. Then imagine all of the juice, together with the negativity it has absorbed, flowing back up into the lemon.

Now lift the ball of white light with the lemon inside it back out of your head and bring it down in front of you. Imagine the ball shrinking down, growing smaller and smaller, with the lemon inside. When the ball is so small you can no longer see it, symbolically blow it away. Ask the Goddess to take the energy and reuse it in more positive ways. Finally, clear and release as always.

· · · ·

Spell for Lesson VI
A Simple Invocation

An invocation is a prayer for the presence and aid of Deity—either Universal Deity or a personal deity. An invocation can be addressed to Universal Deity, to the Goddess and/or the God, or to a particular goddess or god—all are ultimately manifestations of the same Universal Power.

To make an invocation, speak to Deity from your heart, and with love. You should always address Deity with respect, but the particular words you use are not so important as the sincerity behind them. You will learn more about invoking Deity in Lesson VII, but for now we will give you a simple, all-purpose invocation that is good for any use, here presented in the context of a simple house-blessing ritual.

Select your ritual space and set up your altar. You will need a tarot deck to perform this invocation. To begin, clear and release as you always do. Cleanse the space and cast the circle as has been outlined in this lesson. Invoke the quarters as you have learned how to do.

When you have erected the magic circle and called the quarters, you will want to invoke Deity. The following invocation is directed toward Universal Deity:

> *"Holy Mother-Father God, Creator and Sustainer of all things, be with me now and aid me in this my undertaking. Give me your blessing and your guidance, I pray you, with love and gratitude for your aid!"*

Take up the Ace of Swords. Face the east, and see again the column of white light you called up when you invoked the guardian of the east. Now raise the Ace of Swords, holding it out so it too faces the east. Imagine the card surrounded by a ball of white light. Address the guardian of the east with words like these:

> *"Guardian of the east, empower this card as your representative,*
> *so that it may be a lasting bond between us. May this card keep the power of air and the sacred athame always with me! May I always have mental strength, good ideas, and clear communications in this home!"*

Now replace the card upon the altar.

Next, take up the Ace of Wands and face the south. Again see the column of light you drew up when you invoked the quarter. Raise the Ace of Wands, holding it so that it too faces south. Imagine the card surrounded by a ball of white light. Address the guardian of the south with words to the effect of:

> *"Guardian of the south, empower this card as your representative, so that it may be a lasting bond between us. May this card keep the power of fire and the sacred wand always with me! May I always have strength, vitality, and creativity in this home!"*

Return the card to the altar.

Now take up the Ace of Cups and turn to the west. See again the column of light you called up when you invoked the quarter. Hold up the Ace of Cups so that it too faces west. Imagine the card surrounded by a ball of white light. Address the guardian of the west with words to the effect of:

*"Guardian of the west, empower
this card as your representative,
so that it may be a lasting bond
between us. May this card keep
the power of water and the sacred
chalice always with me! May I
always have love, compassion,
and nurturing in this home!"*

Replace the card upon the altar.

Take up now the Ace of Pentacles and turn to the north. See the column of light you brought up when you invoked the quarter. Hold up the Ace of Pentacles so that it too is facing north. Imagine the card surrounded by a ball of white light. Address the guardian of the north with words to the effect of:

*"Guardian of the north, empower
this card as your representative,
so that it may be a lasting bond
between us. May this card keep
the power of earth and the sacred
pentagram always with me! May
I always have wealth, prosperity,
and wisdom in this home!"*

Return the card to the altar. Say to yourself:

*"Behold, I am One with the
Powers of the universe!"*

Now imagine a bright light shining out from your solar plexus, like a sun within you. Place your hands over the four Aces and imagine a bright white light coming from your hands and surrounding the cards. Charge them with words like these:

*"By the powers of air and fire, by
the powers of water and earth,
and by the power of Spirit—
within me—may these cards
be blessed, and may they guard
and bless this house! By my will,
so mote it be, and it is so."*

Now you will give thanks and dismiss, beginning with Deity. Say the following:

*"Holy Mother-Father God,
Universal force of Life that
suffuses and supports all things,
I thank you for your presence and
your Aid! I offer you my love,
and bid you hail, and farewell!"*

Now close the magic circle according to the instructions in this lesson. When you have closed the circle, before you cleanse and release your excess energy, take the four Aces from the altar.

Go to the easternmost wall in your home and place the Ace of Swords there. Hang it with a thumbtack or bit of tape, or affix it in any other manner that seems right to you. Again imagine the card surrounded with white light and say:

"May the Blessing Be!"

Now go to the southernmost wall of your house and affix the Ace of Wands there. See the Ace of Wands surrounded by white light and say:

"May the Blessing Be!"

Go now to the westernmost wall in the house and affix the Ace of Cups there. Visualize the card surrounded by white light and say:

"May the Blessing Be!"

Finally, go to the northernmost wall of your home and affix there the Ace of Pentacles. See the card surrounded by white light and say:

"May the Blessing Be!"

The spell is now complete. Clear and release all excess energy.

• • • •

God for Lesson VI
Descent of the Goddess

In our last four lessons, we have used the God section to speak of the Goddess and her three forms as Maiden, Mother, and Crone. The Goddess is the principal focus of much of the Wiccan religion, but she is not alone. There is also the God. In future

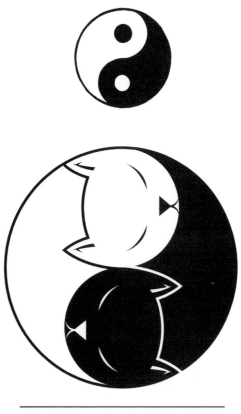

Yin-yang symbols: standard version, top, and stylized feline version, below

lessons, we shall use the God section to speak more about the nature of the God and his four major forms. In this lesson, however, we wish to speak of the interaction between the Goddess and the God, and what it means to the Wiccan.

Most students will be familiar with the YIN-YANG symbol, which has its nascence in TAOISM. This famous symbol portrays the union of yin and yang energies. Yin is the feminine, reactive, spiritual energy—the Goddess. Yang is the masculine, active, physical energy—the God. In the yin-yang symbol, these two polar forces are shown wrapped around each other in a swirling sphere of motion.

What we see in this ancient and venerable symbol is that the polar energies—yin and yang, Goddess and God, spirit and matter—are not separate and opposing forces, but rather conjoined and complementary powers. In Wicca, we portray this concept through the romantic union of Goddess and God, polar powers bound together through love and mutual passion.

Moreover, in the yin-yang we further see that each of the polar powers contains the seed of the other. In the dark, feminine power of yin, we see the bright seed of yang. In the light, masculine power of yang, we see a spot of yin's dark essence. Each by nature leads back to the other.

In Wicca, we say that the Goddess gives birth to the God: the bright seed of yang energy grows within her until she gives it birth. Thus, we say that material existence comes forth from spirit. And since the God, like all of us, comes from the Goddess, her essence is always within him—his soul, if you will. Thus, the essence of yin is ever-present in yang, for it is yang's origin: matter comes from spirit and carries spirit within it.

These two powers—Goddess and God, yin and yang, spirit and matter—cannot be truly separated. They are as opposite sides of a coin. Though there is an obverse and a reverse, still there is only one coin. This is what is meant by the sacred formula used in the consecration of the GREAT RITE:

The Goddess is not Greater than the God
Nor is the God greater than the Goddess
But Both are equal
And Neither is complete without the Other.

And just as the polar forces cannot be considered separately from one another, so too we can never be separate from them. We are not observers of the cosmic forces, but aspects of them. We are their living union—spirit in matter. We can no sooner be separate from the Goddess and the God than a molecule of air can be separate within the firmament. Distinct within it, yes, but separate from it, never.

You may have noticed by now that the Wiccan religion is rich in symbolism. It is not, however, rich in myth. The central myth of Wicca is the Descent of the Goddess. This myth takes many forms and can be interpreted on many levels, but it always speaks to the relationship between the two polar forces.

The myth of the Descent of the Goddess is simple in format. The Goddess creates, gives birth to, or marries the God. The God dies, either literally or symbolically.

The Goddess resolves to have the God back and follows or pursues him. Finding the God, the Goddess resurrects or otherwise reunites with him. From these acts, an eternal cycle of involution and evolution is established, on which the order of the universe is based.

There are many versions of this myth. It is at least as old as human memory—and, in reality, surely older. Sometimes the Goddess and God are shown as mother and son, more often as lovers. Sometimes they are portrayed as being of the same gender, as in the story of Demeter and her daughter Persephone, or the story of Kastor and his brother Polydeukes. None of these details change the basic meaning of the myth.

The Descent of the Goddess can be taken on many levels. At its simplest and most accessible level, the myth is the story of the origin of the seasons and the establishment of the eternal cycles of time and of the earth. On another level, the Descent of the Goddess speaks to the immortality of the soul and to the cycle of death and rebirth, to which we are all subject through so many lifetimes. On still another level, the myth tells the story of creation and of spirit's descent into matter through the soul, its journey of birth and rebirth, and its ultimate return to its divine origin.

All of these meanings and many more express themselves through the many variations of this sacred myth. You have already encountered one version of the Descent of the Goddess in the creation story from the *Vangelo delle Streghe*. Here we see the Goddess create the God out of herself and pursue him when he falls into matter. Reunited with the God by her own entry into matter via the many souls, the Goddess sets up the cycles of existence, symbolized as her spinning wheel, which the God turns.

Below follow several other versions of the Descent of the Goddess:

Cybele and Attis

A Mother goddess of Phrygia (in what is now Turkey), Cybele came to be identified with the Roman Magna Mater, or Great Mother. The worship of Cybele was very popular in the imperial period and attracted many followers. According to her myth, Cybele was the first being to exist, having created herself. In this dawn of existence, Cybele was ANDROGYNOUS, being equally male and female—for she contained the seeds of all things and was the perfect union of the polar forces of spirit and matter. In time, Cybele decided to separate the two forces, thus creating the manifest Universe. She did this by castrating herself—thus separating out the masculine, or physical, elements. From the severed penis, the God, Attis, grew. Attis became Cybele's consort, and they

loved one another deeply. But Attis came to be killed when he was gored by a wild boar—a frequent symbol of death. Journeying to the land of death, Attis became the favorite of its queen, Persephone, who made him her consort. Meanwhile, the grief-stricken Cybele wanted Attis back, and she resolved to bring him back from the land of the dead. Cybele journeyed to the land of death and struck an arrangement with Persephone whereby they would share Attis's favors: each year, Attis would spend six months in the world of the living with Cybele and six months in the world of the dead with Persephone. During the six months Attis spent with Cybele, the earth bloomed with life; this is summer. During the six months Attis spent with Persephone, life withered and fell away from the earth; this is winter. Attis was often represented by a tree, and each year his rebirth was celebrated by decorating sacred trees; this is one of the origins of the Yule Tree. Another notable feature of their worship is that Cybele and Attis were served by a transsexual clergy: men who imitated the Goddess's example of self-castration and thereafter lived as priestesses.

Demeter and Persephone

Demeter, whose name means "the Mother," is a Greek goddess of the earth and agriculture. Demeter had a beautiful daughter called Kore ("the Maiden"), whom she loved more than anything. Together, Demeter and Kore tended the earth, causing it to bring forth all manner of vegetation and foliage. The god of death, Hades, also became consumed with love for Kore—though of another kind. Hades abducted Kore and bore her away to the kingdom of death, where he made her his queen, and she became known as Persephone. Not knowing what had happened to her daughter, Demeter was plunged into the deepest grief. As the Great Mother wept, the first snow fell, plants withered and died, and the earth fell into the first winter. Demeter searched everywhere, but she could not find Kore or anyone who knew anything about her disappearance. At last, Demeter turned to the great Hekate, the Crone, who alone was able to tell her what had happened—for Hekate knows all. Demeter stormed into the kingdom of the dead to confront Hades and reclaim her daughter. After much ado, an agreement was reached whereby Demeter would have her daughter with her for six months of each year, during which she would be Kore, the Maiden. This would be summer, and during this time the two goddesses would cause the earth to thrive. The remaining six months Kore would spend with Hades in the kingdom of death, as Persephone. During this time, the earth would experience winter as Demeter returned to her grief. And thus the cycle of the seasons began. Demeter and Kore/Persephone returned to the earth at Eleusis, near Athens, and here the two goddesses established their sacred Mysteries, which were enacted yearly for many centuries. These ELEUSINIAN MYSTERIES were considered the most sacred rites of the ancient world, and they included many famous initiates. Seeing the devastation caused by the first winter, Demeter created agriculture, and she selected the Eleusinian prince Triptolemus to disseminate the knowledge of cultivating and preserving grain throughout the earth, so that humankind need not suffer too much during her period of grief.

Inanna and Dumuzi

Inanna was the patron goddess of the ancient Sumerian city of Uruk (or Erech) in Mesopotamia. Dumuzi was Inanna's mortal consort, who served her as king of Uruk. Inanna loved Dumuzi greatly, and his life as her consort was very sweet. But Dumuzi came to be killed by a wild boar and then descended into the land of death. Inanna was wild with grief when she heard of Dumuzi's death, and she resolved to follow him to the land of the dead and bring him back out of it. Inanna was sure that she could persuade Ereshkigal, the queen of the dead, to release Dumuzi, for Ereshkigal was Inanna's sister. But as she ventured into the realm of death, Inanna came to seven gates. At each of the seven

gates, Inanna was compelled to surrender one item of clothing or jewelry, until at last she entered the land of the dead naked—just as one enters the land of the living. Though the details vary in different versions, Inanna managed to free Dumuzi and return with him to the world of the living, thus establishing the cycle of rebirth. In later versions, the two goddesses agree to share Dumuzi, who must spend half of the year with Inanna (summer) and half of the year with Ereshkigal (winter). In time, Sumerian civilization came to be dominated by the Semitic peoples. The Semites kept the myths of the Sumerians but gave the deities Semitic names. Thus, Inanna was later known as Ishtar, while Dumuzi came to be known as Tammuz. Ereshkigal the Semites called Allat ("the Goddess"). Later still, the Greeks came to rule Mesopotamia. They identified Ishtar with Aphrodite. Tammuz the Greeks called Adonis ("the lord"), while they identified Allat with Persephone.

Isis and Osiris

Isis and Osiris are the Greek names for the ancient Egyptian deities Aset and Asar, whose worship dates from the earliest historical times. Children of earth (Geb) and sky (Nuit), Isis and Osiris ruled over Egypt in love and peace, teaching the Egyptians all of the arts and sciences of civilization. But their brother Set grew jealous of Osiris

and resolved to kill him. Set invited Osiris to a great feast and proposed a contest, producing a marvelous painted chest made in the shape of a man. Set offered the chest to whichever man fit in it exactly. All of the male guests tried to fit in the chest, but Set had deliberately had it made so that it would only fit Osiris. When Osiris's turn came, he fit in the chest exactly, and Set slammed down the heavy lid and sealed it; this was the first MUMMY CASE. Then Set threw the mummy case into the Nile so that Osiris drowned. Thereafter, Set made himself king of Egypt. Set wished to have Isis as his queen, but she turned herself into a white bird and flew away. Overcoming her grief, Isis searched all over Egypt for the mummy case that contained her husband's body. At last, she found the mummy case caught in the roots of a great tree on the island of Byblos. Obtaining the mummy case, Isis performed powerful magic to resurrect Osiris from the dead, and she conceived a child by the revivified Osiris. Thereafter, Osiris became the lord of the dead, and Horus was born as his son and reincarnation on earth. There are many versions of the story. In some versions, Set hacks Osiris's body into fourteen parts, and Isis must reassemble it before she can resurrect Osiris. Sometimes the two versions are put together. The most popular and enduring of all Egyptian deities, Isis was called the "Lady of Ten Thou-

sand Names." Her followers stressed that all deities were manifestations of a single spiritual truth. Isian religion was very popular in the Roman Empire. Today, the principal center of Isian worship is the Fellowship of Isis, or *Aset Shemsu*, which is the largest Goddess-centered organization in the Western world.

Izanagi and Izanami

In this Japanese Shinto version of the myth, the sexual polarities are reversed, and the God pursues the Goddess. Izanagi ("the inviter") and Izanami ("the invited") are the Japanese creator couple. In the beginning, Izanagi struck his spear into the ocean. The head of the spear shattered, becoming the Japanese islands. Izanami danced around the spear, and Izanagi pursued her. At length, Izanagi caught Izanami, and they became consorts. Izanami and Izanagi were very happy and had many children. But Izanami's last child was the god of fire, and she was burned so badly during his birth that she died. Izanagi was grief-stricken, and he resolved to follow his wife into the Afterworld and bring her back. Izanagi entered the land of the dead and, finding Izanami, begged her to come back with him. But Izanami refused. Izanagi pressed her, and Izanami revealed that her outer form had begun to decay. Shamed by this admission, Izanami chased Izanagi out of the realm of the dead at the head of a band of spirits. Even more grief-stricken than before, Izanagi went to a nearby river to ritually purify himself after his contact with the dead. As he performed his ablutions, several new deities were born, notably the sun goddess Amaterazu. Though Izanagi could not bring Izanami back into the world of the living in her old form, Amaterazu might be thought of as her mother reborn, thus completing the mythic cycle.

· · · ·
Glossary for Lesson VI

androgynous—The term *androgynous* means to have characteristics of both sexes. Many Pagan deities have androgynous forms, including Ishtar, Cybele, Shiva, and the famous Hermaphroditus, to name only a few. This refers to the idea that spirit and matter—represented as female and male—are not truly separate, but rather two aspects of the same force.

asperse—To asperse something is to sprinkle it with blessed water for the purpose of cleansing, blessing, or consecrating it. The water may be the type of holy water you have learned to make in these lessons, or it may be any of several other kinds of blessed water commonly used in magic. You will learn more about other kinds of blessed water that may be used for aspersing in future lessons.

battery—A battery is a repository from which additional resources may be drawn as needed. In daily life, we most commonly think of the term *battery* in terms of the electrical batteries used to power appliances. In magic, we often create energy constructs to act as psychic batteries, drawing spiritual energy from them to assist our workings. This sort of battery is basically an artificially created energy vortex that increases the amount of energy available for use.

Ceremonial magic—Ceremonial magic, or Ceremonialism, is a magical tradition derived from Hermeticism and alchemical thought. It is followed by both Pagans and Judeo-Christians. The Ceremonial Tradition has much in common with Wicca in its practices, but it also reflects much difference. Ceremonialism tends to be very precise and dogmatic, with a strong emphasis on the use of particular words, actions, and tools. Ceremonial magicians tend to see magic as compelling outside forces to act in their interest, whereas Wiccans tend to access their own powers or the ambient energies around them. The two groups are closely related and have often interacted. Many Wiccans have also been Ceremonials, and vice versa. For this reason, you will find many Ceremonial elements in modern Wicca.

circle dance—The circle dance is one of the most ancient forms of ritual expression, dating back as far as anyone can guess. People joining hands and moving in a circle is as simple, yet as profound, a way to raise energy as one could ask for. At one time, this sort of dance was called caroling, and the songs used to accompany it still bear that name when used in Yule celebrations. In his famous, if rather slanderous, picture of "The Witches' Sabbat," De Lancre shows several kinds of circle dance apparently used by medieval Witches. Today, there are many forms of circle dance used in Wicca, but the most popular remains the simplest: simply dancing around the circle, hand in hand.

devoke—To devoke is to release an energy construct you have created or an aspect of Deity you have invoked. In common usage, the term *devoke* is used to describe the process of giving thanks to Deity, taking down the quarters, and opening the circle.

Eleusinian Mysteries—The Eleusinian Mysteries were considered the most sacred religious rites of the Greco-Roman world. Held annually at Eleusis, near Athens, these rites honored the goddess Demeter and her daughter Kore-Persephone. There were Lesser Mysteries held in the spring and Greater Mysteries held in the fall. The Greater Mysteries lasted for many days and involved complex ceremonies and lavish processions. Would-be initiates were instructed in sacred ritual by experienced *Mystagogues* and led through the Mysteries' *Epopteia*, or secrets, by the *Hierophantes*. The Mysteries included many famous initiates, but not one ever revealed the inner details of the rites.

energy constructs—Energy is the basic substance from which the universe is made. It responds to thought and emotion, which give it shape and form. In magic, we often use thought and emotion to shape energy into useful forms, such as the Quarter Towers. The resulting creation—a ball of white light, for example—is called an energy construct. Energy constructs have many uses: the magic circle, for example, by containing energy intensifies it. Most commonly, energy constructs are used as "batteries"—that is, to add extra energy to our workings (see below).

Fellowship of Isis—Founded at the spring equinox of 1576 Pisces (AD 1976), the Fellowship of Isis is the largest Goddess-centered organization in the Western world. FOI members come from many religions, but they share a common reverence for and love of the feminine aspect of Deity. The fellowship was founded by the Most Reverent Honorable Olivia Robertson and her brother and sister-in-law, the late Baron and Baroness Robertson of Strathloch. It is headquartered in the family's ancestral home, Huntington Castle, in Clonegal, Ireland. Many of the leadership of the Correllian Tradition are also members of the Fellowship of Isis.

finger—Fingers are, of course, the digits found on the hand. They are very useful in magic. In many ways, tools such as the athame and the wand are only extensions of the finger, and as such the finger can readily be used in place of the tool. Which finger do you use? Usually, you will use the index finger, the middle finger, or both together. Each finger has a meaning of its own. The index finger represents the Goddess and the feminine polarity. The middle finger represents the God and the masculine polarity. Both together represent divine union, and thus the combination is commonly used for blessings.

Great Rite—In Wicca, the term *Great Rite* is given to the physical representation of the union of the Goddess and the God. In symbolic terms, this union is represented by the insertion of the athame, representing the God, into the chalice, representing the Goddess. The Great Rite may be celebrated in other ways as well, including in some cases the physical union of a priestess and priest. Another term for the Great Rite is the Greek *Hierogamos*, or "sacred marriage." The Great Rite is considered one of the most sacred ceremonies of Wicca.

magic circle—Used from ancient times, the magic circle is a common feature of most magical traditions. In Wicca, the magic circle is erected before most rituals and many magical workings. The magic circle is an energy construct that serves to amplify energy and also to confine and thus intensify it. Like all magical undertakings, the erection of the magic circle may involve certain physical actions, but it truly takes place inside the person doing it—on an astral, or energetic, level.

mummy case—A mummy case, as you might imagine, is a casket prepared to hold a mummy. A mummy is a corpse preserved through drying. This can happen accidentally or through human art. The ancient Egyptians perfected the art of mummification as a means of preserving the bodies of their dead, which they regarded as sacred. The process of mummification and the complicated rituals that accompanied it took several months. The internal organs of the deceased were removed and placed in special Canopic jars, sacred to the four

directions. The mummy itself was placed in a mummy case: a human-shaped casket, often richly decorated, which bore an effigy representing the dead person's face. Then, if the family could afford it, the mummy case would be placed in a stone sarcophagus, similar to today's concrete vaults. According to Egyptian legend, the first mummy case was the chest in which the god Set trapped and killed his brother Osiris. Many mummy cases have come down from the Egyptians, some humble and others exquisite exemplars of the jeweler's art. The most famous mummy cases are the four nesting mummy cases made of gold and gems for the pharaoh Tutankhamen. Today, with the modern revival of the art of mummification, this sort of elaborate mummy case is again being made, but on a much-reduced scale.

sacred space—Sacred space is space that is used for magical work or worship. Sometimes it is specially prepared by cleansing or other magical operations whose purpose is to change the vibration of the energy. In some instances, this change in vibration takes place as an automatic consequence of the activity taking place. In all cases, it is not the physical area itself that is sacred, but rather the special nature of the energy that has been raised in this way that creates "sacred space."

Shinto—Shinto is the indigenous religion of Japan. Centered around the worship of the *Kami*, or deities, Shinto is strongly focused on nature and the natural cycles. The principal Shinto deity is the sun goddess Amaterazu No Kami, who is the mythical ancestress of the Japanese royal house. Shinto places great emphasis on the worship of the ancestors and on the importance of ceremony. It is an intensely local religion that varies from place to place and from temple to temple.

Taoism—Taoism is the name given to the popular form of Chinese Paganism. The religion takes its name from the word *Tao*, meaning "the Way," referring to the natural movement of energy in the universe. Though legend attributes the founding of Taoism to the sage Lao Tsu, its roots lie far back in Chinese prehistory. Taoism is a magical religion with a strong similarity to Wicca. For many centuries, Taoism was one of three major religions that coexisted in China, the others being Buddhism and Confucianism.

yin-yang—The symbol used to portray the nature of the union of the two polar powers. The yin-yang originated in Chinese Taoism and has a long history in Asia, but today it is used as a popular symbol around the world. The yin-yang shows the polar powers as two comma-shaped segments wrapping around each other within a circle or sphere. Yin, the feminine or spiritual force, is shown as dark, while yang, the masculine or physical force, is shown as light, and each contains a small portion of the other.

Study Questions for Lesson VI

1. With what tool do you cast the magic circle, and what can you use if you don't have one?

2. What is meant by negative energy?

3. What are the four quarters? Which one do you invoke first?

4. When do you normally invoke Deity during ritual?

5. Why is it a bad idea to leave the circle during ritual?

6. How do you cut a door in the circle?

7. What does it mean to dismiss the circle?

8. In which direction do you move when opening the circle?

9. Which finger represents the Goddess?

10. What is an energy construct?

11. What is a Ceremonial? How does Ceremonial magic commonly differ from Wicca?

12. What do we mean when we call an energy construct a "battery"?

13. What is the last thing you should do in any ritual?

Lesson
VI

137

Lesson
~ VII ~

Invocation

An invocation is a kind of prayer addressing Deity, or a particular aspect of Deity, and asking for Deity's presence or aid. In Correllian Wicca, we have two basic ways of looking at Deity: UNIVERSAL DEITY and PERSONAL DEITY.

Universal Deity is conceived of as being everywhere, in everything. Universal Deity is the divine consciousness behind the energy that forms and gives life to all that exists—and in Correllian Wicca, we believe that anything that exists lives. Universal Deity is above and beyond all individual aspects and manifestations, including the universe itself. Universal Deity is the Creator, Sustainer, and Essence of all things.

Universal Deity is beyond any form of depiction, is neither masculine nor feminine in character, and in truth is so far beyond our understanding that we can only try to imagine its full nature. To illustrate this, we often refer to Universal Deity as "Mother-Father God," showing that Universal Deity includes the concepts of both the Goddess and the God within itself.

In addition to Universal Deity, we also have personal deities. A personal deity is any aspect of Universal Deity with which we can make an emotional connection. We call them "personal" deities because we relate to them in a personal manner, as opposed to the more abstract nature of Universal Deity.

As described in earlier lessons, we can think of Universal Deity like a diamond. The diamond is only one stone, but it has many facets. Look at the diamond closely from any one angle and you will discover patterns in the facets that are not apparent from a greater distance. Examine the facets with a jeweler's loupe and you will discover formations within the stone that you would never see when looking at the diamond as a whole. Similarly, Universal Deity is one force—or "One Power in the Universe"—but it has many facets, which are personal deities. Through the many individual conceptions of personal deity, we can learn things we would never understand through the abstract nature of Universal Deity. Personal deities translate the abstractions of Universal Deity into human terms that people can understand and identify with. The nature and cycles of Universal Deity are interpreted through the mythology of personal deities, and in this way we can

identify with and internalize them through the emotional connections we make with these separate aspects of Deity.

Universal Deity is without any form of limitation. Any attempt to depict or define Universal Deity limits our conception, making that conception a personal deity, or a limited aspect of Universal Deity. There are more personal deities—that is, limited aspects of Universal Deity—than it would ever be possible to count. Personal deities range from the great powers of the universe (Goddess and God) to deities who aid specific functions (Asphalta, goddess of the roadways) to the Higher Self of everything that exists—for everything that exists is a limited aspect of Universal Deity.

In general, Deity might be thought of as a single universal power having increasingly limited points of reference, some of which include:

Universal Deity: All That Is

Goddess and God: The polar powers, yin and yang, spirit and matter, and so on

The Seven Great Powers: The seven principal archetypes of Deity

Specific-purpose deities: Patrons of various activities, such as arts, sciences, and so on

The Higher Self of all things: The individual spirit of any creature or thing

We interact with Deity at all of these various levels and others. When we wish to formally initiate that interaction—as at the beginning of a ritual or ceremony—we invoke that deity. *Invoke* comes from the Latin *vox*, or "voice," and means "to give voice to" our prayer—but that doesn't mean that an invocation always has to be said out loud. An invocation can be made silently, in the heart, as well: Deity, being inside us all, will hear.

An invocation formally invites the deity to be present and often requests a specific blessing or aid. Many times, an invocation will describe the qualities of the deity being addressed. An invocation can also express thanks for past blessings from the deity. Invocations are often quite beautiful. They can be poetic and are sometimes highly artistic. But the best invocation is one that honestly conveys heartfelt emotion toward the deity.

In any religion, and certainly in Wicca, your personal relationship to Deity is of primary importance. We have many forms of Deity, but we know that they, like we ourselves, ultimately reflect a single power that flows through all things. That single power—Universal Deity—is ultimately loving, creative, and always acting toward the good; consequently, all personal deities are also ultimately loving, creative, and acting always toward the good. Everything you experience has a reason whose purpose

is good. You may not always see that good, but it is always there.

You never need to fear Deity in Wicca. Deity does not judge you or persecute you; Deity will only ever wish to help you. Though our actions come back to us through karma, this is not a "divine judgment" so much as a necessary balance: it is there to help all beings grow. Deity may give us difficult lessons in life, but this too is motivated by love, to help us grow—never to "punish" us. Whatever may afflict you, Deity wishes to help you move past it, for Deity wishes you only growth and happiness in whatever personal form you picture Deity.

. . . .
Aspects of Deity

There are as many forms of personal deity as we could ever imagine, for any image can serve as a personal form of Deity if that image can embody an aspect of Deity for *you*.

All forms of personal deity will correspond to one or more of seven basic archetypes, sometimes called the "SEVEN GREAT POWERS" or various similar names. You will see deities grouped in larger numbers—often in groups of twelve—but these will only tend to duplicate the seven basic forms.

Most of the world's cultural PANTHE-ONS include dozens or hundreds of deities,

Cultural Correspondences

Archetype	Maiden	Mother	Crone	Hero	Lover	King	Sorceror
Planet	Venus	Moon	Saturn	Mars	Sun	Jupiter	Mercury
German	Freya	Frigga	Hella	Tyr	Baldur	Thor	Odin
Irish	Brigid	Boan	Morrighan	Ogmios	Aengus	Nuada	Dagda
Greek	Aphrodite	Hera	Hekate	Ares	Apollo	Zeus	Pluto
Roman	Venus	Juno	Carmenta	Mars	Apollo	Jupiter	Saturn
African	Oshun	Yemaya	Oya	Ogun	Shango	Obatala	Ellegua
Egyptian	Hat-Hor	Isis	Sekhemet	Horus	Ra	Amon	Osiris
Hindu	Durga	Lakshmi	Kali	Ganesha	Visnu	Brahma	Shiva

The Seven Archetypes

Archetypes of the Goddess: Maiden, Mother, Crone

Archetypes of the God: Hero, Lover, King, Sorcerer

Lesson VII

duplicating the seven basic archetypes many times over. This is because smaller local cultures and their pantheons come together and grow into larger, heterogeneous cultures while retaining their distinct original traditions. In the chart above, we have not attempted to deal with all of the deities of a given culture, but rather with the major deities of these cultures and their correspondences to the seven basic archetypes.

• • • •

Patron Deities

The reason we have so many forms of personal deity is so that people can make a personal, emotional connection to Deity. The abstract nature of Universal Deity is difficult for most people to comprehend or form an attachment to. A personal deity, on the other hand, portrays aspects of Deity in terms that are very easy for humans to understand and that have strong emotional appeal for us. We have many, many personal deities, because each person is different and has different needs for Deity to fulfill. Deity is all things to all people;

consequently, Deity must have very many personal forms.

The particular aspect of Deity that a person best interacts with is called a PATRON DEITY. The patron deity is the form of Deity you work with most. For some people, the relationship with their patron deity will be intense and highly emotional. They will receive dreams and visions from the patron deity and may learn to channel oracles from the patron in time. For other people, the patron acts as an inspiration and an example, helping the DEVOTEE to develop the qualities the patron personifies. There are deities whose principal qualities are virtues like wisdom, courage, or magical ability, and the devotees of these deities hope to develop these same traits by choosing them as patrons. Other deities have virtues like creativity, happiness, or self-expression, and their devotees also hope to gain these qualities by choosing one of them as patron.

Not every person will have one particular patron deity, nor does having a patron deity mean you do not interact with other deities. All forms of personal deity are aspects of Universal Deity, and therefore they can never conflict—though people can surely conflict over them, and they can appear to conflict if *you* believe they must.

Many people will have several patron deities. Sometimes all of these will be given equal status; other times there will be one principal patron deity and other lesser patrons. This is not unusual, and it works perfectly well.

· · · ·

How Do I Choose a Patron Deity?

Actually, your patron deity will choose you. The deity will do this in one of several ways: You may be drawn to the name or image of the deity and not really know why. The image of the deity or its attributes (such as a totem animal) may show up in your life repeatedly. You may have a vision of the deity. You may just "know." Or you can choose a patron because you admire that deity or wish to acquire its qualities.

You can have as many patron deities as you need, or you can have no patron deity at all—it is not required. As time passes, you can add or change patron deities. They are there to help you, not to bind you.

· · · ·

Care and Feeding of Your Patron Deity

Once you have a patron deity, you should talk to it, pray to it, and make offerings to it on a regular basis. A good offering is the light of candles. Other good offerings are items that represent sustenance or devotion. A bowl of water, a bowl of flour, a bowl of salt—these are typical offerings for some devotees. Incense, flowers, candy—all of these are good offerings too. What is offered really doesn't matter so much as the attitude of the devotee: the offering should be made with love and genuine devotion. We expect to receive blessings from our patron deity, and we make offerings back to it not because the deity needs them—it does not—but rather to show our gratitude and our own willingness to give back and share.

Remember, your patron deity is an aspect of Deity, so interact with it in the manner you consider appropriate to Deity. The deity will take its cue from you: if you treat it as being aloof, it will respond in kind, because it sees that's what you want from it.

• • • •
Other Kinds of Patron Deities

Not only do people have individual patron deities, but professions and other activities may have patron deities as well. There are many patron deities for education, for example, and for music. These too will correspond back to the Seven Great Powers; for example, Sesheta, ancient Egyptian goddess of writing and education, is a Maiden goddess.

Moreover, individual festivals also have patron deities. Commonly, these will be one or more of the Seven Great Powers, any of whose individual forms will do. For example, the Crone is patron of Samhain and may be invoked simply as the Crone or in the individual forms of Hekate, Morrighan, or Hella, as well as many others. The Maiden Goddess is the patron of Candlemas and can be invoked as the Maiden or in individual forms, such as the Irish Brighid.

• • • •
What Is an Invocation?

An invocation, then, is basically a kind of formal prayer. It may be directed to Universal Deity or to a personal deity or patron deity. Regardless, it should come from the heart and reflect genuine emotion.

When you invoke a deity, you should imagine that deity strongly. You may visualize the deity in your mind or imagine it manifesting before you. Some people visualize the deity as amorphous light or as a ball or column of light. They may also imagine the light of Deity descending into a statue or picture of the particular deity. All of these are good, as is any other visualization that helps you to focus on Deity's presence as you invoke it.

• • • •
Exercises

At this point in your development, you should be doing Exercises 7, 8, and 9 on a daily basis, plus Exercise 10 periodically. You should be finding your capacity for the exercises greater, your time faster, and your visualization clearer. Chakras are like muscles: the more you use them, the stronger they get and the more you can do with them. That is why it is important to do these exercises on a regular basis and to take them in order: in this way, you will build up the strength of your chakras gradually and in a consistent manner.

The next exercise is meant to be added to the daily routine following Exercise 9. On days when you do Exercise 10, it would follow this exercise.

Exercise 11

You may feel a bit like you're back where you began, because Exercise 11 is meant to strengthen the palm chakras, as were the first three exercises in these lessons. Exercise 11, however, is much more intense than Exercises 1, 2, and 3, and using it will bring your capacity to handle energy to a much higher level.

Do Exercises 7, 8, and 9 as usual, opening your chakras and turning them first white and then violet. When you have done this, let the image fade, just as before the Lemon exercise. When you open your chakras this way, you greatly increase the energy you can access for what you are doing.

Now raise your hand; either hand is fine. Lift your hand so that the palm is vertical and facing a wall, preferably five to six feet away. Imagine a thin beam of red light coming out from the center of your palm and going to the wall, rather like a laser beam. See the beam of light as clearly as you can, with the red as bright as possible. Hold this image as long as you feel you comfortably can. Now imagine that beam of red light retracting back into your palm.

Do the same thing with the other hand. Whenever you exercise one palm chakra, you should make sure to do the other too. This is because you will often need to use them together, and both should be equally developed.

When you've finished both hands, you may do Exercise 10, if you wish. If you feel fatigued, Exercise 10 will help revive you. If you're not doing Exercise 10, then you're ready to close. Imagine again your seven balls of violet light at the chakras, and close them down normally as per the instructions in Exercise 7. Finally, clear and release as always.

Do this exercise for a few days, or until you can do it easily, and then replace it with Exercise 12.

Exercise 12

As so often happens in these exercises, Exercise 12 begins just like Exercise 11 does. Do Exercise 11 just as you normally would, up to the point where you have created the beam of red light from your hand to the wall.

Here, keeping the image of the beam of light clear and strong, begin to move it. You do not need to move your hand to do this, but rather just let the beam pivot where it connects to the palm. Use the beam to draw simple designs on the wall. Imagine the designs being made in the same red light of which the beam is composed. Try to hold the image of each design even as you go on to draw the next one. This will become easier as you go, and if you can't do it at first, don't worry about it; it will come.

When you have mastered simple designs, you should try using the beam of light to write words, using cursive letters. This will increase your skill with the technique. When you feel you have done enough, retract the beam of light into your palm and let the image of the designs you have drawn dissipate. (Remember to do both hands.)

You may now do Exercise 10 if you wish. If not, go straight to shutting down your chakras as described above, and then clear and release as always.

Do Exercise 12 until it becomes easy for you. Do not feel you must always use a wall; you can try drawing the designs in midair as well. If you like, you can try Exercise 12 separately from the other exercises: on the bus, in the store, outdoors, or anywhere you wish. Simply send out your beam of light and start drawing. Be sure to clear and release afterward, though. Also, understand that this would be in addition to, not in place of, your daily session.

When you feel that you are ready, go on to Exercise 13.

Exercise 13

Exercise 13 is exactly like Exercise 12, except that instead of using red light, you will use multicolored light. By multicolored light, we mean that you should see many different colors in the light at once, rather like a psychedelic tie-dye. Using this multicolored light, do Exercise 13 just as you would otherwise do Exercise 12.

· · · ·

The color of the light—that is, energy—we use is extremely important. Color reflects the vibration of the energy, and thus its individual nature. In general, energy is perceived as being white in color in its natural state. White light thus is a good, all-purpose energy to use for just about anything you might want to do. Like clear quartz crystal, white light amplifies what you put in without adding anything of its own. For many purposes, this is good. When you transform the balls of colored light you have opened in your chakras, you are strengthening and amplifying the energy of the chakra.

Sometimes, however, it is best to use colored energy, as the color's particular quality may help in what you are doing. For example, when you transform the balls of light in your chakras from white to violet, you are attuning them to the level of violet energy. Violet energy is extremely spiritual and comes from the highest level of the being, thus causing each chakra to attune to its own highest nature and greatest good.

In these exercises, we have been using red energy. Red adds strength and vitality. We are using it here to add a needed push to help us use a chakra in a new and unaccustomed way. Thus, red energy makes the exercise easier by giving you extra energy with which to do the exercise. The multicolored energy used in Exercise 13 serves to help develop all aspects of the given chakra at once, and it follows the same principle as the rainbow we used in Exercise 3.

You will learn more about color as you go on, as well as about how it affects energy. Not everyone perceives the color of energy in quite the same way, just as not everyone sees color exactly the same way with their physical eyes; consider the colorblind, for example. Some people develop highly individual methods of interpreting the vibration of energy through color. The system we are using is the most common. If your own experience varies, that's OK—it's just different. You should still be able to do the exercises with the colors as described.

Spell for Lesson VII
The Witch's Bottle

The Witch's Bottle is a very ancient type of spell, and it has countless variations. The idea of performing a spell and sealing it in a jar is as old as the manufacture of jars, and it may be regarded as a portable version of burying a spell in the earth— the jar here representing the womb of the Mother.

Many examples of this sort of spell have been found by archeologists, though modern versions tend to be rather different from ancient ones, partly due to the difference in materials readily available for magical working. In ages past, anthropomorphic jars were especially popular for this sort of working, the jar itself then taking on the character of a spirit helper to aid the spell's unfolding. Sometimes the whole jar would be made in the likeness of a human being or animal, and sometimes only the face would be shown. The so-called BELLARMINE JARS, bearing the likeness of the Old God, often in triple form, were commonly used for this sort of undertaking and are strongly associated with it.

Today, we use any sort of jar or bottle that appeals to us or is convenient. Decorative jars are often favored, but ordinary glass jars and bottles, either plain or self-decorated, serve just as well.

For this particular Witch's Bottle, you will need the following materials:

- A small jar, such as a baby-food jar or a medicine bottle
- A larger jar, such as a canning jar or a decorative canister
- A bit of paper and ink; red ink would be preferable
- Some herbs; a combination of parsley and sage might be a good general choice
- A bit of essential oil; vanilla might be a good choice
- Some stones; aquarium gravel would be good, as it is small and easy to handle
- A quantity of water

Choose a time when you will be able to work unhindered. If possible, it is best to make the bottle during the waxing moon. First, assemble your materials. Begin, as always, by clearing and releasing. It may be beneficial to light some candles for extra energy. You may even want to cast a full circle, now that you know how, but that isn't really necessary.

Take up your piece of paper. It can be any kind of paper you wish: ordinary writing or typing paper will do, but you may find that a bit of nice stationery or parchment helps to set the mood better, thus assisting the needed shift of consciousness.

On the paper, write what it is you wish the spell to accomplish. Because the bottle is a sturdy artifact that can be kept as long as you wish, it is especially useful for long-term desires, such as prosperity, peace in the home, balance, and so on.

Write your desire on the paper in the form of the following incantation:

"There is One Power
in the universe,
And I am a perfect
manifestation of that Power.
As such, I create for myself
[insert your wish here].
I manifest this in accordance
with the free will of all,
And with harm toward none.
By all the power of
three times three,[ii]
As I do will, so mote it be."

As you write this, try to concentrate on the thing you are desiring. Focus on it. Imagine yourself having this thing, as if it were already accomplished—already yours. Feel confident, and know that it will come about.

· · · ·

ii If you remember reading about Pythagoras in Lesson V, you will recall that three in numerological theory represents magic and the art of creation. Three times three, or nine, represents creation unfolding into infinity. Since ten reduces back to one, nine represents the furthest extent of creation before returning to the Creator.

Now, fold the paper until it is small enough to fit easily in your smaller jar.

Say to yourself:

"Behold, I align myself to the powers of the universe."

Imagine a stream of white light coming down into you from above your head, filling your body. This is the light of Spirit—the Goddess. She will help you with your working.

Hold the paper in your hands, and imagine it surrounded by a ball of bright white light.

Again focus on your wish. Imagine it already yours, already accomplished. Speak the incantation out loud:

"There is One Power
in the universe,
And I am a perfect
manifestation of that Power.
As such I create for myself
[insert your wish here].
I manifest this in accordance
with the free will of all,
And with harm toward none.
By all the power of
three times three,
As I do will, so mote it be."

Now place the paper into the smaller jar and seal the lid. Say:

"Even as I seal this jar, so too I use my will to seal my wish just as tightly into manifestation."

Now place the smaller jar into the larger jar. Fill the space between the outside of the small jar and the inside of the large jar with rocks, about halfway up. (This is why aquarium rocks are good: they are small and easily handled.) Now add water until the larger jar is filled. Add three drops of oil to the water, and now sprinkle it with the herbs.

Imagine the larger jar filling with white light. See that light shining forth from within it like a miniature sun, sending out energy in all directions. Now say something to the effect of:

"Earth supports water. Oil feeds fire. Air feeds herbs. May the powers of all the elements feed my spell and carry it forward in their eternal dance. As I do will, so mote it be."

Seal the larger jar tightly, and never open it again. End by clearing and releasing as always.

Put the jar in your home—in an obvious place if it is decorative, or out of the way if it is not. Leave it there and allow it to bring the quality you have manifested into your life. Alternatively, the jar may be buried or left outdoors.

God for Lesson VII
The God

As we see in the *Vangelo delle Streghe*, in Wicca the God is perceived as an emanation of the Goddess. Created by her, the God is the Goddess's son. Created from her, the God is the Goddess's brother. United with her, in the embrace that creates and sustains the universe, the God is the Goddess's lover.

On the level of personal deity, the God and his many forms are deities who can be accessed and worked with just like the Goddess. On the more abstract level, the God represents the principle of manifestation. The Goddess is the Creator, and the God is the Creating; together they are the Creation. Goddess is essence, and God is form. Goddess is spirit, and God is matter. Goddess is eternal, and God is temporal cycles. Goddess is life, and God is living. The union of the two produces the world we know.

Because the God is connected to physical manifestation, he is often associated with light, for the physical world is made of energy, or light, slowed down in frequency and vibration. Often, therefore, the God is represented by the sun, while the Goddess is represented by the moon.

The God governs the quality of time. For this reason, the Goddess and the God are sometimes thought of as Mother Nature and Father Time. It is as lord of time that the God is considered lord of the Dance of Life: time, the sequencing of events, is what allows the dance. It is through time that energy can be slowed enough to become matter. The nature of time is illusory, being more a matter of perception than reality, but through it events are structured and take on ordered meaning, allowing change and growth to occur. In the *Vangelo delle Streghe*, the Wheel of Fortune (fate and karma) is described as the Goddess's spinning wheel—the Goddess is spinning the thread, but the God is turning the wheel. This is because the universe proceeds from the spirit but is carried forward by time.

In this same way, the God governs the Wheel of the Year: the Goddess gives it form, but the God moves it forward. As lord of the year, the God has two basic forms: the Young God of life, lord of summer and of day, and the Old God of death, lord of winter and of night.

God of summer, lord of life, strength, and creativity, the Young God represents the sun at the height of its powers in the Light half of the year and the God in his evoluted or outward-turning state, when he focuses on growth and expansion.

God of winter, lord of death, dreams, and magic, the Old God represents the sun in its waning state in the Dark half of the year and the God in his involuted or inward-turning state, when he turns from physical to spiritual pursuits.

In ancient times, people pursued farming in the Light half of the year, under the patronage of the Young God (who embodied the fertility of the fields and the nurturing power of the sun). In the Dark half of the year, people had to rely on their stored food and on what they could catch by hunting, under the patronage of the Old God. The Wheel of the Year eternally rotates between these two principles.

In mythology, the God is sometimes portrayed as a single figure who grows from the Young God to the Old God, spending summer as the Young God with the Mother Goddess in the land of the living, and winter as the Old God with the Crone Goddess in the Otherworld—as in the myths of Adonis, who spends summer with Venus but winter with Persephone, and Tammuz, who spends summer with Ishtar and winter with Allat. Sometimes he is portrayed as two separate figures, with the Goddess being the one to spend part of the year with the Young God and part with the Old God—as in the myth of Blodeuwydd, who spends summer with Lugh and winter with Hafgan. Both variations tell the same story: in the Dance of Life, the soul is moved forward through a continual cycle of death and rebirth.

Beyond this, these two aspects of the God further break down into four archetypes. The Young God breaks down into the Hero and the Lover, while the Old God breaks down into the King and the Sorcerer. All forms of the God will fall under one or more of these four archetypes, just as all forms of the Goddess fall under either Maiden, Mother, or Crone.

The Hero is the champion who overcomes all obstacles and embodies creativity, vitality, and self-expression (astrologically, Mars). The Lover is the consort of the Goddess, the dying and reborn God who embodies all virtues (the sun). The King is the god of justice and cosmic order, prosperity and expansion (Jupiter). The Sorcerer is the divine fool, the magician who rules over magic, prophecy, and the Otherworld (Mercury). The Sorcerer is also called the Horned God, because he is often shown with horns or antlers and is identified with the forest (as a symbol of the Otherworld).

• • • •

Glossary for Lesson VII

Bellarmine jars—Bellarmine jars were large jars decorated with the face of a bearded man, said to be one Cardinal Bellarmine. Often, the jar actually had three faces of the same man, sometimes conjoined. It is believed that the faces actually represent the Horned God. Bellarmine jars were particularly favored for bottle magic.

devotee—A devotee is a person who is particularly devoted to a personal deity who is their patron. A person can be a devotee of more than one deity at a time.

pantheons—A pantheon is a grouping of deities associated with a particular time or culture: for example, the Egyptian pantheon or the Roman pantheon. The deities of these pantheons usually began separately, as local variations, and then grew together over time. For this reason, though the deities of a given pantheon will correspond to the Seven Great Powers, they will appear to duplicate each archetype many times. Some people prefer to work with one or another pantheon exclusively; this is a matter of personal preference. Other people believe that you should never mix deities from one pantheon with deities from another pantheon; this is a superstition, and experience shows that it is simply not true.

patron deity—A patron deity is the particular goddess or god with whom one feels most at home. Some people have more than one patron deity, but usually one will predominate. Any deity that you are drawn to can be your patron deity. One's patron deity is prayed to for guidance, visions, blessing, and so on.

personal deity—A personal deity is any one of the many faces we ascribe to Universal Deity to make Deity easier to understand. Whereas Universal Deity is all-encompassing and abstract, personal deities are individual aspects of Deity portrayed in very human terms. Personal deities are there to help us understand Deity and make a personal, emotional connection to Deity.

Seven Great Powers—The Seven Great Powers are the seven basic archetypes to which personal deities tend to correspond. They are also likened to the seven planets of Ptolemaic astrology. The archetypes are as follows: Goddess—Maiden, Mother, Crone; God—Hero, Lover, King, Sorcerer.

Universal Deity—The different faces of Deity are ways of understanding Universal Deity. All of the faces of Deity in the end reflect the same universal power, as in fact do we humans and all of the rest of creation. That universal power is infinite and beyond our power to know in its totality, so we make understandable images through which we may interface with it. That infinite power is Universal Deity—the spirit of Deity that is beyond all names and images.

Study Questions for Lesson VII

1. What is an invocation? Why would you make one?

2. What is Universal Deity?

3. What is a personal deity? Name any three. Can you name a personal deity not listed in this lesson?

4. What are the Seven Great Powers?

5. What are the archetypes of the Goddess? Which of these has most personal significance to you, and why?

6. Explain the archetype of the Sorcerer. Name three personal forms of the Sorcerer. Can you name one not given in the lesson?

7. What is a pantheon? Should you ever mix pantheons? What will happen if you do?

8. Should you ever be afraid of Deity? Why or why not?

9. In Pythagorean numerology, what does the number nine represent?

10. What is a patron deity?

11. How do you choose a patron deity?

12. Why is the color of energy important? Why would one use violet-colored energy?

13. Explain the relationship between the Young God and the Old God. What do they have to do with the concept of evolution?

Lesson
VIII

Garb

In preceding lessons, we have discussed the nature of the universe and of magic. We have talked about how we purify our space, cast our circle, call the quarters, and invoke Deity. Now for the most crucial question of them all: what to wear?

What is the well-dressed Witch wearing these days? Well, the most common answer to that is, the same thing everyone else is. At rituals, gatherings, private workings, and all manner of occasion, most Wiccans wear street clothes, the same clothes they might wear to do any other activity. Granted, they might choose special "romantic" or "Witchy" clothes—big swirly skirts, exotic fabrics, or interesting jewelry—but these would be things they could wear elsewhere too.

Overwhelmingly, for most Wiccan events people wear pretty much anything they want to. There are, however, some exceptions.

• • • •

Robes

Many groups like to wear robes. Sometimes only the presiding clergy will be robed. Sometimes everyone will be robed. The robes may all match to stress the temple's *esprit de corps,* or each person's robe may be different and individual. These are all decisions that are up to each individual temple.

People wear robes for several reasons:

1. They look cool.

Robes, like other accessories, can act as KEYS to the Higher Self. Robes can help us to feel magical, and that helps us to shift our consciousness and become magical. This is probably the best reason for wearing robes.

2. They create a sense of "belonging."

Having a special garment, such as a robe, that everyone in a group wears creates a feeling of "specialness"—of belonging to a distinct and individual group. Like any uniform, wearing a robe creates a sense that we are doing something different from everyday life. And when everyone is wearing a robe, there is a sense of solidarity—that "we're all in this together." This is another good reason for wearing a robe.

3. To aid the flow of energy.

In times past, people sometimes felt that clothing restricted the flow of psychic energy. It was believed that anything tied around the body or anything intricately constructed—such as stitching—slowed down or stopped the flow of energy. (You can see a vestige of this belief in the Christian Amish, who still believe buttons, zippers, and—Heaven forbid!—Velcro are harmful, even though the Amish have forgotten the original reasons for the belief.) Perhaps at an earlier point in human development this may have been true, but few people believe it today. The Gardnerian author Doreen Valiente has pointed out that if psychic energy can't be stopped by walls, a thin layer of clothing should be no impediment to it.[iii]

Still, many people feel that their energy moves better when they are wearing less restrictive clothing. For this reason, they advocate loose robes or other simple clothing that doesn't bind the body. People in this camp would say that a loose, comfortable robe with little or nothing underneath makes it much easier to do magic or psychic work, as there are no tight waistbands or complicated structures to impede the flow of energy. While we would not take the view that clothing restricts energy, we certainly would agree that wearing loose, comfortable clothing makes pretty much anything easier, including magic. Obviously, comfortable clothing is easier to relax in, and being relaxed helps us to work magically or psychically. Nothing impedes

• • • •

iii Doreen Valiente, *An ABC of Witchcraft Past and Present* (Blaine, WA: Phoenix Publishing, 1988)

Lesson
VIII

the flow of energy like tension; that's why we clear and release before every working.

For all of that, few things are more comfortable than a robe, or less restrictive of movement. As long as we treat it as a preference and not a necessity, this too is a good reason to wear a robe.

· · · ·

Types of Robes

Whether we belong to a temple that wears robes or we just want one for our own personal use, our next question is, "Where do I get one?"

The answer, usually, is that we make it.

There are stores and companies that sell commercially manufactured ritual robes. Usually, however, these companies' primary business is selling medieval or Renaissance garb for historical recreationists, Renaissance fairs, and theatrical production companies. Some of these robes are very nice, but they also tend to be very expensive.

Making your own robe is both cheaper and more personal. By doing it yourself, you put your own energy into the robe, thereby attuning it to yourself from the start. When you make your robe yourself, it is uniquely and truly your own.

Of course, for many people, not knowing how to sew can be a bit of an impediment to this process. But most robe patterns are very simple; a couple of straight seams and a hem will usually do it.

In making a robe, you will want to consider several things, as discussed below.

Fabric

Choose a fabric you can work with. Silky fabrics feel great, but they can be hard for a beginner to sew. Stretchy fabrics are hard to sew too. A cotton or cotton blend is often your best bet.

Also, consider how the fabric will feel. Rituals are often held indoors, and many involve dancing, so you don't want a fabric that's going to be too hot. Though a velvet robe might be magnificent to behold, it may also give you heatstroke. A lighter fabric is usually preferable, unless you are making a robe specifically for outdoor use.

Cut

There are many styles of robe, but the most common type is the simple "T" style favored by the ancient CELTS and passed on to the medieval period. This style is simple to make and easy to move in. Another popular style is the caftan, a very unconstructed robe whose simplest versions rather resemble a long poncho sewn up the sides. This was a pretty universal garment in antiquity and can be very striking. Some people prefer a more Greco-Roman style of robe. These often feature a PEPLOS, a decorative fold of fabric hanging down from the shoulders. Some Greco-Roman styles of robe are simply pieces of fabric wrapped and pinned in place.

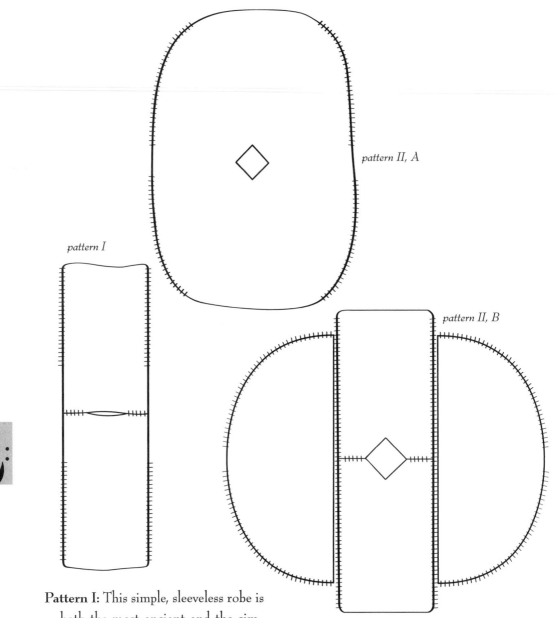

pattern II, A

pattern I

pattern II, B

Pattern I: This simple, sleeveless robe is both the most ancient and the simplest style of sewn robe. Take a rectangle of fabric measured and cut to the appropriate length and width to fit you, double it, and sew two-thirds up each side, leaving the last third as a sleeveless hole. Cut a hole for the neck. Hem sleeves, neck, and bottom.

Pattern II: The caftan is one of the most dramatic styles of robe. Shown are two patterns, one simple, one more complex.

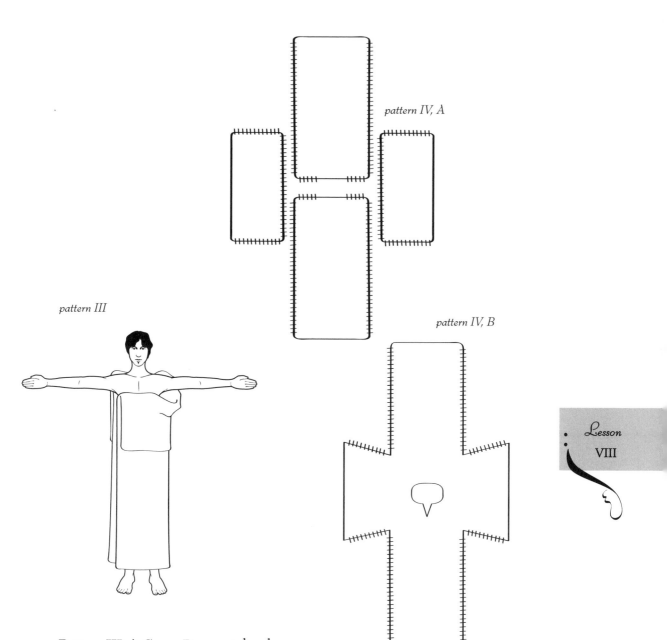

pattern IV, A

pattern III

pattern IV, B

Pattern III: A Greco-Roman style robe may be no more than pieces of fabric attractively draped and pinned over one shoulder. Or it might be a formal Greek chiton, as shown in the pattern.

Pattern IV: The most common style of robe is the medieval "T" robe. Shown are two patterns, one simple, one more complex.

There are many, many styles of robe, and in choosing one—unless we belong to a temple that asks its members to wear a particular style of robe, as some do—our primary consideration is what style makes us feel the most spiritual and magical.

Color

Again, there are many colors for robes, and what color we choose largely depends on whether we belong to a temple that requires specific colors or whether we have only ourselves to please. All colors have symbolic meanings, and every color is appropriate for some ritual, if not necessarily for all. Many temples, however, will require a certain color for robes—often black or white.

It is very common for a temple to wear black robes at new moon and white robes at full moon, or to wear black robes in the Dark half of the year and white robes in the Light half. Other temples may have a single specific color for robes; all their robes will be made in that color, regardless of the occasion. Another common color scheme is for members to dress in the quarter color associated with their astrological sign.

If we are not affiliated with a particular temple, or if our temple doesn't ask for a particular color scheme, then we can choose pretty much whatever color we want.

Decoration

Many people decorate their robes to make them more individual. Even when we belong to a temple that asks for a specific color of robe, we may still be able to decorate it as we wish.

There are many ways to decorate a robe. The most common is to add a border at the hem of the sleeves and skirt. Sometimes people will also place metaphysical symbols on the body of the robes: astrological, elemental, runic, or seasonal symbols, for example. All manner of material can be used to decorate a robe: beads, seashells (especially cowry shells), ribbon, embroidery, fabric paints, and many more. The only limit is your creativity.

Decoration can add greatly to the beauty, symbolic value, and individuality of your robe. But don't overdo it, as too much decoration may tend to be distracting.

Other Details

In making a robe, there are also certain practical considerations we should pay attention to. These are as follows:

- Make sure the neck hole is big enough to get your head through.
- Don't make the sleeves or hem so long or wide as to be dangerous. Remember, there are likely to be candles, and you don't want to set yourself on fire, nor do you want to

trip over your hem while dancing. Few things will disturb the solemnity of a ritual like someone taking a pratfall in the middle of it.

- Make sure the robe is wide enough to move in. Remember, you will want to be able to dance in this garment and to move comfortably and easily. The look of the Morticia Addams fishtail skirt is not necessarily what you're going for here.

· · · ·
The Tabard

Moving on from the robe to other kinds of ritual garment, a tabard is a simple rectangle of cloth that hangs down the front and back of the body but has no sides. The tabard is an ancient Celtic garment that is essentially a very narrow poncho. In Celtic times, they were worn (1) to give extra warmth to the torso, when made of a heavy fabric; (2) as an apron, to protect one's clothing, when made of a cheaper fabric; and (3) for added decoration on a formal occasion, when made of a dressy fabric. In later times, tabards were primarily used to display the insignia of an organization to which one belonged, rather like a kind of uniform. The most famous example of this with which most people would be familiar are the tabards worn by fiction's Three Musketeers.

In Wiccan ritual, it is not uncommon to see tabards used to indicate who will perform certain roles—as, for example, who will call which quarter. They are also sometimes worn to indicate rank, though if a temple is indeed using them to indicate rank, they will tell you. Other times, tabards are worn purely for decoration.

Tabards are easy to make, and you can use one to dress up a basic robe or wear one over street clothes in place of a robe.

· · · ·
The Stole

The stole is a narrow band of fabric worn around the neck, hanging down in front. It may be quite decorative, but it is never worn just for decoration. Only certain traditions use the stole, but if you see one, you can be sure that it has a meaning beyond just being pretty.

In some groups, the stole will be worn only by the chief priestess or chief priest. In others, it may be worn by all initiated clergy. In the Correllian Tradition, the stole is worn by all initiated clergy, dedicants, and full OUTER COURT members, especially for more formal ceremonies. It is used to indicate membership, and its color and markings indicate rank. Initiated clergy wear purple stoles, honorary clergy members wear lavender stoles, dedicants wear white stoles, and Outer Court members wear green stoles.

Many different Pagan traditions use the stole, as do some of the BOOK RELIGIONS, though they will do so for very different reasons. Christians use the stole as the last vestige of the Roman toga. The TOGA, originally a large, cloaklike garment worn wrapped around the body, assumed the form of the stole during the BYZANTINE period, in the opening centuries of the Age of Pisces. Certain Pagan traditions of Mediterranean origin wear the stole for this same reason.

Usually, however, Pagans wear the stole not as a modern version of the Roman toga, but as a modern version of the TORC. The torc was a metal necklace used by the Celtic peoples as a symbol of initiation. It represented death and rebirth. The torc looks rather like a horseshoe, and it is believed that the practice of hanging horseshoes in a house to bring good luck may have come about as a replacement for the earlier practice of hanging a torc. In this sense, then, the stole represents initiation and rebirth and the continuation of the ancient past.

The stole is cognate to the collar. Another modern version of the ancient torc, the collar is a band of cloth worn around the neck, just as the torc once was. The collar may be worn when the stole is too cumbersome.

· · · ·
Vestments

A vestment is a sacred garment that is worn only for ritual or other religious occasions. It is believed that by wearing the vestment only for religious purposes, its ability to act as a key to aid in the shift of consciousness is increased. This is because if we wear the vestment only for magical and spiritual activities, then every time we put it on, our Inner Self will know that we're going to do something magical and spiritual, and it will automatically shift the consciousness to align with the Higher Self.

In some groups, all robes and other garments used for ritual are considered to be vestments and as such are worn for ritual purposes only—never for anything else. Though each Correllian temple is free to establish its own policies, as a tradition Correllianism takes the position that a robe is a garment, like any other garment, and that the only actual vestment is the stole. It may be bad form to wear certain robes for nonreligious purposes, but only the stole has a sanctity unto itself.

· · · ·
State Robes

State robes are robes that are worn to indicate rank, and they should be worn only by persons who possess that rank. Full Correllian state robes are rarely worn.

Each part of the state robe has a meaning: a red tabard, for example, is worn by a Third Degree high priestess or high priest, a gray tabard by an elder of the tradition, and a purple tabard by the heads of the tradition when acting in that capacity. A black Clavis, or narrow tabard, is worn by heads of temples.

The most commonly used part of the Correllian state robes is the stole, whose color and symbols indicate the rank of the wearer. Outer Court members wear green stoles, clerical dedicants wear white stoles, and clergy wear purple stoles. Honorary clergy wear lavender stoles. This system was devised by Reverend Traci Logan-Wood.

• • • •

Jewelry

There are several pieces of jewelry that are associated with Wicca. All manner of necklaces, bracelets, and rings are readily available with Wiccan or Pagan themes or symbols, and these can be worn by anyone. In addition, some temples have special medallions, pins, or rings that are available only to their members and that may or may not symbolize rank. The exclusivity of such symbols should be respected, as a matter of good manners.

There are two particular pieces of jewelry that are commonly used to symbolize rank. The first is the GARTER. The garter

is a piece of fabric or leather tied or buckled just above or below the knee or elbow. There are many variations on how the garter should be made, what color it should be, and so on. These details vary according to the tradition one is dealing with. Some traditions use the garter to indicate a variety of ranks. Most often, however, the garter represents the Third Degree, or High Priesthood, and should be worn only by its members.

The second item is the coronet or tiara. The coronet also represents the Third Degree, and so it should be worn only by Third Degree clergy or Second Degree temple heads. Many kinds of wreath or headband are worn for many reasons by many people in Wicca, especially floral wreaths. But the coronet is something distinct, usually made of metal and mounted with a moon, sun, or other symbol. Sometimes a coronet may be worn by someone taking part in a specific ritual or mystery play because of the role they are playing, but in that case the coronet belongs to the role, not to the person. Usually, however, the coronet is the reward of many years of study and service, and it should be left to those who have earned it.

• • • •

Skyclad Ritual

Another ancient, but somewhat misunderstood, form of ritual garb is going "skyclad"—that is to say, naked. This practice

arises from the idea that psychic energy is restricted or inhibited by clothing, especially tight or binding clothing. As we have said, most people no longer believe this, but it was once taken very seriously.

Another reason for the idea of skyclad ritual is that since we are born naked, we are only truly "pure" when in that state. If we approach Deity nude, we are laying aside the preconceptions and prejudices of the physical world to reveal our inner, spiritual selves. By going without clothes, we operate outside of the social distinctions and self-deceptions clothing often represents, opening ourselves to the light of the Goddess. This aspect is especially clear in the skyclad SADHUS of India: holy people who go naked to show that they have moved beyond the outer form to the inner essence of being. On a more pragmatic level, the kind of clothing that was worn in earlier times was not very practical for dancing or dealing with fire.

Skyclad ritual is a very ancient custom, but it is not very common in modern Wiccan practice. Many Wiccans go skyclad only when they are working alone or with a romantic partner. There are certain distinct advantages to skyclad ritual, however, and it can be very good to experience it at least once. Most people have many issues about their bodies, and working skyclad can help you to become familiar with your body and to accept it as it is. Clothing and

fashion impose many false and unrealistic ideas on our relationship with our bodies. By accepting our bodies as they are, we can break free of these socially imposed ideas. Also, many people use clothing as a mask, placing their physical self-esteem in external items of dress. But external items are purely illusory and not always under our own control, and by accepting our bodies as they are, we can put our self-esteem where it truly belongs: within.

You are not going to encounter skyclad ritual in most temples, but in your own personal practice you may find it very liberating.

• • • •

Exercises

At this point in your development, you should be doing Exercises 7, 8, 9, and 13 every day, plus Exercise 10 periodically. The exercise below is meant to follow Exercise 13 directly.

Exercise 14

When you have finished Exercise 13—the beam of light from the palm chakra—instead of closing down as usual, turn your attention to your third eye.

The third eye is located in the forehead. Because each chakra is actually a collection of many points, the exact location may appear to vary from person to person according to their individual development.

Your third eye may be centered in the middle of your forehead, placed toward the top of your forehead, or located between your eyebrows. If you have a strong feeling for any of these places, use it as the third eye; otherwise, we recommend using the approximate middle of the forehead.

From your third eye, send out a beam of clear red light, just as you have learned to do with your palms. Project that beam out to a wall approximately five or six feet away. Imagine the beam as clearly as possible, with the light as bright a red as possible, and hold it there for as long as you are comfortable, just as you did with the palm in Exercise 11. Then retract the beam of light back into your third eye.

You may find that this gives you a headache. In most people, the third eye is not used to getting much exercise, and it may hurt a bit. If this happens, there is a simple solution to it, one that may be used for any other chakra as well: run yellow light through it. Imagine a ball of yellow light in the third eye, as clear and bright as possible. Continue to see the yellow light until the headache dissolves.

After this, you may do Exercise 10 if you like, or you may go straight to closing down the chakras as usual.

Exercise 15

When you have become comfortable extending the beam of red light from your third eye, you may replace Exercise 14 with Exercise 15.

As you might imagine, Exercise 15 is just like Exercise 14 up until you have extended the beam of light from the third eye. Now use that beam of red light to draw simple designs on the wall, just as you did with your palms in Exercise 12. And just like in Exercise 12, when you have mastered simple designs, try writing words with the beam of light, using cursive letters. As you get better, try drawing the designs in midair and at different distances. When you have finished, retract the beam of light into your third eye, do Exercise 10 if you wish, and then close down your chakras as always and ground and release.

This will exercise and develop your third eye, which is extremely important. And, as with Exercise 12, you can do Exercise 15 anytime you wish: on the bus, at the store, or outdoors, for instance. Just remember that this exercise comes in addition to, not in place of, your daily exercises.

Exercise 16

Exercise 16 is (you guessed it) just like Exercise 15, except that instead of using red light, you will use multicolored light; this increases the effect of the exercise. In all other respects, do it in just the same way as Exercise 15.

Spell for Lesson VIII
The Shadow Knows

In Lesson VIII, we have talked at length about what people wear for ritual. Near the end of this lesson, we discuss the idea of ritual nudity—the idea of wearing nothing at all during ritual. Ritual nudity is an ancient custom based on the desire for freedom of movement, an unencumbered flow of psychic energy, and the belief that when we are nude—as we were born into this world—we are most honestly who we are, as well as closest to Deity.

In modern Wicca, ritual nudity is very rare. It is generally reserved for solitary ritual or for ritual between romantic partners. Many contemporary Wiccans are not comfortable with the idea of ritual nudity at all, except in the most abstract sense. This is because so many people have been taught to feel badly about their bodies. Non-Pagan segments of society tell people that they are too fat or too thin, that their breasts are imperfect or their buttocks sag, that their penises aren't big enough or their noses are too big, that they smell bad, that they are too hairy or not hairy enough, that they're too old . . .

Society tells us these things to control us. No matter what you do, you can't get away from your body. If you feel badly about it, you feel badly about yourself, and if you feel that you aren't good enough,

then you will be susceptible to others who can convince you they are better.

Society does the same thing with our sexuality. And our psychology. And our financial and social position. If we can be made to feel badly about these things, we will feel badly about ourselves, and when we feel badly about ourselves, we can be controlled.

All of these things are part of our SHADOW. Our shadow is the part of us that we do not normally think of but that holds us back. The shadow is made up of all the fears, anxieties, and insecurities we carry around with us. The shadow is composed not only of what society does to us and what our families do to us, but also, and most significantly, what we do to ourselves.

Working to heal the shadow is one of the most important parts of the Correllian Wiccan path. No amount of knowledge or ability has any benefit for you if you are controlled by your shadow. Luckily, the shadow can be worked with.

In Wicca, it is not our goal to suppress or repress the shadow. Rather, we seek to heal it. Healing the shadow is an ongoing process that gets progressively deeper as we grow. If you have been doing the spells given in these lessons, you have already been working on this: as early as Lesson I, the spell for the lesson dealt with releasing aspects of the shadow.

Shadow work always has an effect, although sometimes it must be done several times to completely heal an aspect of the shadow. The further you progress in Correllian Wicca, the more you will heal of the shadow.

The following spell is for working with the shadow aspects of our self-image. To do it, you will need:

- A black candle
- A red candle
- A mirror, preferably a large one
- Time to be alone
- Two sheets of paper
- A burning dish
- A stick or knife to maneuver the burning paper
- Some drawing utensils—crayons, markers, or colored pencils are ideal

Begin by completely undressing. Look at yourself in the mirror. If it is a hand-held mirror, hold it at every angle. Study every part of yourself. Look at things you don't normally look at.

Now take your paper and drawing implements and find a comfortable position. Draw yourself. That's right: draw yourself—nude. Be honest. Show yourself as you really are. Include all the lines. All the sags. All the things you don't like about your body. Include the good things too, but this is meant to focus on what you are not comfortable with.

Don't worry about the quality of the drawing. This is for a spell, not an art show. Put into the drawing what you see and what you feel about yourself, and don't worry what anyone else would think about it.

When you have finished your drawing, think about all of the things you don't like about your body. On the edges of the paper, around the drawing, write these things down. Now write down everything else you don't like about yourself: bad habits, behaviors you wish to change, things that make you insecure, and so on. Put all of these things down on the paper.

Now take the drawing to your altar, and clear and release all excess energy. Light the black candle; black here is for releasing. Hold the sheet of paper in front of you and visualize a ball of white light around the paper. Concentrate on all the things you have written.

Now make an incantation to this effect:

"There is One Power
in the universe,
And I am a perfect
manifestation of that Power.
And as such I release
all of these things
which I have drawn
and written on this paper,
that they may limit me no more.
May they be healed
and transformed

and their energy reused
by the Mother
in new ways as she sees fit.
By my will, with harm toward none,
so mote it be."

Now touch the paper to the candle flame. Continue to imagine the paper surrounded by white light as it burns. Concentrate on releasing all that the paper represents.

When the paper is aflame, set it in the burning dish. Use the stick to lift it so that it can burn underneath. Let it burn until it is completely gone.

Make a final affirmation like:

"And it is done."

Extinguish the black candle. Remember not to blow it out, but rather to snuff it out to show respect. Finally, clear and release all excess energy.

Now go back to your comfortable position. Take up the second sheet of paper and draw yourself again, still nude. This time, focus on the things you like about your body. Think about all of your best traits and abilities. Write these down around your drawing. Now add traits and abilities you wish to develop or to strengthen.

Go back to your altar, and clear and release again. Light the red candle; red here is for manifestation. Visualize the paper surrounded by a ball of white light.

Repeat the incantation, but this time say something like:

"There is One Power
in the universe,
and I am a perfect
manifestation of that Power.
And as such I will that these things
which I have drawn and
written on this paper
will grow in strength and
increase in my life.
May they come to me as surely
as the river goes to the sea,
as surely as the rain comes
to the ground.
By my will, with harm toward none,
so mote it be."

Let the paper burn as before, but now focus not on releasing but on increasing those things the paper represents. Let the paper burn itself out.

Make a final affirmation as before, if you like, and then extinguish the candle and clear and release.

The spell is done. You may not immediately feel all of its effects, but they will rise to the surface in the days to come. And it may be that some of these things may require additional healing; the spell may be repeated as needed. But you will find a pronounced effect that only deepens with time.

God for Lesson VIII
The Hero

The God has two basic forms: the Young God of life, growth, and evolution, and the Old God of death, transformation, and involution. Each of these in turn has two forms as well: the Young God is the Hero and the Lover, and the Old God is the King and the Sorcerer. These might be thought of as the temporal and spiritual polarities of the two God forms. The Hero is the temporal aspect of the Young God, and the Lover is the spiritual. Similarly, the King would be the temporal aspect of the Old God, and the Sorcerer the spiritual.

The Hero, then, is the temporal or outward aspect of the Young God's energy. The Hero is the god of the spring, of dawn, and of beginnings. His festival is the spring equinox, and he is associated with the astrological sign Aries.

The Hero God represents independent young manhood. Energy, vitality, and growth are his attributes, as well as courage and strength. In former times, the Hero was often thought of as a warrior, but he is also an athlete, an adventurer, and a follower of quests. The Hero is idealistic and virtuous, brave and true. He is noble and chivalrous, a protector of the weak and a defender of the just. The Hero is the bearer of new life and the bestower of knowledge. He is the opener of new doors and the blazer of new trails. The Hero subdues and overcomes all problems.

The Hero represents the energy that pushes against all odds and eventually succeeds. He is the spirit in the seed pushing up through the soil, the green leaves unfolding their tender buds for the first time. He is the river water breaking through winter's ice, the animals emerging from their burrows—the spirit of life reawakened.

Like the Maiden Goddess, the Hero God is a patron of the arts and sciences, a disseminator of knowledge. He is the "culture hero" who teaches humankind the skills of civilization. It is the Hero God who brings to humanity the Goddess's gift of agriculture: for example, the Greek Triptolemus, who receives the gift of grain from Demeter, and the Cherokee Inagi, who brings the world the corn and beans that Selv Tvia has produced from her own body.

The Hero God is the son of the Goddess, and her champion. He carries life back to the world with the spring at his mother's behest.

In the story of King Arthur, in which the ancient gods are portrayed as people, it is the Hero God in his form as Percival (or in some versions Galahad) who successfully quests for the Grail and then brings it back to heal the stricken king. Here, the Hero uses the energy of the Goddess,

symbolized by the Grail, to renew the earth after winter.

Often, little distinction is made between the Hero and the Lover. Frequently, they are seen not as different aspects but as different phases of the Young God. Still other times, the two forms may seem wholly different from each other. We will discuss the Lover God in the next lesson.

Below follow several examples of the Hero:

Apollo

Venerated by the Greeks and Romans, Apollo is the god of life force and vitality, creativity, and self-expression. Apollo is the god of beauty and the master of all arts and crafts. He is the lord of prophecy and healing and patron of both physical and spiritual medicine. Apollo is also god of music, which to the Greeks had mathematical significance and represented cosmic order. In later times, Apollo was viewed as the sun god and lord of the year. In one legend, he is made to win a musical contest with a satyr named Marsyas, representing the triumph of spring over winter. In later times, his polar opposite is Dionysus, lord of satyrs. Brother of Artemis/Diana, Apollo will readily be seen to be the god portrayed in the *Vangelo delle Streghe* as the lord of light, master of the physical world.

Green Man

The Green Man, also called Green Jack or Green George, represents the spirit of vegetation that returns to the earth in spring and flourishes in summer. He is particularly associated with the spring equinox, but also with the growing season generally. The Green Man represents the life of the forest and of the fields, and the God as the flowering of the material world. The Green Man is represented in various ways. Often, only his face is shown, surrounded by foliage, which in some versions he is breathing out of his mouth. Sometimes he is represented by a tree or a man in a tree costume. Frequently, the Green Man is shown with his tongue extended, representing the God's sexuality and vital energy. The Green Man represents the God energy growing forth from the Goddess, just as the green vegetation grows from the earth.

Mars

Although usually thought of as a god of war, the Roman god Mars is actually much more than this. Mars represents the summer season, the growing crops, and the warmth of the sun that fertilizes the earth. He stands for courage, strength, and action—the ability to accomplish goals and move forward. Mars also represents strength and honor, as well as virtue and personal integrity. Mars is associated with

Venus and Vulcan in a seasonal myth in which Mars is the summer season, Vulcan the winter season, and Venus the earth that forever moves between the two. Mars is a god of personal achievement, action, and success.

Percival

Percival, or Peredur, figures in the legend of King Arthur as the knight who finds the sacred Grail, which restores the stricken king to health. In the earliest versions of this ancient tale, it is not King Arthur but the Fisher King whom Percival must heal. In the castle of the Fisher King, Percival witnesses a sacred procession. Two men, dressed in polar colors, carry a huge spear, which drips blood. Behind comes a maiden carrying a chalice with an image of a head (the Celtic symbol of the soul) inside it. When asked what this procession means, Percival remains silent. He is later told that had he answered, the Fisher King would have been cured of his lameness—that is, the Old God of winter would have been reborn as the Young God of spring. The secret of this procession, which Percival did not speak, is this: the blood-dripping spear is the God-force, overflowing with life, that comes out of the Goddess, represented by the head in the cauldron, which also represents the consciousness of the womb of creation.

Thor

Originally called Thunar, or "thunder," Thor is the Germanic god of storms and fertility. Son of the earth goddess Jord, Thor embodied the vitality of the life force and the masculine virtues of courage and integrity. He was pictured as a red-bearded man carrying the sacred thunder-hammer Mjollnir, or in some versions a sacred thunder-axe. With this magical implement, Thor made thunder and lightning and sent the fertilizing rains upon the earth, his mother. Thor was also strongly linked to sacred trees and sacred groves, and he was sometimes represented by a tree.

· · · ·

Glossary for Lesson VIII

book religions—According to Orpheis Caroline High-Correll, progenitor of the Correllian Tradition, there are two religions in the world: Native (or Pagan) religions and book religions. Pagan religions are living religions that grow out of people's direct experience of Deity through Nature and metaphysical experience. Pagan religions change and develop as culture and people's abilities develop. The book religions descend from the Bible and Koran and believe themselves to be "revealed religions"— that is, that they are perfect in origin and must never be changed.

Lesson
VIII

Byzantine—The Byzantine Empire is a term used to describe the last phase of the Eastern Roman Empire. Toward the end of its long history, Rome broke into two portions: the Western Roman Empire, with its capital at the ancient city of Rome itself, and the Eastern Roman Empire, with its capital at the city of Byzantium, also known historically as Constantinople and today as Istanbul. Although the Western Empire fell at the dawn of the Age of Pisces (AD 400), the Eastern Empire continued for another thousand years, falling to the Turks in 1092 Pisces (AD 1492). From the Western Roman Empire developed the Roman Catholic Church, and the Eastern Roman Empire created many Orthodox Christian churches. Because of the extreme animosity between these churches—typical of the book religions—the people of Western Europe preferred to call the Eastern Roman Empire "Byzantium" and considered it Greek rather than Roman, which the latter considered insulting.

Celtic—The Celtic people are believed to have developed in central or Eastern Europe sometime around 700 BC (500 Aries), and they spread through Western Europe all the way to the British Isles. (Some scholars believe their origin to be much earlier.) Interbreeding with the preexisting peoples of Western Europe, the Celts developed a distinctive and highly mystical culture. Absorbed by the Roman Empire, Celtic culture had a strong influence on medieval Europe and consequently the modern world. The Druids, the Celtic priesthood, have been a subject of fascination for subsequent generations and are believed to be a major contributing strain to modern Wiccan thought. The great Greek philosopher Pythagoras cited the Druids as a primary source for many of his teachings as well.

garter—A band of cloth, leather, or metal worn around the leg just above or below the knee or on the arm just above the elbow, the garter is an ancient garment still in use as an item of dress. The garter is also used by Wiccan high clergy in certain traditions as a symbol of rank. There are many variations on exactly how a high priestess's or high priest's garter should be made, and these vary with the tradition. Perhaps the most famous example of the garter from history comes from the reign of England's Edward III. Tradition has it that a noblewoman, perhaps the countess of Salisbury or the "Fair Maid of Kent" (consort of the Black Prince) dropped her garter at a royal ball. The king picked up the garter, saying, "Let none think ill of it," and proceeded to found the Order of the Garter in honor of the event. It is believed that the lady was a priestess of the Old Religion, and that in doing this the king extended his protection to her. According to Margaret Murray, there are many things to suggest the active promotion of Pagan religion by England's Plantagenet dynasty.

keys—Keys are outer forms (items or concepts) that are used to help a person to shift their consciousness and connect with the Higher Self. Anything that makes a person feel more spiritual or magical can serve as a key. Robes, incense, and many kinds of atmospheric trappings are commonly used as keys, as are all of the techniques and ingredients of spellcraft. Keys are very useful, especially to the beginner, as they help people to make shifting consciousness easier and more automatic. Fully realized magic users, however, require no external stimuli to aid in their work, though they may still enjoy using them.

Outer Court—Many temples have both an Inner and an Outer Court. In such temples, the Inner Court is made up of the actual clergy of the temple, while members of the Outer Court are free to attend temple ceremonies but are not expected to train for the clergy.

sadhu—A sadhu is a kind of holy person in certain sects of the Hindu and Jain religions, one who pursues a life of meditation and spirituality. Often, Sadhus wear little or no clothing, which symbolizes that they are dealing with the inner essence rather than the outer form. A famous example of such a holy person is Mahatma Gandhi, who adopted a loincloth as his principal item of dress. In the Jain religion, founded by Mahavira, holy people go completely naked, eschewing even a loincloth, after Mahavira's own practice. It is Mahavira who coined the term *skyclad*.

shadow—*Shadow* is a term we use to describe feelings that we do not normally think of but that function as limitations in our lives. The shadow is made up of all the fears, anxieties, and insecurities we carry around with us.

toga—The Roman Empire dominated ancient Europe during the Age of Aries, collapsing just before the advent of the Piscean Age. Beginning as a republic, Rome gradually slid into despotism over the course of centuries. A garment that could be worn only by Roman citizens, the elite of the empire, the toga was a length of white cloth worn wrapped around the body and fastened over the left shoulder. The toga took different forms in different periods, beginning as a relatively simple cloak and ending as a version of the stole, a long, thin piece of fabric wrapped around the body or worn hanging over the shoulders.

torc—In Celtic religion, the torc, a circular metal necklace, was a symbol of initiation and the Divine Mysteries. The torc's circular shape reflects the cyclical nature of reality and the ancient concept of Ourobouros: the snake swallowing its own tail, representing the idea that all things ultimately return to their source. Sacred to Cernunnos-Secculos-Dagda, the Celtic lord of the dead and of the spirit realms, the torc not only was worn as a symbol of initiation but was also used as a symbol of all things magical and spiritual. It was frequently hung up in a house to confer protection, in which use it was later replaced by the horseshoe. Suppressed first by the Romans and then by the Christians, the torc survives today in many altered forms, not least of which is the stole, a narrow band of cloth worn around the neck as a symbol of priesthood.

Study Questions for Lesson VIII

1. What do people usually wear at a Wiccan ceremony?

2. Name a reason people wear robes.

3. Who is Doreen Valiente? To what Wiccan tradition does she belong?

4. What is an Outer Court?

5. Give an example of a common color scheme that a temple might use for robes.

6. Where did the Celtic people come from?

7. In the state robes of the Correllian Tradition, what color symbolizes the Third Degree?

8. What is a vestment? What does the Correllian Tradition recognize as a vestment?

9. What color is a Correllian stole? Why do you think that is?

10. What is a torc? What does it mean?

11. What is a garter? Who can wear it?

12. What does the term *skyclad* mean?

13. Name one potential benefit of skyclad working.

Lesson

IX

Symbols, Omens, and Divination

Symbolism is extremely important in Pagan religion and probably has been since the beginning. Symbolism is the use of an easily recognized creature or object to represent a more abstract or elevated concept. Thus, a serpent may be used to represent psychic power and connection to the Divine; a feather may represent truth, purity, or the element of air; and the chalice may be used to represent the womb of creation and the Goddess's all-pervading, all-sustaining Spirit.

In Wicca, as with all things in life, everything is exactly as it seems on the surface, yet below that surface lie many other levels. Through the use of symbolism, even seemingly simple images and acts take on rich deeper meanings. The casting of the circle and the calling of the quarters symbolically portray the creation of the universe and the interaction of elements that continues it—from thought (air) and action (fire) to emotional reaction (water) and understanding and integration (earth). The conjoining of the cup and sword portrays the eternal interaction of the Goddess and the God, spirit and matter, death and life.

So too the rich symbolism of animals, plants, and abstract motifs can be used to convey important spiritual ideas in the decoration of simple objects. A chalice decorated with lotuses speaks of the growth of spiritual enlightenment, for the lotus is rooted in the mud and grows up through water to bloom in the open air, just as our consciousness is rooted in physical perception, grows up through emotional and mental understanding, and blooms in spiritual enlightenment. An athame decorated with the head of a stag refers to the magical qualities of the Old God, while oak leaves refer to the strength and vitality of the Young God.

The use of multiple symbols to convey complex spiritual ideas is called allegory. It has been said that allegory is the crowning achievement of Pagan thought. Allegory allows a single artwork, story, or symbolic action to convey many meanings at once, on many levels. Allegory allows subtle ideas to be conveyed through simpler, blunter forms, so that they may be more easily understood.

Thus, a myth such as the DESCENT OF THE GODDESS, which appears so simple

on the surface that it could be taken as a children's tale, speaks not only to issues of life and death, but also the interaction of spirit and matter, the nature of reality, the energetic system of the chakras, and the cycle of the seasons—all at once.

Symbolism is important because, though intelligible to the conscious mind, it also speaks directly to our subconscious and can be absorbed on that level. Often, the conscious mind can absorb in symbolic fashion complex ideas that it could not grasp easily in abstract form. In this way, we can make an emotional connection to information that we might otherwise find too complicated to identify with intellectually.

• • • •

Omens

An omen is a symbolic message from Spirit—that is, the Goddess. Omens come in many forms and can show up at any time. Probably the most famous example of an omen is the black cat crossing one's path. Commonly understood as bringing bad luck, this omen would be better and more accurately described as a warning to be careful and avoid unnecessary risks.

Omens have been with us since the beginning. Some people think omens are SUPERSTITIONS, but if you understand that your connection to the Goddess comes from within, then the idea of receiving messages from the Goddess should not seem odd. And since the Spirit of the Goddess is within all things, all things can serve as her messengers.

There are many traditional meanings for omens, and we have referred to some of these in this lesson. But in interpreting an omen, it is more important to pay attention to what a symbol means to you than what it may have meant to others. Since your connection to Goddess comes from inside, she certainly knows what things mean to you as an individual, and she will use this knowledge to communicate with you. Thus, though tradition says that a spider seen in the morning warns of difficulties ahead, if you particularly love spiders or are a devotee of a spider goddess such as Arachne or the Native American Grandmother Spider, the spider may have positive meaning for you no matter when you see it.

To take best advantage of the Goddess's ability to speak to you through omens, you should familiarize yourself with a wide variety of traditional symbols, as well as with things that have symbolic value for you individually. Once you have developed a rich inner language of symbols that you will understand as omens, the Goddess's ability to communicate with you in this way is greatly expanded, whereas if you have only a few symbols to use, or a fuzzy understanding of what those symbols mean

to you, your ability to receive omens will be greatly lessened.

When people speak of omens, they are usually thinking of messages that come unbidden. But you can ask for an omen in response to a question too; this is divination.

· · · ·

Divination

Divination is the term for systems of symbols we use to help us speak to Deity or to our own Higher Selves, which are of course emanations of Deity (see Lesson II). If you ask for an omen in response to a question, you are practicing divination.

Say, for example, that you're in a park or in the woods. You might ask the Goddess to give you an answer to a question by the omen of the next animal you see. You might specify, for example:

"O Goddess, if the answer to my question is yes, may the next bird I see be brown. If the answer is no, may the next bird I see be black."

Or you might leave the omen open-ended, especially if you're asking how a given situation will go. For example:

"O Goddess, may the next animal I see tell me how I may expect this situation will progress."

Lesson IX

177

NUMBER CHART FOR DIVINATION

Number	Meaning
one	self-reliance, personal ability, and one's own capabilities
two	partnership, assistance, and peace
three	growth, expansion, fertility, creativity, and good luck
four	practicality, stability, life lessons, and working things through
five	communication, movement, and speed
six	love, home, and pleasure
seven	spirituality, psychism, and spiritual aid or guidance
eight	intensity, extremity, and great success or failure
nine	compassion, helping others, and group projects
ten	completion and unity

COLOR CHART FOR DIVINATION

Color	Meaning
black	protection, safety, grounding; also wisdom, learning
red	strength, vitality, passion
pink	love, compassion, nurturing
orange	creativity, self-expression
yellow	pleasure, happiness, success
green	healing, growth, abundance, money
blue	communication, focus, willpower
indigo	psychic ability, spiritual guidance
violet	spirituality, connection to Higher Self, Goddess
white	all purposes, unity, purity

If the next animal you see is a dog, it could mean a happy outcome to the situation. If the next animal is a spider, it might indicate a need to meditate and seek inner guidance.

Or, in another example, you might be walking on the street or riding a bus and say to the Goddess:

"O Goddess, if the answer to my question is yes, then may the next person I see be wearing a warm color. If the answer is no, may they be wearing a cool color."

This sounds very simple, and so it is. But you must be psychically open to do it, so you will want to clear and release before you begin. Also, like anything else, practice makes perfect. If at first you don't receive good results, work with it. If you have been doing the exercises that accompany these lessons, you should not have any trouble with this, as you will have opened and strengthened your psychic abilities. If you have not been doing the exercises, you will find psychic work harder.

There are many more formal kinds of divination that can be used to get more detailed answers. Among the most famous of these forms are TAROT CARDS, TEA LEAVES, and RUNESTONES. These forms of divination use complex systems of omens to divine very specific answers to questions.

The answers come because Deity speaks to us from within, through the medium of whatever symbolic language we understand. This, again, is stated in the ancient maxim of Hermes Trismegistus: "As above, so below." Because all of the universe is an emanation of the Goddess, and all of our souls ultimately connect to her, the totality of the DIVINE PLAN can be seen reflected in all of its parts, for nothing that exists is separate from the rest. Because this is so, anything that exists can be used for divination.

In this lesson, we have discussed several different forms of divination, some of which you might like to try. But remember, again: practice makes perfect. If at first you don't get good results, keep working. You'll get better. Also remember that you have free choice. Any form of omen or divination shows you not what must be, but what will be if circumstances remain unchanged. Use the information you get to help you make the conditions you want, not to limit your choices. Nothing in a spiritual path should ever limit or bind you; rather, everything can help you to open and grow.

. . . .

Exercises

By this point in your development, you may find yourself feeling very drained after doing your exercises. This is because you're using psychic "muscles" you're not used to using, and this unaccustomed activity makes them sore—just as your physical body will be sore if you begin a new exercise regimen that uses muscles you have not been using otherwise.

Happily, just as there are salves and medicines for the physical body, there are ENERGETIC restoratives for your psychic muscles. Not only after doing psychic exercises, but also anytime you feel your energy is low, these techniques can help you restore your natural balance. Use these techniques anytime you feel you need them, but especially if you find yourself feeling tired after doing any kind of psychic work.

Like the Lemon exercise from Lesson VI, these techniques are not meant to be permanently added to your daily routine, but rather to be used occasionally as they are needed.

Exercise 17: **The Pearl**

This exercise is intended both to replenish energy and to soothe frayed nerves. Thus, it is very good to use this if you are feeling nervous tension or exasperation as well as fatigue.

Place your hands in front of you, and between them imagine a ball of white light about one foot wide. Now add detail to this ball of light: imagine it as a giant pearl, softly iridescent and gently glowing.

When you have the image of this giant pearl clear in your mind, imagine the inside of the pearl filled with a thick, viscous amber light, the color and consistency of honey. This honey-colored light is translucent and glowing softly from within.

Lift the pearl up over your head and bring it down upon the top of your head. As it comes into contact with the top of your head, imagine the pearl rupturing and all of the thick, rich, honey-colored energy pouring into your body.

Visualize the honey-colored energy going down into your body, coating every part of it—and soothing frayed nerves and rough edges everywhere it goes. Let the honey-colored energy distribute throughout and settle in your body, going wherever it is needed. When you are finished, clear and release as always.

Practice this exercise every day for one week to get the hang of it, and then use it only as needed. Periodic use of the Lemon exercise and the Pearl exercise will help keep you open and unblocked as you continue your other exercises.

Exercise 18: **The Silver Ball**

After practicing the Pearl exercise for one week, you will be ready to try the Silver Ball. Like the Lemon and the Pearl, this exercise is meant to be used as needed, rather than as a permanent addition to your daily psychic exercises. The Silver Ball is intended to increase or restore energy. The exercise uses a stronger energy than you may be used to, one with which it is good to become familiar.

As with the Pearl, you will begin by forming a ball of energy between your hands. Imagine this ball not as white light, however, but as a sparkling silver light—rather like the silver glitter used in craft projects. Imagine the light composed of thousands of constantly moving, glittering silver particles. You might think of it as being filled with tiny silver stars in swirling motion.

When you have this image clear in your mind, bring the ball of swirling silver glitter up over your head. Then bring the silver ball down through the top of your head and into your body, stopping at the heart chakra.

Now imagine this glittering silver light beginning to expand beyond the ball: moving out into your body, going into every part of your body, and filling you completely until you are saturated with it. Let the light circulate within your body for a while. Then clear and release, allowing the excess light to run out of you.

Do this exercise every day for one week to become familiar with it. Thereafter, use it only as needed. This is a very powerful form of energy, and very useful. If you continue your studies beyond the First Degree, you will learn much more about how to use it.

Exercise 19: The Golden Ball

After you have spent a week with the Silver Ball exercise, you are ready for the Golden Ball. As you might imagine, the Golden Ball is very much like the Silver Ball, except it is gold. This may seem like a small change, but in reality it is not: though the exercise is very similar, the energy is very different.

Again, place your hands in front of you and create a ball of light between them—this time, a ball of glittering golden light. Imagine the light as if it were composed of thousands of particles of swirling golden glitter. When the image is clear, you will bring the ball of golden light up over your head and thence down into your heart chakra, just as you did with the silver ball of light.

Also as you did with the silver light, allow the golden light to expand throughout your body, filling it completely so that you are saturated and suffused with the sparkling golden light. Allow this energy to circulate for a time, and then release.

As with the other exercises in this lesson, practice the Golden Ball for one week and then use it only as needed. This golden light is a very powerful form of energy, one which you are only touching on here, and it is not at full strength in this form. If you continue your studies, you will in time learn much more about it.

Lesson

IX

Spell for Lesson IX
Merlin's Rune

This month's spell comes to us from Merlin the Enchanter, head of the House of Lawrence and proprietor of the Lawrence Museum of Magic and Witchcraft, established in 1537 Pisces (AD 1937).

This is an old spell that makes use of runes. RUNE is a Germanic word for a magical symbol or marking. The term is used especially to refer to the ancient Germanic alphabet—also called FUTHARK—that was used for magical workings, but it can also be used to refer to other magical markings or SIGILS.

This spell is intended to work with one of several general goals. The specific details of how the goal will come to pass are left to the universe to decide. This is usually for the best. If for some reason you must be more specific, then instead of the rune, or along with it, use a written word or a symbol of your own design that represents your goal.

Select the rune that represents your goal. Below are several traditional magical runes to choose from:

Healing (yellow): ᛉ

Protection (white): Ⴤ

Love (red): ᚷ

Prosperity (green): ᚾᛉᚾ

Each rune has an accompanying color. You will need to acquire a piece of paper and an accompanying candle in that color. Any eight-inch to ten-inch candle will do, but a knob candle separated into nine segments is ideal. On the bottom of the candle, carve the rune you have chosen. This represents the foundation of your working.

Now take your piece of paper—it needn't be large—and draw the rune that represents your goal at the four quarters of the paper. This will represent the dispersing of your intent to the universe, through the four quarters. Also, if you are doing the spell for another person, write that person's name in the center of the paper.

Now you can set up your altar for the spell. You can either use your regular working altar or create a special altar specifically for the spell. Either way, be aware that the process of this spell will take nine days, during which the candle should not be moved, so bear this in mind as you decide where and how to set it up.

You will need the following things:

- The candle in the appropriate color with the rune carved into the bottom
- The paper in the appropriate color with the rune written at all four quarters
- A fireproof burning dish, as discussed in Lessons II and IV

- Matches or a lighter
- A coin

Begin, as always, by clearing and releasing excess energy.

You may choose to dress your candle (see also Lesson IV). If so, you would do that now. You might use lavender for healing, cinnamon for protection, rose for love, or vanilla for prosperity. To dress the candle, put a little of the oil in the palm of your left hand. Now rub your two hands together so that they are coated with the oil. As you rub your hands together, visualize white light shining out from between them, and see this white light expand and grow into a ball of light around your hands. Now take up your candle, holding it by the middle. Slowly work the oil up toward the top of the candle, a little bit at a time, and then down toward the bottom. As you do this, imagine the candle filling with white light and concentrate on the goal you have chosen. Coat the whole candle with oil, including the wick, and then return it to the altar.

Now place the coin directly in front of the candle. Light the candle.

As the candle burns, focus on your goal. Imagine the goal strongly, and picture it being fulfilled. Imagine what it is like to have achieved this goal in your life. For example, if you are working for healing, see yourself being healed and healthy, and if you are working for prosperity, imagine yourself surrounded by money or by items that represent prosperity to you. The more strongly you concentrate on your goal, the better.

Now take up your paper. Imagine the paper surrounded by a ball of white light, shining with energy in every direction. As you visualize this ball of light, continue to focus on your goal so that the energy becomes strongly impregnated with it.

Touch the paper to the candle flame so that it ignites. As the paper begins to burn, imagine a ball of white light around the flame, growing larger and stronger as the flame grows. Focus strongly on your goal and speak the following incantation:

*"Behold, there is one power
in the universe, and I am
a perfect manifestation
of that power. And as such
I will that
[insert your goal here]
will come to me.
It will come to me
in the best and most positive way
and with harm toward none.
I will it. I draw it to me.
I manifest it. I accept it.
I receive it. And I give thanks
for it. By my will, so mote it be."*

Lesson
IX

183

As the fire begins to consume the paper, you will want to place it in the burning dish, where it can burn safely. Continue to concentrate on your goal and visualize the burning paper surrounded by a ball of white light, until the paper is reduced to ashes.

When the fire goes out, sit and meditate before the still-burning candle for a few moments. Focus on the goal and upon the flame of the candle. Meditate for about ten to fifteen minutes, and then extinguish the candle. If you are using a knob candle, let it continue to burn until the first segment is completely gone. Remember to snuff the candle flame rather than blow it out, and as you do so, say:

"By all the power of three times
three, as I do will, so mote it be!"

Now clear and release. Scatter the ashes of the paper outdoors so that your intent is symbolically released to the universe.

Each day for the next eight days (making a total of nine), you will light the candle again. Imagine the flame surrounded by white light. Repeat the incantation given above, and then meditate on your goal for ten to fifteen minutes. If you're using a knob candle, let one full segment burn away each day. Then extinguish the candle, saying:

"By all the power of three times
three, as I do will, so mote it be!"

After the nine days, you should have only a stump of the candle left, with the original rune still on the bottom. Take this candle stump to a tree you are particularly fond of, or to any tree that is tall and strong. Take the coin that has been sitting with the candle all this time too.

Make a little hole at the base of the tree and place the candle stump in it. Place the coin in the hole as well, as an offering to the tree spirit. Cover the hole over and say something to the effect of:

"O tree, even as you grow,
may the power of this my working
grow likewise. I thank you for
your aid. So mote it be."

This is a very ancient act based on both the idea of SYMPATHETIC MAGIC—that is, the idea that like creates like—and the idea that the spell's power will grow and flourish because the tree grows and flourishes, and the two have been mystically bound.

Now leave the tree, knowing that your goal will continue to grow and unfold in your life and trusting that it shall come to pass.

Lesson

IX

• • • •
God for Lesson IX
The Lover

The Hero is the temporal aspect of the Young God—that is, the Hero, who brings life back to the world in the spring, expresses the energy of the Young God in a physical way. The Lover expresses that same energy on a more spiritual or cosmic level.

The Lover represents the God as consort of the Goddess. She is spirit and he is matter. She is yin and he is yang. Their union creates and maintains the physical world, which arises from her and is carried out by him.

The Lover God represents the principle of the God at its greatest power. This is the yang or outgoing principle, symbolized by the sun. The Lover represents the flowering of physical life and the material plane. The festival of the Lover is the summer solstice, when the sun reaches its greatest strength. Astrologically, he is associated with the lunar sign of Cancer, symbolizing his union with the Goddess. The principal myth of the Lover is the story of his death and rebirth, for the sun begins to diminish as soon as the summer solstice is past. For this reason, he is also sometimes called "the Dying God."

The Lover achieves his union with the Goddess and then dies, becoming the Old God of winter. In spring, he will be reborn again to repeat the cycle. The Lover is the spirit of earthly life, which is constantly dying and being reborn, transforming and assuming new forms that carry it forward from life to life. Thus, though the earth turns to winter, it always returns to spring. Though day gives way to night, a new dawn always follows. Though our bodies die, we are eternally reborn in new and different forms, even as we have already lived many lives before this birth. The union of the Lover and the Goddess symbolizes this eternal and perfect cycle.

As a personal deity, the Lover embodies all of the strengths of the sun, life, and balance. He is the master of every art and skill. He is beautiful beyond words. He embodies all virtues and expresses the highest ideals of a given culture.

The Lover is the ideal consort of the Goddess, and he acts from a fully activated heart center: his emotions are positive and harmonious. He is the patron of poetry, music, and dance. He is a god of love, beauty, and joy. The Lover represents the joy of life and the exuberance of being.

Bear in mind that while the Hero and the Lover are sometimes conceived of as separate forms of the God, at other times they are seen more as phases through which the God moves. It is not uncommon for a single form of the God to be both the Hero and the Lover. Some gods, like the Egyptian Osiris, combine all four aspects

Lesson

IX

of the God among their attributes. However, each of these four main aspects—Hero, Lover, King, and Sorcerer—are inherently distinct in themselves, and understanding them separately helps to clarify their nature even when a single personal deity combines them.

Below are several examples of the Lover:

Attis

Attis is the consort of Cybele, a Mother goddess whose worship originated in Asia Minor (modern Turkey) and later became popular throughout the Roman Empire. According to a central myth, Cybele was the first being to come into existence—Primordial Deity. Both male and female, Cybele contained within herself the origins of all things. But Cybele was lonely and desired a companion, and so she cut off her masculine genitals and used them to create Attis, lord of the physical world. Thus, Primordial Deity divided herself between female (spirit) and male (matter), just as in the *Vangelo delle Streghe*. The physical world took form, and Cybele and Attis lived happily in it. But in time, Attis came to die, gored by a wild boar, and he then went into the land of death to become the consort of Persephone, goddess of the dead. Grief-stricken Cybele struck a deal with Persephone, allowing Attis to spend half the year with each of them, thus establishing the seasons and the cycle of death and rebirth. Attis is therefore seen to be the world of matter, eternally moving between life and death—or evolution and involution. The yearly death and resurrection of Attis were marked by elaborate rites in which he was represented by a tree, like the European Green Man. Cybele and Attis were served by a transsexual clergy who sought to unify both sexes within themselves, as does Primordial Deity.

Horus

In Egyptian mythology, the god Osiris taught the Egyptians all arts and sciences and ruled them as their king. In time, Osiris was murdered by his brother Set, who coveted both Osiris's kingdom and his wife, Isis. Unwilling to yield to Set, Isis fled from Egypt and resurrected Osiris through magic, becoming pregnant with a child, Horus. Thereafter, Osiris became ruler of the Otherworld, and Horus took his place in the world of the living. Though the Egyptians looked upon Horus as the son of Osiris, he still fulfilled the role of the reborn deity who triumphs over death. Growing to adulthood, Horus engaged his uncle Set in battle, and they became polar opposites. In earlier traditions, the struggle of Horus (life) and Set (death) was eternal, and they were more or less equals. In later traditions, Horus defeated his uncle Set and banished him. Identified with the sun and with the concept of Light, Horus was often pictured as a falcon or a falcon-headed man. The disk of the sun—that is, its physical form—was the *Utchat*, or "Eye of Horus."

Lugh

Also called Lugus and Lleu, Lugh is the Celtic version of the dying and reborn God. Born of the sky goddess Arianrhod ("Silver Wheel"), Lugh was raised by his uncle Gwydion, god of sorcery. Because the magic of his mother prevented Lugh from marrying any mortal maid, Gwydion used his magic to create a bride for Lugh from nine kinds of flowers. This was Blodeuwydd ("Appearance of Flowers"). For a time, Blodeuwydd lived happily with Lugh, and the world abode in summer. But after some months, Blodeuwydd fell in love with Hafgan, and together they plotted Lugh's death. But the same magic Arianrhod had used to prevent Lugh's marriage to a mortal woman also made him impervious to any injury, either upon land or in water, indoors or outdoors, mounted or on foot, clothed or naked. And so it was necessary for Blodeuwydd and Hafgan to go to some lengths to bring about the god's death. So Blodeuwydd prepared a bath for Lugh under an outdoor pavilion. When the time came for him to get out of the bath, Lugh found the tub was too high to easily step out of. So he wrapped himself in a towel

and had a nearby goat brought over to use as a stepping stool. As Lugh stepped out of the bath—balanced with one foot on the goat, the other on the rim of the tub, and wearing only a towel under an open pavilion—Hafgan struck, running him through with a spear at that brief moment when the god was vulnerable. Thereafter, the world fell to winter. Grief-stricken Gwydion searched for Lugh for many months. At last, Gwydion found Lugh reincarnated as an eagle, perched in a tree. Gwydion used magic to restore Lugh to his former self, and the world returned to spring, thus inaugurating the cycle of the seasons.

Tammuz

According to an ancient Mesopotamian myth, Tammuz was the king of Uruk and husband of the goddess Ishtar. Killed by a wild boar—an animal often used to represent the deity of the Otherworld—Tammuz crossed into the realm of death, which was ruled by the goddess Allat, sister of Ishtar. Stricken with grief, Ishtar resolved to go into the land of death and reclaim her beloved consort. Descending through seven symbolic gates, which represent the seven planes of existence and the seven chakras, Ishtar arrived at the realm of her sister Allat. Through means that vary in different versions, Ishtar convinces Allat to release Tammuz and all the other spirits of the dead, thus inaugurating the cycle

of death and rebirth. The myth speaks on several levels to the mysteries of death and rebirth, the cycle of the seasons, and also the spirit's entry into the world of matter. Ishtar, Tammuz, and Allat are the Semitic names of deities whom the Sumerians had earlier known as Inanna, Dumuzi, and Ereshkigal. Some people believe that Dumuzi was a real king of Uruk near the end of the Age of Gemini (4400–2800 BC) who became identified with the pre-existing myth.

Xango

Xango is the Afro-diasporic god of fertility. Lord of storms, Xango is accompanied by thunder and lightning and governs the rains that fertilize the earth. Xango is thought of as the epitome of masculine beauty and virtue. He is the god of courage, honor, and skill. Like the Germanic Odin, Xango hung himself from the World Tree and died, only to be resurrected through the efforts of the goddess Oya, thus bringing about the cycle of the seasons and of death and rebirth. Xango's symbol is the two-headed thunder-axe, the *Oshe Xango*.

• • • •

Glossary for Lesson IX

Descent of the Goddess—The Descent of the Goddess is one of the most important Wiccan myths, one that has meanings on many levels. The Descent of the Goddess is used to illustrate ideas of reincarnation and the cyclical nature of time. More importantly, the Descent of the Goddess speaks to the nature of spirit and matter and the way in which they interact to form the universe, and the purpose behind this all. The Descent of the Goddess tells how the God "fell into matter"—that is, when the Goddess separated the physical parts of herself from the spiritual parts, creating the God, the physical aspects solidified, becoming the material world. To redeem these, the Goddess entered into matter herself, in the form of the millions of souls, and reunited with the God in this way. In time, these souls, combining both material and spiritual aspects, will return to their origin, just as the earth returns to summer after each winter and the soul is reborn after each lifetime.

Divine Plan—The term *Divine Plan* refers to the idea that nothing happens accidentally or randomly, but rather everything is united as part of a single divine whole, all of whose parts have meaning. The Divine Plan is an intrinsic part of Deity that is contained within everything that exists, since everything that exists is ultimately a manifestation of Deity. The Divine Plan can be accessed through the monadic level of the being, which, though separate from Deity, retains all of the essential nature of Deity at the core of the individual soul. The idea that the totality of the Divine Plan is present in all things, and can be seen through them, is the ultimate meaning of "As above, so below," the ancient maxim of Hermes Trismegistus.

energetic—The term *energetic* as used here refers to things pertaining to psychic energy. Thus, *energetic healing* refers to healing by means of psychic energy, the chakra system is part of one's *energetic body*, and the movement of energy between chakras is through *energetic circuits*.

Futhark—*Futhark* is a modern term used to describe the ancient Germanic runic alphabet. *F-u-th-a-r-k* are the first six letters of that alphabet, hence the name we use for it today. In recent years, there has been a great interest in using the runes of the Futhark for magic and divination, and so the term *runes* is most commonly used in reference to these. There are several variations of the Futhark alphabet, including Scandinavian, Saxon, and German forms. Some Celtic peoples also adopted the Futhark alphabet in certain periods. The Germanic peoples were very superstitious about the Futhark runes and considered them very powerful. People who worked with runes, magically or otherwise, were

called *Witca*—a word closely related to the modern *Witch*.

intent—We do magic by consciously focusing energy. We shape that energy through thought and emotion. The energy takes its direction from the intent we set into that thought and emotion. Intent is your goal or purpose— what you wish to achieve. And it is very important to be clear in intent. When you concentrate on your intent during a magical working, you are imprinting the energy with your intent so that the energy will shape itself to bring your intent to pass.

runes—Runes are magical symbols that are used to communicate ideas or messages. The term refers specifically to simple line symbols that are or that resemble letters of an alphabet. Most commonly, the term refers to the Germanic Futhark alphabet, but it can also be used to describe other magical alphabets as well, notably the Theban magical alphabet, the letters of which are also called Witches' Runes. In addition to alphabetic symbols, a number of pictographic symbols have been traditionally termed "runes." These pictographic symbols were used to represent ideas such as prosperity, as well as professions, marital status, and degrees of kinship. In traditional German half-timbered

189

buildings, one can often see this sort of runic symbol built into the facade of the house; this makes a statement about the people who lived there or was used to attract something the family needed.

runestones—Runestones make up a system of divination based on a series of stones or plaster markers inscribed with the letters of the ancient Germanic Futhark alphabet. They are read in a number of ways, most commonly by drawing one or more stones from a bag and interpreting the message based on the meaning of the runes inscribed upon the stones.

sigils—A sigil is a magical symbol representing a deity, spirit, or concept in picture form. A sigil is usually very abstract and easy to draw, so that anyone can use it. Sigils are very important in magic, both because they convey complex ideas in simple forms and because in former times people who used magic often could not read, and so relied upon pictographic forms to convey ideas much more than people tend to do today.

superstitions—The great Pagan philosopher Plutarch, in his book *De Superstitiones*, defined the difference between religion and superstition in this way: religion is based on love of Deity, and superstition is based on fear of Deity.

Superstitions are practices based on a fear of consequences that do not in reality come about; thus, they are illogical and senseless ideas. For example, no one ever broke their mother's back by having stepped upon a crack in the sidewalk. An omen is not a superstition. Rather, an omen is a message from Spirit that can help you to improve or correct a situation; thus, it is wholly positive and is to be welcomed rather than feared.

sympathetic magic—Sympathetic magic is based on the idea of sympathy—that items that have similar qualities can be used to represent each other and can be used to affect each other magically. Thus, because growing plants are green, green is the color of growth and increase, and therefore you burn a green candle to bring prosperity. Because fire brings transformation—changing raw food to cooked and wood and other materials to ash—burning a magical charm on a piece of paper can bring transformation to a situation. In reality, these are keys, or symbolic tools that we use to focus our energy and intent, which is what really makes the change.

tarot cards—Tarot is a system of divination based on a series of allegorical images drawn or printed upon cards. The deck is shuffled and specific cards are drawn, from which messages are divined. Tarot cards appear to have been created in the AD 1300s (900s Pisces) or a little before, drawing upon very ancient and traditional symbols. Contemporary tarot decks have seventy-eight cards encompassing twenty-two Major Arcana cards and four suits of Minor Arcana cards. The suits of the Minor Arcana correspond to the four sacred tools of Wicca—Wands, Swords, Cups, and Pentacles—as well as to the four suits of common playing cards, which descend from them.

tea leaves—In former times, tea was not made from tea bags, but rather from loose tea leaves. These would leave residue in the cup when the person had finished drinking the liquid. Skilled diviners interpreted this residue by means of the pictures it seemed to form and by their placement in the cup. The same technique was also used to read the residue left in the cup by coffee grounds. Once widely popular, the reading of tea leaves is now a rather rare form of divination.

Study Questions for Lesson IX

1. What is an omen? From what source do omens come?

2. Why are the traditional meanings of symbols important? Can you make up your own? Give an example.

3. In Wicca, what does the Great Rite symbolize?

4. What is allegory? What's so good about it?

5. What is divination? Give an example of one kind of divination that people commonly use.

6. Can you make up your own kinds of divination? Why would they work?

7. What is the Divine Plan? From what level of your being do you access it?

8. What does the number four symbolize? What does this have to do with Pythagoras?

9. What are tarot cards? How are they used?

10. What is the difference between superstition and religion?

11. What is sympathetic magic? Give an example of a sympathetic element one might use in a spell.

12. What is Futhark? Who used it?

13. What are the Witches' Runes?

Lesson

X

Basic Energy Work

• • • •

Blessed Be

What does it mean to give a BLESSING? Is a blessing no more than a nice prayer or a wish for good things to come to someone? Does a blessing really do nothing more than show respect or affection?

We sometimes use the word blessing to mean no more than friendly good wishes or a vague acknowledgment of divine love. When we use the phrase "Blessed be" in daily conversation, we often mean no more than this. Yet in its truest form, a blessing means much more.

A blessing is a transfer of energy. When we give a blessing, we transfer a bit of energy from ourselves to the person or thing receiving the blessing. We do this by CHANNELING the divine energy to which we are connected through our Higher Selves. The divine energy passes through us to the one being blessed and helps to activate the divine energy within them.

Such a blessing has an actual physical and spiritual effect on the one being blessed. The blessing can open doors in the psyche, activate latent talents, and stimulate healing. Or it may simply impart a pleasant feeling and help to strengthen the person's connection to Deity.

In these lessons and their accompanying exercises, we have talked a great deal about how to focus and direct energy within your own body and how to send energy out of your body to create energy constructs, such as the magic circle. More difficult but equally important is the ability to send energy to another person or to receive it yourself. This is called energy transfer.

• • • •

Energy Is Everything

As we said in Lesson I and have frequently restated since, the universe and everything in it is composed of energy—swirling, constantly shifting energy that assumes complex patterns in reaction to our thoughts and emotions, creating an illusion of solid matter. In every moment of our life, we shape this energy unconsciously—it takes its form from us. In magic, we learn to shape it consciously.

Our body is composed of energy, as is our soul. Like the shell of a snail, the body is an emanation of the soul, even as the soul itself is an emanation of the Goddess. Thus the divine energy of the Goddess is always present at the center of our being, and we can learn to consciously access it through the practice of psychic and magical arts.

When we look at the physical form of a person or thing, we are seeing only the external shell of the soul, and this shell conceals much more within. By accessing the inner being—the soul—we can greatly affect the seemingly solid exterior. We do this by transferring energy—that is, sending energy from one person or thing to another. We use energy transfer for a number of reasons, which include the following:

Healing: Energy healing is used to promote spiritual or emotional healing or to aid in physical healing. In healing, we access a person's energy, remove blockages or negative energy, and inject positive, healing energy. In the hands of an accomplished practitioner, energy healing can be as complex and precise as physical surgery.

Blessing: As previously discussed, blessing is an injection of divine energy meant to strengthen spiritual connection or foster spiritual opening or growth.

Communication: Energy can be used to share communication as well: a message or messages are placed into energy, which is then used to communicate it directly to the recipient, bypassing the conscious mind entirely. This is how we receive messages from our ANCESTORS or SPIRIT GUIDES. We can send information in this way as well.

With any of the above methods of energy transfer, the recipient may or may not have a conscious reaction to the event. Some people will feel the slightest variation in energy, while others will not feel even the strongest energy work. It depends on how psychically open the person is and how sensitive they are to energy. So if you are doing energy work on a person and they don't feel it, don't let that bother you; it doesn't mean you're doing it wrong, it just means the recipient is not psychically able to pick up on it.

· · · ·

How It Works

The body is composed of energy. This energy is regulated by energy centers, commonly called CHAKRAS or PLEXI. There are thousands of such chakras throughout the body, and they are connected by MERIDIANS, or energy pathways. When several of these small chakras work together, they form a larger chakra with several levels. There are many of these larger chakras throughout the body as well.

In doing energy work, you may work with any of these smaller or larger chakras, but you are more likely to work with one of the seven so-called major chakras, which we have described in earlier lessons. Each of these major chakras is actually a network of many lesser chakras that have been grouped together to form a single unit. Because of this, the major chakras have many different levels, and these levels may be developed differently in different people, depending on their experiences.

Energy flows from one chakra to another by means of the meridians. The ways in which energy flows through the chakras are called ENERGY CIRCUITS. There are several such circuits, and these have different qualities and purposes.

We have already spoken, in Lesson III, about the solar circuit. The solar circuit, based in the solar plexus chakra, is the energy system that keeps the body's basic functions going. The solar circuit is fueled by the inexhaustible energy of the soul, and it runs automatically, like breathing. We don't have to do anything to get or keep the solar circuit going, but we can inject extra energy into it, usually through the heart chakra.

The second energy circuit we will discuss is the lunar circuit. Based in the root chakra, the lunar circuit is the circuit commonly studied by Hindu systems, and it is sometimes referred to as the KUNDALINI

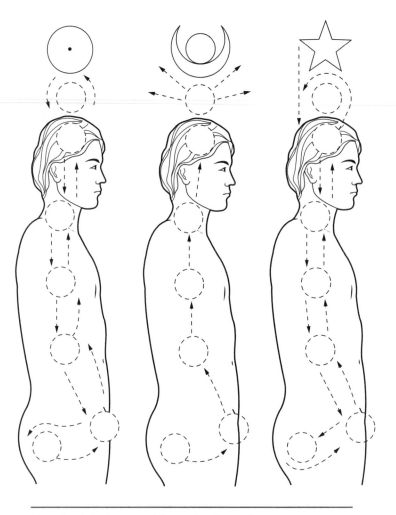

The solar (left), lunar (middle), and stellar (right) circuits

system. Unlike the solar circuit, the lunar circuit is not automatic, and it can be engaged only through study and training. The lunar circuit is used to perform high-level magic, or "miracles," and is capable of achieving incredible results, but it can also be very dangerous and hard to handle, and as such should only be used with care. Unlike the solar circuit, the lunar circuit

must be deliberately started and stopped; it does not run constantly but rather is only used for short periods of time.

The third energy circuit of the body we'll look at is called the stellar circuit. The stellar circuit is primarily used to receive energy into the body. Based in the crown chakra, the stellar circuit can be used to receive many kinds of energy, but especially energy programmed for communication. This is the circuit by which channeled messages are received and through which clairvoyance operates; it is particularly important for dealing with ancestors and spirit guides. Like the lunar circuit, the stellar circuit is not automatic but rather must be specifically started and stopped. The stellar circuit is also often used for healing.

Whenever you put energy into another person or receive it into yourself, the energy will enter one of these circuits. At a beginner level, it is not especially important that you know which circuit is being used, as the energy will naturally go where it is needed. Later, you will learn to differentiate between the different circuits.

The energy of the soul goes well beyond the boundaries of the body. Most commonly, this is perceived as an AURA, or an envelope of energy surrounding the body. A healthy aura extends several feet in all directions around the physical body, but it is easiest for the beginner to detect it within a few inches of the skin. An accomplished clairvoyant can tell a great deal about the state of a person's energy by the colors and patterns in the aura. For the beginner, the temperature and sensations associated with the aura will be more easily detected. It is through the aura that we can locate blockages in the chakra system.

A common technique for energy work is to fill the aura with light. The color and qualities of the light used determine the nature of the effect. This technique can be used for shielding, strengthening, healing, cleansing, and many other uses. If you have been doing the exercises that accompany these lessons, then you will have learned how to do this for yourself—and through energy transfer, you can do it for others as well.

• • • •

How to Do It

Now that we've talked about how energy transfer can be used and a bit about how it works, you probably want to know how to do it. Energy transfer is accomplished by projecting energy from your body into someone else's. The energy is pulled in from the universe and channeled through your body to the recipient. Commonly, the hands are used, and the energy is focused through the palm chakras. If you have been doing your exercises, you will already know how to focus energy through your palm chakras. Imagine the energy projecting from each of your palms as a beam of light. Focus intensely on this, and imagine it as clearly as possible. You are now transferring energy.

Energy can be injected through the crown chakra or through any other chakra. To determine where to send energy, you

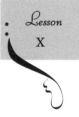

will want to scan the person's body. Certain places will feel "different," and these are the ones that need energy work. Also, if a person is sick or injured in a certain area and just wants healing energy, you can send it directly into the place that hurts.

Energy can also be removed from the body. You do this by pulling the energy out, rather like a vacuum cleaner does. In the Exercises section below, you will find more detailed instructions for doing this kind of energy transfer. Like with anything else, practice makes perfect, and you should not expect to be proficient at once. Keep working with it, and you will master the technique.

Because energy transfer is not normally thought of as a First Degree skill, our purpose here is only to review the basic ideas involved and provide an idea of what energy transfer is about. The techniques given in this lesson are very basic and introductory. You will learn much more about energy working if you go on to study for the Second Degree; you could also study energy working independently.

· · · ·

Exercises

The exercise included in this lesson is not part of the ordinary regimen of exercises you have learned, but rather is a totally separate exercise on the subject of energy transfer. Continue your ordinary exercises

as you have been doing them, and try this one separately.

To try this, you will need to work with another person. If you cannot find another person to work with, you can use a plant or animal, as these too have energy systems to which the exercise is applicable.

To begin, clear and release all excess energy, as always. Now stand to the side of your working partner, so that they are in profile to you; it will be easier to determine what you are feeling from this position. Starting at the top of your partner's head and working your way down, pass your hands over them, about two or three inches from the surface of their body. Pay attention to what you feel. The first time you try this, you may not feel anything, but if you continue to work with the technique, you will soon develop the sensitivity needed.

Pay attention for a sense that any part of the body feels "different." How you perceive that difference may vary: it may feel warmer than the rest of the body, it could have a feeling of static, it may seem to "pull" you, or it may take some other form. But one way or another, you will find that parts of the body have a different feeling from the rest; these are BLOCKAGES. Pay close attention to where these blockages are. When you have finished scanning the whole body, return to the places where you found blockages. Place one hand over the area of the blockage—again, several inches from the body. You will find that one hand or the other is better for doing this with, but whether it is the right or left varies from individual to individual, so you will want to experiment with both until you find out which is stronger.

Visualize a ball of white light coming from your palm chakra. Imagine the negative energy of the blockage being sucked into this ball. Concentrate strongly on this and "pull" the negative energy with as much effort as needed. Now slowly pull the ball of white light with the negative energy inside it away from the body. More negative energy may be pulled along with the ball, extending behind it rather like a rope. Discard the ball and continue pulling the rope of energy out of the body until none is left. As you pull this negative energy out and discard it, imagine it turning to purple-colored light. This is called TRANSMUTING; it recycles the energy so that it may be reused for more constructive purposes elsewhere in the universe.

When you have removed and transmuted all of the negative energy, place both hands over the area you have been working with. Imagine white light flooding into you through the top of your head and passing out through your hands into the person you are working on. Continue to do this until no more energy will go in.

You have now accomplished a basic energy healing. Clear and release as always, and you are done.

Spell for Lesson X
The Witches' Ladder

The Witches' Ladder is an ancient technique for working a spell, and it is quite simple to do. Before you make your Witches' Ladder, you must first be clear on what it is you wish to accomplish. The Witches' Ladder can be used for any purpose, but it is best used to bring about something that will be accomplished through an ongoing process—such as increasing prosperity, learning a particular skill, or losing weight—rather than something that can be accomplished in a single event. As always, remember the Wiccan Rede, "Do as you will, but harm none," and start out with reasonable goals: skill is built through practice.

To perform this spell, you will need a length of cord. Silk cord is nice, but anything will do—a piece of string, a shoelace, a tie, or a scarf, for instance.

Begin by placing yourself in a comfortable position, and then clear and release. Now imagine a ball of golden light in your heart chakra. Say to yourself:

*"Behold, I am One with the
powers of the universe."*

Now imagine that ball of light growing larger and brighter, radiating out in all directions like a sun inside you. Let the ball of light grow to fill your chest, getting stronger and stronger as it does so.

Lesson
X

199

Now take the cord (or whatever other items you may be using, if you are doing either of the variations given below for this spell) and place it before you. Make three tuathail (counterclockwise) circles above the cord with your hand. Say something to the effect of:

"Behold, I cleanse and purify you,
sending out from you any
impurities that may lie within."

Imagine the cord surrounded by a golden light. Imagine it shining brightly, and then let the image fade.

Now make three deosil (clockwise) circles above the cord and say something like:

"Behold, I bless and consecrate
you to this purpose!"

Imagine the cord surrounded by a brightly shining blue-white light. Again hold the image for a moment, and then let it fade.

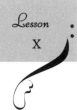

Now take the cord in your two hands, or hold your hands to either side of it (with your palms facing it). Imagine a ball of white light between your hands and surrounding the cord. Concentrate on the goal you wish to bring about through this spell; focus as hard as you can on the goal for several minutes. Imagine the goal, or some image that represents the goal, inside the ball of light. See the goal as you want it to be when it is already accomplished and complete. If your goal is to gain a skill, for example, imagine yourself already proficient in that skill. As you imagine this, know that this goal is already accomplished and only needs to be drawn into physical manifestation.

Now let the image of the goal and the ball of light fade, and take up your cord. Continue to focus on your goal, seeing it already accomplished. Still concentrating on the goal, take the cord and tie a knot near one end of it. Say:

"By knot of one, the spell's begun."

Imagine yourself one step closer to having your goal.

Now tie a second knot a short distance from the first, and say:

"By knot of two, no power undo."

Focus even more strongly on the goal, knowing that each knot draws it closer.

Tie a third knot, and say:

"By knot of three, so mote it be."

With each knot, know that your goal comes closer to you; imagine it more strongly and know that it is truly yours.

Now tie the fourth knot, saying:

"By knot of four, open the door."

Then the fifth:

"By knot of five, it comes alive."

The sixth:

"By knot of six, the spell is fixed."

The seventh:

*"By knot of seven, the
boon is given."*

The eighth:

"By knot of eight, decreed by fate."

And lastly, tie the ninth knot:

"By knot of nine, now it is mine!"

Now once again imagine white light all around the knotted cord, and place your hands above or beside the cord with your palms facing it. Again imagine the image of your goal very strongly. Then release all of your focused energy and concentration directly into the cord. Do this just as you do when you clear and release before or after any working: imagine the energy flowing out of you in the form of light or water.

When all of the energy has flowed from you into the knotted cord, take it and seal it in a safe place. It is best to bury it in the earth, and it is especially good if you can bury it at the foot of a tree. This symbolizes the physical manifestation of the goal.

In some cases, you may wish to keep the Witches' Ladder in your house rather than bury it outdoors. You can do this by placing it in an earth pot—a pot filled with soil and kept on the altar or in a special place—or by making a special box or bottle for it. In any of these instances, you will fill the receptacle with soil and then bury the completed Witches' Ladder in it.

Variations on the Witches' Ladder

The simple technique used to make the Witches' Ladder has many variations. These can add to the efficacy of the spell by deepening your connection to it. This deepening is accomplished by appealing to the Higher Self through symbolic means, or keys. We have discussed keys in Lesson I and throughout: keys are aesthetic or symbolic elements that help you to make the shift in consciousness and access your Higher Self, thus facilitating magical work. Anything that appeals to your creativity or your subconscious and puts you in a more "magical" mood can be a key.

Variation I: Make your Witches' Ladder using not one but several cords of differing colors. For example, to do a prosperity spell you might combine a green cord, for fertility and abundance, with a yellow cord, for success. Or, for psychic development, you might select a dark blue cord, for

Lesson
X

201

psychic ability; a pale blue cord, for communication and learning; and a violet cord, for spiritual guidance.

Variation 2: Instead of simply tying a knot, tie something *into* the knot. You might use beads, twigs, or feathers, to give just a few examples. Then tie one into each knot as you work the spell. The use of feathers comes from a particularly old version of this spell; examples have been found dating back hundreds of years.

• • • •

God for Lesson X
The King

King, father, counselor, judge—of all the forms of the God, this is the one with which most Wiccans have the greatest difficulty. Centuries of Christian rule have caused the King archetype to be identified with PATRIARCHAL domination and the ruthless suppression of the weak by the strong. Distorted images of the "King of the Gods" capriciously interfering in human life and moving people around like chess figures have left a sour taste in the Wiccan mouth. But these images have more to do with the Christian Jehovah than with any Pagan god.

In Pagan mythology, the King is a positive figure, empowered not in his own right but by union with the Goddess. His wisdom and strength are an aid to her and a blessing to us. He does not "rule" but rather works to advance his family and community, whose welfare are his responsibility. The God has sacrificed himself at summer solstice, giving his life force for the greater good, and it is as King that he carries this out, pouring out his love for the world through constructive action.

The King is the god of the harvest. He is the sun that has begun to dim following the summer solstice, and who in dimming nurtures the crops that ripen in the fall. He is the spirit of the crops, literally sacrificing his life so that others may live. The King is the God passed from warrior to leader, nurturing family and community rather than merely self. He is the father who has given up the independent life of a child to be part of a family and who has given up his separateness to help in the raising of his children and the running of the community.

The King is the protector of the people, the keeper of the peace. He is the god of honor and of law, of honesty and civility. He is the god of contracts and agreements, and guardian of the SOCIAL CONTRACT— the agreed-upon terms by which we live together in peace. The King is a judge, but his judgment is not the careless imposition of capricious will, but rather the willingness to tackle and resolve difficult situations, to abide by and uphold agreements,

and to keep the peace. The King is the god of balance and justice, which makes it especially appropriate that his festival should come on the fall equinox, when the sun enters Libra, the Scales.

The King is the temporal or outward aspect of the Old God, the Sorcerer being the spiritual or inward aspect. As such, the King is the god of structure and form. The King puts the physical world to order and establishes solid forms and systems, while the Sorcerer overcomes the illusion of solid form through magic. Where the Hero is expansion and growth, the King is stability and prosperity: he makes the good things of life plentiful and sustainable by the application of organization.

He is the aspect of the God who turns the Goddess's spinning wheel, the WHEEL OF FORTUNE, so that she may spin the thread of existence. He puts her will into action and protects and upholds her. He is her stalwart supporter, her champion and helpmeet. She has birthed the world, and he protects it with her, just as the father bird protects the mother and the nestlings.

Below follow several examples of the King:

Atlas

Atlas is one of the Titans, the gods of pre-classical Greece. A god of the sky, Atlas's consort is the goddess Pleione, whose daughters are the Pleiades. Atlas was associated with the west, and the Atlantic ocean is named for him, as is Mount Atlas. Most of Atlas's mythology was lost with that of the other Titans, but enough survives to draw some conclusions. Atlas is a god of cosmic order, and he separated earth from sky and bore the sky upon his shoulders: an act of self-sacrifice that enabled the universe to assume its present form. He was a patron of law and government and a culture hero. According to Plato, Atlas was the founder of the kingdom of Atlantis, creator of its culture, and progenitor of its royal house. Atlas was the father of the Hesperides, the three goddesses who guarded the apples of immortality at the far western edge of the world.

Jupiter

Roman king of the gods, Jupiter is related to and identified with the Greek Zeus, but the two are not identical. Jupiter is above all a god of law and government, justice, and wisdom. To the Romans, Jupiter embodied all of the qualities of a good father, including sobriety and impartiality. Jupiter is associated with prosperity, expansion and growth, self-confidence, and optimism. Jupiter's consort was Juno (originally the Etruscan moon goddess Uni), and their daughter was the goddess Minerva, also Etruscan in origin and identified with the Greek Athena. Long after the fall of Rome, Jupiter remained an important deity in alchemical, astrological, and Hermetic systems.

Lesson
X

Nodens

A god of the ancient Celts, much of the mythology of Nodens is lost. He was king of the gods and is associated with prosperity and expansion. Nodens was a god of law and protection and a patron of government. As he was a god of water, offerings were made to Nodens by dropping them into his sacred wells. According to mythology, Nodens was obliged to turn over the divine kingship to Lugus after losing an arm in battle. Nodens's lost arm was replaced with a silver arm, indicating a connection to the German Tyr. Nodens is also a god of healing and medicine.

Ra

Falcon-headed god of the sun, Ra was considered chief among the gods of Egypt for many centuries. Ra is the god who maintains the cosmic order, reigning in the sky by day and under the earth by night. Nightly overcoming the serpent Aapep (chaos), Ra embodied and maintained the cycles of existence. Ra is a god of justice, honor, civilization, and law. According to one myth, Ra created humankind from his tears of compassion. In another myth, the great goddess Isis won the deepest secret of magic from Ra by means of enchantment. A typically syncretic Egyptian deity, Ra was identified with the creator god Temu and with the great southern deity Ammon.

The center of Ra's worship was the city of An, called Heliopolis by the Greeks.

Yu-Huang-Shang-Ti

The "Supreme August Jade Emperor," the Chinese king of heaven, Yu-Huang-Shang-Ti maintains the balance and order of the universe and the eternal progress of its cycles. Patron of government and law, he is a god of justice and honor, duty and responsibility.

· · · ·

Glossary for Lesson X

ancestors—Our ancestors are the spirits of those who have gone before, who are consulted for advice and direction, and whose example helps to define who we are. Usually, we think of the ancestors as members of our family, but any person or group to whom we are connected can serve as our ancestors. Ancestors are a class of spirit guides (see below), to whom we are connected throughout this life.

aura—The term *aura* describes the halo of energy that appears to surround the body, which is visible to clairvoyants. The aura, part of the energy of the soul, is normally visualized as a large ball or egg of light, enveloping the body to a radius of several feet. The more developed a person's energy, the larger their aura is likely to appear. There are several techniques for "reading" the colors of the aura, from which a skilled reader can decipher issues of health, mood, or general personality.

blessing—In blessing, we access divine energy, channel it through our body, and impart it to another person or thing. For example, when we bless the chalice in ritual, we impart divine energy into the wine, through which the energy then enters all who partake of the wine. The divine energy will either interact with the recipient in a predetermined manner (as in an initiation) or act on its own to give the recipient whatever they need most (as in a general blessing).

blockages—Blockages are obstructions in the body's energy system. When energy becomes trapped in a chakra—usually in reaction to a mental or emotional trauma—it forms a blockage. Sometimes energy will block up the meridians as well. The blockage prevents energy from moving naturally through an energy circuit, and when this happens a variety of problems can result. The longer the energy remains blocked, the more solidified it becomes. A skilled energy healer can sometimes tell the age of a blockage by the texture of the energy, as very old blockages are quite hard and rigid. If the blockage is

removed, the energy can resume flowing naturally.

chakras—Chakras are the energy centers of the body. *Chakra* is a Hindu term meaning "wheel," which is used because the energy centers are commonly visualized as balls or wheels of light. Many different peoples have developed systems for working with the chakras, and these different systems have many variations: for instance, some identify more or fewer chakras than the seven major chakras commonly used today, or identify their locations differently. This is because knowledge is constantly developing as we continually learn more. Also, different people's chakras tend to be developed differently, depending on how they have worked with them. Like the physical body, the energetic body develops individually, and charts and systems only provide general guidelines.

channeling—Channeling is a method of communication by which messages or information are imparted to a person (called a *channel* or *medium*) by energy transfer from spirit guides, ancestors, or Deity. The energy enters through the person's crown chakra and passes through their brain, where it takes a form they can understand. Sometimes the message comes in words, sometimes in pictures, and sometimes by just

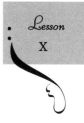

Lesson
X

205

"knowing." Often, the channel will have no conscious memory of the message. This person is also called an oracle.

energy circuit—The term *energy circuit* refers to a course that energy follows as it travels through the body. Energy flows along one of these circuits, moving through the meridians and between the chakras. It is through the circuits that the chakras receive their energy. There are three main circuits that are commonly used; these are termed the solar, lunar, and stellar circuits. These three are not the only circuits that exist, but they are the ones you will work with the most.

energy transfer—A transfer of energy from one person or thing to another. The transferring of energy is used in many ways, including healing, blessing, and channeling. Energy transfer is a powerful tool for transformation and teaching. Because everything that exists is composed of energy, energy can be transferred between any two things that exist, in one direction or the other.

kundalini—The term *kundalini* is used to refer to the kind of energy used in the lunar circuit. In Hindu thought, the Kundalini takes the form of a serpent that sleeps at the base of the spine. When activated, the Kundalini serpent rises through the seven major chakras, uniting

them to form a kind of "super-chakra." Through this technique very high levels of manifestation are possible.

meridians—Meridians are the pathways that energy follows as it flows between chakras. When chakras are blocked, not only the chakras themselves but also the meridians clog up with energy, which can cause a variety of physical difficulties. Meridians are most commonly studied in connection with healing techniques such as acupuncture or moxillation.

patriarchal—Patriarchy is a system of rule in which all power is in the hands of the father, with other family members having no right to oppose his will. Similarly, in patriarchal societies all power is held by the government, with the people having no right to question or oppose it. Patriarchy is marked by a strict social and racial hierarchy, rejection of the body, and an often ruthless enforcement of law. The chief proponents of the patriarchal system today are the book religions. Wiccan religion, on the other hand, follows a matriarchal, or mother-centered, principle. In matriarchal systems, the mother is the head of the family, or both parents are equal. Matriarchy is marked by racial and sexual equality, acceptance of the

body, and an emphasis on the rights of the governed.

plexi—*Plexus* (plural *plexi*) is the Latin term that the Hindu word *chakra* has mostly superseded. The study of the plexi goes back many hundreds of years in Europe, and a detailed system had been developed for interacting with them. When Europeans encountered the superior Hindu system for working with the body's energy centers, the plexus system was largely discarded. The last familiar vestige of the plexus system is the term *solar plexus*.

social contract—*Social contract* is a term used to refer to the laws by which a society lives. We call it a social contract because law is an agreement of society that is created by society. Law is a codification of the terms under which we are willing to avoid fighting with one another and to respect our neighbors. The book religions have claimed that law is a matter of divine revelation and have used this claim to destroy other societies. Even today, some of them want to impose Bronze Age values on a Space Age society, claiming that divinely revealed law cannot change. But Wiccan religion recognizes that law is a creation of humankind, one which grows and changes as our understanding expands. We call it a contract because to be just, law must be a

two-way street between government and people—an equal agreement. A just law must be agreeable to both government and society, and neither church nor state should impose laws without the consent of the people.

spirit guides—Spirit guides are spirits who work with us as guides and advisors. Every person has a number of spirit guides to whom they are connected. The guides work to help the person, even though the person may not be aware of their influence. For some people, the guides appear as humans; for others, they appear as animal spirits. Most often, the guides are spirits you have known in this or other lifetimes. It is beneficial to talk to the guides frequently and to work to build a relationship with them. One can also learn to receive messages from one's guides. In Judeo-Christian religions, spirit guides are called guardian angels.

transmuting—To transmute something is to change it from one state to another. In energy working, this term usually means to raise the vibration of energy, restoring it to a purer form from which it may go on to new uses. Energy removed from blockages associated with disease or negativity is commonly transmuted; its vibration is raised so that it may release the negative pattern. This

is often done by visualizing the energy turning to a clear purple light. However, energy that has been removed from a negative pattern will usually transmute on its own fairly quickly, so this practice is performed as a safeguard rather than as a necessity.

Wheel of Fortune—Fate, or karma, is often portrayed as a wheel. The *Rota Fortuna*, or Wheel of Fortune, represents the eternal cycles of existence, which bring back to us the results of our efforts, for better or worse. In the *Vangelo delle Streghe*, the Wheel of Fortune is portrayed as the Goddess's spinning wheel, from which she spins the threads of fate as the God turns the wheel. This is an allegorical way of saying that fate originates with Spirit and is brought about through the cycles of material existence.

Lesson
X

Study Questions for Lesson X

1. What does it mean to give a blessing?

2. What is the origin of divine energy?

3. What is an energy transfer? Give an example.

4. What do we mean by channeling?

5. Why do we use channeling?

6. Through what part of the body does channeled energy enter?

7. What is a spirit guide? Who can have a spirit guide? How do you get one?

8. What is a plexus? What is it more commonly called? Where does the term come from?

9. How many chakras are there in the human body?

10. What is an aura?

11. How does a chakra become blocked?

12. Name the three main energy circuits of the body.

13. What is the lunar circuit used for? What is another word for it?

Lesson
XI

Herbs, Oils, and Incense

No treatise on Witchcraft would be complete without a section on the subject of herbs. The image of the Witch as HERBALIST is deeply ingrained in our culture and in the Wiccan religion.

In former times, knowledge of herbs was very important. For most people, herbs were the principal form of medicine. Skillful use of herbs for flavoring or for scent made a hard life sweeter, and the metaphysical properties of herbs were used to promote the things one desired and draw them into one's life.

From ancient times it has been believed that certain plants have specific metaphysical qualities. By using the principle of SYMPATHETIC MAGIC—the idea that like attracts like—people have long used these plants to promote the development of their given qualities in their lives.

Though the term *herb* specifically refers to only certain plants in modern usage, for the purposes of this lesson we shall apply the term to any plant used in sympathetic magical practices.

Herbs can be used in many different ways, but they will always be used for the same purpose: the idea is to impart the qualities of the herb to a person or object in order to affect or change it. Sometimes this is done externally, through such media as oils or incense or through the use of the whole plant in the form of a sachet, bouquet, or wreath. Other times this is effected internally, by consuming the herb—as in a tea, for example—though you should never consume an herb unless you are absolutely certain that it is safe.

The simplest way to make use of herbs is to use the fresh plant in a room or on one's person. The quality of the plant will affect the vibration of whoever or whatever is around it. An example of this practice is the use of flowers at weddings. Though people are less conscious of it than they were a generation or two ago, the kinds of flowers commonly favored for weddings have specific metaphysical purposes: roses, for example, which have always symbolized both romantic and divine love, or orange blossoms, which symbolize emotional openness and harmony. The use of these flowers affects the vibration of the energy of the event, coloring it with these qualities. Certain kinds of flowers are traditionally favored for funerals for the same reason. This is also the purpose behind the use of foliate wreaths to symbolize certain offices, such as the champion's crown of bay laurel and the emperor's circlet of oak leaves.

The most common way to use herbs, however, is in various preserved forms. People learned to preserve herbs because the fresh plants were not available all year round. In time, people learned that preserving herbs not only made them available off-season, but also in many cases intensified their metaphysical and aromatic qualities, making them more desirable. For this reason, preserved herbs—that is, oils and incenses—are more commonly used today than the fresh plants themselves.

• • • •

Herbs as Oils

Among the most common forms of preserving herbs is as an oil. Oils are made from many different plants. The oil absorbs the qualities of the plant from which it is made, and it will then impart these qualities to any person or object to which it is applied. In this way, the oil is used to promote such qualities as prosperity, romance, protection, creativity, psychic opening, and so forth.

This same technique can be used to create oils from crystals or gemstones. In this case, the oil absorbs the qualities of the stone, and it is otherwise used in the same manner as an herbal oil.

Once made, an oil can be used in many different ways. It can be applied to the skin as a cologne or dabbed on a handkerchief and carried, to let its metaphysical qualities surround a person. An oil can also be used to anoint a doorway or a piece of furniture, or added to a floorwash, to bring the oil's qualities to a home or place of business. The oil can be applied to a wallet, a letter, a sign, or another object to impart the oil's qualities to that object, increasing its effectiveness or output. In ritual, oil is used to dress candles and ritual objects and to anoint participants, and it is sometimes dropped on hot charcoal as incense.

How to Make an Oil

Good oils are readily available from most metaphysical stores, as well as from some stores that sell bath products or health foods. Commercially available oils are inexpensive, are of high quality, and come in almost any variety you could ask for. For these reasons, you are best advised to purchase rather than make oils.

Commercial oils are available both as pure ESSENTIAL OILS, which are often too strong to use directly on the skin, or as blends, in which the pure essential oil has been diluted with a secondary oil, called a base oil.

If you buy pure essential oils, you will want to dilute them yourself. To do this, fill a small sterilized glass jar with base oil. There are many base oils you can use. The most traditional is virgin olive oil, but other vegetable oils may also be used, such as sunflower or coconut oil. Many people, however, prefer jojoba oil, as it will keep fresh longer than the other oils mentioned. Now add your pure essential oil one drop at a time with an eyedropper or similar instrument, until it reaches the desired strength. Do not stir the oils to mix, but rather swirl the jar in a deosil motion until the oils gently blend. Obviously, if the oil is already diluted, this is not necessary.

Commercial oils are available in single scents and also as mixtures of several scents. If you like, you can purchase several scents and create your own mixtures, combining them until you have the recipe you want. You can also "heighten" the power of your oil by adding to the bottle bits of the plant from which the oil is made or by adding a sympathetic stone whose qualities complement the oil.

If, however, you feel you must make your oil by hand, the easiest way to do it is as follows. Select a base oil just as you would to dilute an oil; again, jojoba is recommended because of its staying qualities. Put the base oil in a pan and add a quantity of the desired herb or herbs to it. Slowly heat the oil and herbs, stirring gently, until they are warm. Do not get the oil hot— warm is what you're going for here. After it is good and warm, remove the mixture

from the heat and let it cool. Repeat this process several times during the course of a day, reducing the plant material further and further. When the mixture has cooled for the final time, strain it into a sterilized glass jar and seal.

Unless you are exceptionally crafty, if you try this you will understand why we suggest that you would do better to buy your oil and then mix or augment it rather than make it yourself.

. . . .

Herbs as Incense

In contrast to oils, incenses are very easy to make. Though many excellent commercial incenses are available to use, there is no reason to feel limited to them. An incense is simply an aromatic plant that is dried and burned. It may be burned in a fire or, more commonly, over charcoal. If a binding agent is used, the incense may be shaped into sticks or cones and burned on its own. All manner of plants are used to make incense, including the common kitchen spices you probably have in your home for use in cooking, like cinnamon or cloves.

The simplest kind of incense to make is powdered incense. In a powdered incense, the dried plant is reduced to very small pieces or ground to a powder in a mortar and pestle. The resulting powder is then sprinkled over lit charcoal, as described above. It is best to use a self-lighting charcoal of the sort made specifically for incense; this is readily available at most metaphysical stores. Charcoal prepared for incense is not as dense as the cooking charcoal you might use for a barbecue; it is much easier to light and burns much more quickly.

Powdered incense is by far the oldest and most dramatic form of incense. This form gives you more direct control over how much incense you use, and if you choose to use a lot, it will create billowing clouds of scented smoke that are very atmospheric. However, you will need an incense burner to safely hold the charcoal, which gets very hot.

Commercial incense is also available in solid form, as cones or sticks. Solid incense gives you less control but more convenience: once a cone or stick is lit, it will keep burning at a steady rate until it is gone, with no further effort from you. Solid incense is commercially available in so many varieties and scents that you would never have to make your own. But you can make your own if you want to.

To make a solid incense, you begin with a powdered one: assemble the dried plant materials you wish to use and powder them in a mortar and pestle. Now mix the incense powder with a binding agent—gum arabic or acacia gum being good choices readily available from many art-supply stores.

Mix them thoroughly and mold the paste into the desired shape on a piece of waxed paper. Either form the incense into cones, like those commercially produced; roll it into a layer a quarter-inch thick and cut it into cubes; or mold the mixture onto a broom straw for stick incense. Then leave the pieces to dry on the waxed paper.

• • • •

Herbs in Waters

In addition to being used fresh or dried, in oils or in incenses, herbs can also be used in waters. This is commonly done by making a tea or tisane. To do this, you boil the herb so that it imparts its special qualities to the water. The water, thus impregnated with the qualities of the herb, can then be used in a number of ways. In some cases, it can be consumed as a tea (though again, you should consume *only* what you specifically know to be safe); it can also be used as a concentrate and added to a floorwash or a bath.

Floorwashes are used to ceremonially wash the floor of a temple, home, or place of business for the purpose of imparting the qualities of the herb involved to that location—to give protection, draw prosperity, or stimulate social discourse, for example. Sometimes a floorwash can also be used on walls or to anoint doorways and windows. The use of a floorwash should be preceded by making an appropriate prayer

or affirmation and by concentrating on your purpose while applying it.

An herbal bath fulfills the same purpose as a floorwash but imparts the qualities of the herb to a person. An herbal bath is prepared by adding to warm bath water either a small quantity of concentrated tea or the fresh herbs themselves in a cheesecloth sachet. The person then immerses themselves in the water, even to the point of momentarily immersing their head, so that every part of the body is exposed to the water. Then they remain in the water in a state of meditation for fifteen to thirty minutes. After the person leaves the water, it is considered preferable to take the time to air-dry. The herbal bath should be preceded by an appropriate prayer, and throughout the process of setting it up and taking it, the bather should stay focused on the intent of the ceremony.

Herbal waters can also be used to asperse or anoint people or places. To do this, purify and charge the water as described below. The water can also be put into a spray bottle and dispersed in this way.

• • • •

Charging Herbs

These, then, are the basic ways in which to prepare and use herbs in the form of oils, incenses, and waters. No matter which form you are using, and regardless of whether you buy it or make your own, you

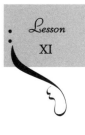

will greatly increase its efficacy by charging it. Below are two simple ways to charge these or any other items.

Method 1

The easiest way to charge any item is to hold it in your hands and visualize a ball of white light around it. As you do this, focus on the purpose to which the item is to be put. Concentrate on that purpose and imbue the item with that energy. In this way, you add greater energy to its native qualities. If you cannot hold the item in your hands, then hold your hands either above, before, or around the item.

Method 2

A more effective but still simple method of charging has already been given to you in Lesson IV, but we will reiterate it here.

Begin by clearing and releasing all excess energy. Place your hand over the item. Make three tuathail (counterclockwise) circles over the item, concentrating on removing any negativity from it. Say something to the effect of:

> *"Behold, I do cleanse and purify you, casting out from you any impurities that may lie within!"*

Imagine yellow-white light pouring down from your hand into the item and forcing out all negativity.

Now make three deosil (clockwise) circles with your hand over the item. Say something like:

> *"And I do bless and consecrate you to this work!"*

Visualize the item being filled with a clear, bluish-white light. Imagine the item filling with this light until it shines as brightly as if there were a blue-white sun within it. You have now cleansed and charged your item.

• • • •

Exercises

In Lesson IX, you learned ways of replenishing your energy after completing your daily routine of psychic exercises. At this point, your daily regimen should include Exercises 7, 8, 9, 13, 14, 15, and 16. In addition, you should be doing Exercises 10, 17, 18, and 19 as needed.

To this we now add two new exercises. These draw on the silver and gold energy that you have begun to use as replenishment since Lesson IX. These exercises should be added into the regimen directly after Exercise 16.

Exercise 20

Imagine a ball of white light centered in your pelvic region. Visualize the light as pure and clear, with no cloudiness or mottling. Imagine tiny silver sparks entering the light—just a few at first, then more. See the light filling with glittering silver sparks until at length the ball of light is completely filled with them—shimmering and scintillating, like a ball of undulating silver glitter.

When this is clear in your mind, imagine the silver energy moving up from the ball and through the middle of your body in a narrow beam. Visualize the silver energy shooting up through the top of your head and showering down on all sides around you, like a geyser. Let this continue for a few moments. Then end your exercise routine as usual, by clearing and releasing.

Add this exercise to your daily routine. When you can do it easily, you are ready for Exercise 21.

Exercise 21

As you might expect, Exercise 21 begins just like Exercise 20, except when you have the ball of white light clear in your mind, you will imagine sparks of golden light entering it instead of silver. Do the exercise in just the same way in all other respects, seeing the ball of white fill with sparks of gold until it is full. Then see the glittering golden light shoot up through your body, emerge through the top of your head, and shower down around you like a fountain of golden glitter.

• • • •
Spell for Lesson XI
Uses of Plants

Instead of a specific spell for this lesson, this section includes a list of plants that can be used to do the things described in the lesson.

The plants can be used in some or all of the following ways: as incense, perfume, an essential oil, an herbal sachet, or potpourri. Plants can be used to anoint a cloth or charm to carry with you, or to anoint a letter you will be sending out. In certain obvious cases, they can also be used for their food value, though only some are edible—if you are not familiar with a plant as food, *do not eat it.*

Each herb has specific uses that can be activated by the various methods you have learned, and as such each might be thought of as a spell in and of itself.

acacia—Blessing, raising of vibration, and protection via spiritual elevation.

agrimony (cocklebur)—Helps to overcome fear, dispel negative emotions, and overcome inner blockages.

allspice—Adds strength to will and gives determination and perseverance. Gives added vitality and energy. Also good for social gatherings: increases harmony, sympathy, and cooperation between people and stimulates friendly interaction and conversation.

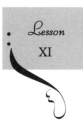

almond—Attracts money. Promotes alertness and wakefulness.

aloe—Promotes patience, persistence, and resolve. Also inner healing and overcoming blockages.

amber—Mental clarity and focus. Protection from harm, outside influences, and psychic attack.

ambergris—Strengthens the effect of anything it is added to or used with. By itself gives strength and vitality. (Substitute: cypress and patchouli mix.)

anise—Psychic opening and clairvoyance. Opens third eye. Favored in Afrodiasporic traditions for use before and during ritual, to aid in perception of and connection to the Divine.

aphrodisia—Passion, sexuality, and romance. Sold by Orpheis High-Correll in red velvet bags to draw love.

apple or apple blossom—Promotes peace of mind, contentment, happiness, and success in all undertakings.

apricot—Encourages sexuality and sensual passion. An aphrodisiac.

asofoetida—Protection and banishing negativity.

azalea—Encourages light spirits, happiness, and gaiety.

banana—Helps to overcome serious blockages or obstacles.

basil—Promotes sympathy, peace, and understanding. Helps to avoid arguments and clashes.

bayberry—Good fortune, blessing, and money and prosperity.

bay leaf (laurel)—Protection and purification. Repels negativity. Promotes good fortune, success, and victory.

benzoin—Use for cleansing and purification. Helps to remove blockages. Promotes strength, confidence, and willpower. Strengthens the effect of anything it is added to or used with.

bergamot—Protection and prosperity. Combine with mint to work faster.

birch—Spiritual and psychic opening, and connecting with spirit helpers. Promotes balance, harmony, and connection to others.

camphor—Increases one's persuasiveness and personal influence. Adds strength to any mixture it is part of. Also used for purification.

Anise

caraway—Luck, good fortune, and prosperity. Also promotes passion and enjoyment of sensuality.

cardamom—Promotes love, sensuality, and sexuality. Also calmness and tranquility.

carnation—Attracts love or friendship and improves or deepens relationships. Promotes feelings of security and confidence. Aids in recovery from illness or difficulties.

cayenne—Cleansing and purification. Repels negativity. Speeds up the effect of any mixture that it is added to.

cedar—Confidence, strength, and power. Protection, perseverance, and lastingness. Spiritual opening.

celery—Promotes sexuality, sensuality, and ecstatic trance.

chamomile—Promotes meditation, tranquility, and inner peace.

cherry or cherry blossom—Happiness, good cheer, and gaiety.

chives—Protection.

chocolate—Adds to one's influence and persuasiveness. Helps others to be receptive to one.

chypre—Draws money and success in gambling. Promotes persuasiveness and eloquence. Made from the rockrose plant.

cinnamon—Luck, strength, and prosperity. Increases the effectiveness of any mixture it is added to. Promotes calmness and tranquility, especially for children. Also used as a strong protection.

cinnamon and sandalwood—Aids meditation and spiritual opening.

citronella—Promotes eloquence, persuasiveness, and prosperity. Draws friends to the home and customers to the business.

Clover

civit—Strength and protection. Promotes confidence and sexual attractiveness.[iv]

clover—Strengthens and deepens existing love.

cloves—Courage, self-confidence, and very strong protection. Dispels negativity and strengthens psychic shielding. Can act as an aphrodisiac.

. . . .

iv Civit is not a plant material, but it is included here as a common ingredient in incense.

coconut—Strengthens confidence and inner resolve. Heightens allure and sexual attraction.

coffee—Grounding and protection from negativity. Peace of mind. Helps to dispel negative thoughtforms and nightmares and overcome internal blockages.

copal—Promotes spiritual opening. Also protection, purification, and overcoming obstacles. Repels negativity.

coriander—Love and healing. Also used for protection.

crab apple—Promotes calm and tranquility and helps settle unrest, conflict, and anxiety.

cumin—Promotes peace and tranquility.

cyclamen—Draws and strengthens love.

cypress—Calm, tranquility, and spiritual opening. Associated with death and mourning, cypress stimulates healing and helps overcome the pain of loss.

dill—Mental strength and quickness. Aids focus and concentration. Also used for blessing.

Dill

dove's blood—Promotes peace and tranquility. Helps to settle disputes and conflict.

dragon's blood—Dispels negativity, gives protection, and helps to overcome blockages.

eucalyptus—Spiritual cleansing, purification, and healing. Helps to overcome spiritual blockages.

fennel—Strength.

fenugreek—Mental clarity and focus. Dispels negativity.

fern—Cleansing and purification. Dispels negativity.

five-finger grass (cinquefoil)—Protection. Also stimulates memory, eloquence, and self-confidence.

frangipani—Attracts love, trust, and admiration. Promotes openness in those around one.

frankincense—Blessing and spiritual opening. Aids meditation.

galangal—Success in court or legal disputes.

gardenia—Promotes peace, repels strife, and protects from outside influences.

garlic and garlic skins—Cleansing and purification. Used to dispel depression, negativity, and obsessive thoughts. Draws money and prosperity. Also used as a strong protection.

geranium—Overcomes negative thoughts and attitudes and lifts spirits. Promotes protection and happiness.

ginger—Draws adventure and new experiences. Promotes sensuality, sexuality, personal confidence, and prosperity. Adds to the strength of any mixture of which it is part, and makes it work more quickly.

ginseng—Asian variety of mandrake. Promotes vitality, strength, and personal power. Heightens sex drive and sexual attractiveness.

grapefruit—Cleansing and purification.

heliotrope—Protection, prosperity, cheerfulness, and gaiety.

honeysuckle—Draws success and money. Aids persuasiveness and confidence and sharpens intuition.

hyacinth—Attracts love, luck, and good fortune. Promotes peace of mind and peaceful sleep. Named for Hiakinthos, Greek god of homosexual love.

hyssop—Promotes spiritual opening. Also used for cleansing and purification. Lightens vibrations.

jasmine—Love, success, spiritual aid, and opening. Connected to the moon and lunar magic.

juniper—Protection, purification, and healing.

lavender—Peace and tranquility.

lemon—Cleansing, purification, removal of blockages, and spiritual opening.

lemon grass—Psychic cleansing and opening.

lilac—Promotes wisdom, memory, good luck, and spiritual aid.

Jasmine

lily of the valley—Soothing and calming. Draws peace and tranquility and repels negativity.

lime—Used for purification and protection. Promotes calmness and tranquility. Also strengthens love.

linden—Draws friendship and love. Also promotes healing and rejuvenation.

lotus—Psychic opening and spiritual growth.

mace—Promotes self-discipline, focus, and concentration. Good for meditation and study.

magnolia—Promotes psychic development. Aids meditation and spiritual opening. Promotes harmony, peace, and tranquility.

mandrake—Increases vitality, strength, and personal power. Heightens sex drive and sexual attractiveness.

marigold—Promotes healing, psychic opening, and clairvoyance. Helps one to focus on what is truly needed, even if one is not conscious of what that is.

marjoram—Cleansing and purification. Dispels negativity.

máte—Grounding, cleansing, and purification. Dispels negativity and helps overcome sadness or loss.

mimosa—Aids psychic development and clairvoyance. Draws prophetic dreams.

mint—Promotes energy, vitality, and communication. Draws customers to a business.

mistletoe—Promotes prosperity and draws customers, money, and business.

mugwort—Promotes psychic opening, clairvoyance, and prophetic dreams.

musk—Increases confidence, self-assurance, and persuasiveness. Draws new situations and prosperity.[v]

mustard seed—Courage, faith, and endurance.

myrrh—Spiritual opening, meditation, and healing.

myrtle—Psychic opening and spiritual aid. Enhances any mix it is added to.

narcissus—Promotes harmony, tranquility, and peace of mind. Calms vibrations.

neroli—Joy, happiness, and overcoming emotional blockages.

nutmeg—Aids clarity, perception, and the ability to see below surfaces. Promotes social interaction, emotional openness, and personal confidence.

oakmoss—Draws money, prosperity, and good fortune.

onion and onion skins—Protection, stability, and endurance. Also prosperity.

orange or orange blossom—Harmony, peace, emotional openness, and love. Attracts prosperity and stability. Also used for purification. Considered very solar.

orchid—Concentration, focus, and willpower. Also strengthens memory.

oregano—Joy, strength, vitality, and added energy.

orris (iris)—Promotes popularity, persuasiveness, and personal success. Aids communications and helps to open dialogues. Also used to draw love and romance.

. . . .

v   Musk is not a plant material, but it is included here as a common ingredient in incense.

parsley—Calms and protects the home. Draws good luck, prosperity, and financial increase. Also gives added energy and vitality.

patchouli—Helps overcome the anger of others, calms strife, draws peace, and helps settle arguments. Promotes prosperity, confidence, and personal strength. Enhances sexuality and sensuality.

pennyroyal—Draws the help of others and promotes cooperation and financial assistance from outside sources.

peony—Particularly sacred in the Correlian Tradition, peony flowers and petals promote good luck, good fortune, prosperity, and business success. The peony seed, however, sometimes called a "jumby bean," promotes dissension and strife.

Peony

peppermint—Promotes strength, vitality, movement, and change. When added to a mixture, it speeds up the effect of the other ingredients. Also used for purification.

pettitgrain—Protection.

pikaki—Draws comfort, prosperity, success, and well-being.

pine—Cleansing and purifying. Promotes clean breaks and new beginnings. Repels negativity. Also promotes prosperity, growth, and increase.

plumeria—Promotes persuasiveness, eloquence, and success in dealing with people. Attracts the notice of others.

poppy—Fertility, abundance, and prosperity.

primrose—Promotes the disclosure of secrets, resolution of mysteries, and revelation of truth. Breaks down dishonesty and secrecy.

rose—Love, peace, harmony, and tranquility. Associated from ancient times with the Goddess, especially in her form as Isis.

rose geranium—Blessing and protection. Averts negativity, especially in the form of gossip or false accusation.

Lesson
XI

rosemary—Used for cleansing and purification and as a strong protection. Also promotes healing and strengthens memory. Said to draw the aid of spirits, fairies, and elves.

rue—Protection. Repels negativity and calms emotions. Grounding. Good for smudging and psychic cleansing. Also draws prosperity by removing blockages.

saffron—Promotes clairvoyance and psychism. Also attracts prosperity and good fortune through spiritual openness.

sage—Used for cleansing and purification and to promote wisdom and psychic opening. Also promotes mental clarity.

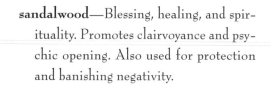

Saffron

sandalwood—Blessing, healing, and spirituality. Promotes clairvoyance and psychic opening. Also used for protection and banishing negativity.

sassafras—Good for legal situations, self-empowerment, success, and overcoming obstacles.

St. John's wort—Protection. Removes negativity and dispels depression and anxiety.

savory—Sensuality, sexuality, passion. Good for sexual magic.

sesame—Opens doors and draws new opportunities, new directions, and hope. Dispels depression and negativity.

Spanish moss—Protection. Dispels negativity and opens blockages.

spearmint—Psychic or physical protection. Repels negativity. Strengthens mental speed and clarity. Increases speed and effectiveness of any mixture it is added to.

spikenard—Blessing, psychic opening, and spiritual elevation.

strawberry—Attracts success, good fortune, and favorable circumstances.

sweet pea—Draws the loyalty and affection of others. Attracts friends and allies.

tangerine—Promotes strength, vitality, and energy.

thyme—Purification, healing, and strength. Attracts loyalty, affection, and the good opinion of others.

tobacco—Used to promote peace, confidence, and personal strength. Promotes love and sensuality. Also used for protection and freedom from outside influences.

tonka bean—Draws love and money and promotes the accomplishment of goals.

tuberose—Serenity, peace, and tranquility. Calms the nerves and promotes romance and sensual love.

vanilla—Joy and good fortune.

verbena (vervain)—Protection. Repels negativity. Promotes peace and tranquility.

vetivert—Protection and overcoming obstacles. Repels negativity. Also draws money and prosperity.

violet—Promotes peace, tranquility, and happiness. Calms the nerves and draws prophetic dreams and visions. Stimulates creativity.

willow—Used for drawing or strengthening love, healing, and overcoming sadness. Lunar magic.

wintergreen—Repels disharmony, negativity, and disease. Promotes good health, tranquility, and peace in the home. *Do not use internally.*

wisteria—Raises vibration. Promotes psychic opening and overcoming of obstacles. Draws prosperity.

wood aloe (lignaloes or lignum aloes)—Protection, success, and prosperity. Often used in consecration.

wormwood—Overcomes negativity and breaks through obstacles. Especially useful for dealing with spirits or the ancestors.

yarrow—Promotes courage, confidence, and psychic opening. Draws love.

ylang-ylang—Increases sexual attraction and persuasiveness.

Yarrow

• • • •

God for Lesson XI
The Sorcerer

Lord of winter, the Old God is also lord of the hunt and of the forests, master of game and of all wild creatures and places.

Lord of death, the Old God is also the patron of shamans, priests, and sorcerers. He presides over omens, dreams, and ecstatic trance. In many ancient traditions, the Old God led the WILD RIDE, in which the souls of the dead were believed to ride forth by night in a great and tumultuous procession, and in which the living could also join through trance and astral projection. This was the central feature of the now-extinct German form of Witchcraft known as the Hexenrai.

The most common name for the Old God you will find in modern Wicca is Cernunnos. Cernunnos is the name of an ancient Celtic form of the Sorcerer archetype, and it means literally "Horned One" (from *cornu*, "horn"). The name of Cernunnos is attested by a number of ancient—mainly Gallic—Celtic inscriptions. It is also preserved in modern folk versions, such as HERNE THE HUNTER and the giant of CERNE ABBAS. Other Celtic names for Cernunnos include Secullos, Dagda, and the Fisher King.

Cernunnos is portrayed in ancient artwork as a middle-aged to elderly man, usually bearded, with antlers or horns mounted upon his head. Often he is shown sitting in a distinctive cross-legged manner reminiscent of the lotus position used in yoga. Cernunnos's animal forms are the reindeer or stag and the horned serpent or dragon. Sometimes this god is also shown with his legs turning into serpents. If you remember earlier discussions of the gods for each lesson, you will recall that the serpent represents the power of Universal Deity in movement: motion, action, time—the Dance of Life.

Patron of Druids and of magical and spiritual knowledge, Cernunnos possessed two important attributes: the Staff of Life and the Cauldron of Plenty. If the god touched any creature with the top end of this staff, it would immediately die. If the god should then touch the creature with the other end of the staff, it would immediately come back to life. This is a metaphor for reincarnation and also for the cycles of time. The staff, sometimes portrayed as a spear or sword, represented the God or male principle—the yang force. Sometimes the staff was exaggerated into the form of a large club; it appears thus on the Cerne Abbas giant and in Irish stories of the Dagda. For the Gallic Secullos, on the other hand, the staff was streamlined to a hammer or mallet, hence the name (*Secullos* means "the Striker"). In modern Wicca, the staff is represented by the athame and the magic wand.

As for the Cauldron of Plenty, it produced a never-ending supply of food and drink. Because of this, Cernunnos was conceived as a giver of plenty, a god of wealth and prosperity. Sometimes in Greco-Roman artwork, the cauldron is portrayed as a cornucopia, and it may also be represented by a bag of fruit or cascading coins. The cauldron represents the Goddess or female principle—the yin force. This is the endlessly creative, nurturing aspect of Deity, constantly bringing forth abundance. The cauldron was also said to bring the dead back to life, thereby representing the womb of the Goddess and her life-giving power. In modern Wicca, the cauldron is represented particularly by the chalice.

In the medieval romance of Percival, or Peredur, the hero travels to the castle of the Fisher King. The Fisher King is lame, representing the slow-moving sun of the Dark half of the year. In the castle, Percival witnesses a sacred procession. Two men dressed in polar colors carry a huge spear, which drips blood. Behind comes a maiden carrying a chalice with an image of a head inside it. When asked what this procession means, Percival remains silent. He is later told that had he answered, the Fisher King would have been cured of his lameness—that is, the Horned God would have been reborn as the Young God and winter would have given way to spring.

The secret of this procession, which Percival did not speak, is this: the spear is the God-force. The blood flowing from it represents the movement of the life force in the universe. The spear is borne by men in polar colors to represent the polarities of life and death, or summer and winter, through which the God continually passes. Remember, the God represents physical existence—the world of action, transformation, and cycles.

The chalice with the head inside it represents the Goddess. To the Celts, the head was the seat of the soul and represented the spirit; thus, the chalice represents the Goddess-force as the origin of the soul and of life. The Goddess represents creation, the life-force, and the soul—the world of spirit, eternity, and essence.

This secret, guarded by the Old God, describes the ultimate nature of life: the Goddess produces life, the soul, and the spiritual world; the God carries this essence into physical manifestation through action and the cycles of time; the world exists through the union of the two.

This ancient allegory was translated into Christian thought as the legend of the Holy Grail. It was venerated by the Knights Templar as the Mystery of Bapho Metis (the "Initiation of Wisdom"). In modern Wicca, it is celebrated through the Great Rite, when the athame and the chalice are

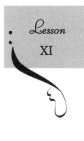

conjoined to symbolize the eternal union of Goddess and God.

The Old God is honored at midwinter, the Sabbat of Yule. After this, he will be reborn as the Young God, but on this shortest day of the year the Old God is at the height of his powers. As lord of midwinter, the Old God is shown as an old man with a long white beard. Commonly, he is dressed in red or green robes and crowned with holly. Portraying this god as "the Spirit of Christmas Present," Dickens interpreted his ancient Cauldron of Plenty as a drinking horn filled with "the milk of human kindness." In his modern form of Santa Claus, the Old God still retains his ancient role as Giver of Plenty—his cauldron transformed into a bag of toys, and his totem reindeer now present at his side on the longest night of the year.

. . . .

Glossary for Lesson XI

Cerne Abbas—The Cerne Abbas giant is a huge chalk carving in the English countryside. The carving shows a naked man sporting an enormous erect penis and carrying a club; it is believed to represent the Horned God, whose attributes include the club or staff, even though this particular example has no horns per se. *Cerne* is believed to be a shortened form of *Cernunnos*.

essential oils—Essential oils are extracted from plant materials through a complicated process that pulls out the plant's natural oils in a very pure form. Pure essential oils can be commercially purchased, but they usually need to be diluted before use, as they may be too harsh to use directly. Sometimes a diluted oil will be sold under the label "essential oil," which can be confusing. You can usually tell the difference by the price: pure essential oils tend to be quite expensive, and the price varies according to the variety of oil in question.

herbalist—An herbalist is a person who studies the medicinal and magical uses of plants. In former times, this was very important, as plants were the principal forms of medicine available to people. Today, herbalism is still used medicinally, though mainly for minor ailments. The magical use of herbalism, however, is more prominent now than ever before. Never has such a wide variety of plants been available around the world for use in magic as is the case today. What were once rare and exotic herbs available only to the very rich—such as frankincense or myrrh—can now be bought at the corner metaphysical store for a small price. Every plant has its own metaphysical qualities, and the purpose of magical herbalism is to harness those qualities and use them to affect a person or place. This is done through many techniques, including the use of incense, oils, and herbal waters.

Herne the Hunter—A famous apparition said to appear in England's New Forest. Christian mythology connects Herne the Hunter with the death of England's King William Rufus, but Pagans see him as the ancient Horned God. Seeing Herne is considered an omen of death, which is not surprising since the Horned God was always connected with death and winter. The name *Herne* is believed to be a shortened form of *Cernunnos*.

sympathetic magic—Sympathetic magic is based on the idea that like affects like—that the metaphysical quality of a plant, stone, or color will stimulate or increase the same quality in the person, place, or magical operation to which it is applied. The same principle is applied to action (as dance, for example), speech, and thought. Thus, to visualize something helps to bring it into reality.

Wild Ride—In certain ancient mythologies, most notably Germanic, the spirits of the dead were believed to ride out in a great procession on certain nights. Some said this ride took place on nights of the full moon; others said it was only on certain festivals. Often the ride was characterized as a "hunt." It was believed that the living could join in this "ride" through astral projection. This was the basis of the German school of Witchcraft known as the Hexenrai, which is well attested to in trial transcripts from the Burning Times. Sometimes the Wild Ride was said to be led by the Crone Goddess. Sometimes the leader of the Wild Ride was the Horned God. There are many interesting descriptions of this Wild Ride in old literature. Odin, Herne the Hunter, Herlichinus (afterward Harlequin), and a variety of other forms of the Horned God were said to lead the ride. The hunt of Diana and her nymphs is sometimes seen as a version of the Wild Ride as well.

Study Questions for Lesson XI

1. Name a way in which people use fresh plants to effect a metaphysical purpose in the modern world. The lesson gives the examples of flowers at weddings and funerals. Can you think of a different example?

2. Give one example of a way in which an herbal oil might be used.

3. What is an essential oil?

4. What do we mean by the term *base oil*? Give three examples of base oils that one might use.

5. How might you use a gemstone in making an oil?

6. How was incense first used?

7. What are the different forms of incense? Which do you think you would prefer, and why?

8. What is your favorite incense? What are its metaphysical qualities?

9. Where might you buy gum arabic? Having bought it, what would you do with it?

10. Why might you use an herbal bath? Name two ways in which an herbal bath might be prepared.

11. If you were asked to prepare an herbal bath to help someone draw a positive new romantic relationship, what herbs might you choose to do this? Name three.

12. If you were asked to prepare an herbal floorwash to bring prosperity to a place of business, what herbs might you choose to do this? Name three.

13. What is the benefit of charging an item, such as incense?

Lesson
XII

Stones and Crystals

Like herbs, stones have been used in magical practices for millennia. Long before people figured out how to cut and polish stones for jewelry, they were carrying rocks for luck and magic. The principle of sympathetic magic assigned meanings to the stones lying about everywhere on the surface of the earth, based on such qualities as color and shape; thus, green stones such as aventurine were used to promote growth and fertility, and red stones such as carnelian were used to promote strength and vitality.

Moreover, people's natural psychic ability helped them to determine how to use stones, as they could pick up on the qualities of the stone's aura. Everything that exists has an aura, or energy field. The aura of something is as distinctive in its features as the physical form, and the aura of each thing that exists has characteristic strengths and weaknesses as well as its own individual variations. These energy fields are not abstract, and they do not exist in a vacuum: auras affect each other when they come into contact, especially when conscious focus is applied. Because of this, the individual characteristics of a stone's aura will affect your own aura when brought into contact with it, thus influencing you in various ways.

There are a number of ways in which people use stones to create a desired effect, including the following:

- The stone can be used to attract or increase (amplify) energies that are in sympathy with its aura, such as wearing rose quartz to increase inner happiness or attract romance, or placing a malachite on top of paper money to stimulate financial increase.

- The stone can be used to focus energy for a particular purpose—rather as a colored gel is used to change the qualities of theatrical stage lights—by visualizing a beam of light passing through, for instance, an amethyst to stimulate psychic opening or a flourite for healing.

- The stone can be used to create or strengthen energy pathways, such as when several pieces of quartz crystal are laid out in a triangle or square to create an energy VORTEX that will aid in psychic or magical work.

Every kind of stone has specific characteristics that determine its best use. Moreover, each individual stone has qualities peculiar to it alone—a personality, if you will. This means that two garnets will not necessarily function in the same way or be equally suited to the same function.

The best way to find the stone you need for your purpose is to run your hand over a selection of stones, passing a little bit above them so that you can feel their energy without actually touching them. The stone you need will feel different from the others. Often it feels warmer, sometimes colder, but always it will feel different.

There are many lists detailing the "meanings" and uses of stones, and this information may help you to determine the type of stone you need. These lists, however, do not always agree on the qualities they accord to the stones. This is because stones work on different levels depending on how you access them. If you seriously work with stones, you may find they interact with you in highly personal ways that are unique to you, because of the manner of your individual interaction. Of course, this is usually how things work, but it is rarely stated. Thus, while we do include a list of uses for common stones, we caution you to be alert for individual variations that will enhance your experience.

Generally, people access stones through their color vibrations (though there are

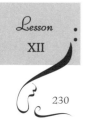

many other ways as well). The clearer a stone is, the purer its basic characteristics will be. The more OCCLUSIONS, striations, or other idiosyncrasies a stone has, the more individual its character will be. This is why clear, bright, crystalline forms such as emeralds or diamonds with few or no occlusions are so highly prized: for their ease and predictability of use. Yet the highly individual stone, if correctly used, may be far more precise and effective.

Not only gemstones, but also perfectly ordinary rocks can be used in this manner, though one must be alert to their individual natures. It is widely held that the most useful stones of all are those that are "found" rather than those that are specifically sought out. Lady Krystel, First Priestess of the Correllian Tradition, maintains on her altar a small river stone that appears to bear the most perfect likeness of the Crone Goddess on one side. Lady Krystel found it on the ground while walking along a perfectly ordinary road, yet in working with it she has found it a powerful stone for psychic and spiritual attunement.

Remember also that synthetic as well as natural stones have auras and therefore are sometimes useful. Many synthetics are extremely shallow, but others, like goldstone or marlenite, have a powerful aura that can prove very effective.

Whatever kind of stone you use, remember that you are not only working with its physical form but with its spirit as well. You may greatly facilitate your working by calling forth that spirit, visualizing it, and interacting with it. You may visualize the STONE'S SPIRIT as a larger, more perfect version of the stone itself that radiates light. Sometimes also the stone's spirit may come to you in human form or as an animal, depending on what is needed in the circumstance. Other times the stone's spirit will give you advice, feedback, or needed information. Always, focus is increased by working with the stone's spirit.

Just as you clear and release after each working, so too stones should be cleansed after being used. Some people cleanse their stones by running them under cold water. Others visualize white or yellow light as a cleansing agent. Many other techniques, such as immersion in salt, are also used. Be alert for what works best for you. Remember to thank your stones for the gifts they bring you, for they too are part of the circle of life and deserve respect.

There are many ways to use stones. They can be carried in a pocket or worn as jewelry to keep their influence around a person. They can be placed upon an altar or just kept in a room to impart their characteristics to that location. They can be used in magical tools to impart their qualities to the energy being focused, or they can be used as magical tools themselves. Among the most common ways to use stones are in the forms of talismans or amulets. You will learn more about talismans and amulets in the spell section of this lesson.

. . . .

Meanings of Stones

amber (yellow, orange, brown)—Helps clear the mind. Gives mental clarity and inner peace.

aventurine (green)—Draws money and prosperity.

bloodstone (green with red flecks)—Promotes creativity, self-expression, and artistry. Also aids healing, especially from surgeries or blood-related diseases.

blue lace agate (light blue)—Healing and overcoming obstacles. Can be used as a "wish stone."

blue stalactite (blue)—Personal power and direction. Helps with finding and staying on the right personal path. Promotes self-knowledge, centering, and connecting to the HIGHER SELF.

carnelian (orange-red)—Promotes personal power, strengthened magic, increased fertility or creativity, and a happy home. Also helps combat the jealousy of others.

chrysacolla (blue, green)—Promotes balance and inner peace.

chrysophrase (green)—Clears blockages in communication and promotes eloquence and persuasiveness.

citrine (golden brown)—Strengthens self-esteem and promotes balance and good cheer.

crazy lace agate (brown stripes)—Awakens hidden talents and abilities and promotes success in career situations.

crystal (clear quartz) (clear)—Amplifies and directs energy. Builds energy pathways. Strengthens the energies of anything it is put with.

diamond (clear)—Earth's hardest stone. Promotes personal growth, spiritual lessons, and perfecting of self. Also resilience, perseverance, and permanence.

emerald (light to dark green)—Protection, success, and prosperity. Also promotes memory and learning.

flourite (comes in many colors)—Promotes healing. The focus of the healing may be emotional, physical, spiritual, and so forth, depending on the color of the flourite.

garnet (dark red, wine)—Personal power, focus, and protection. Also aids in healing, especially with blood-related diseases.

goldstone (brown with gold flecks)—Used to draw money, especially through commerce or the collection of monies owed. Goldstone is a synthetic stone, but it is made with real gold.

haematite (silvery black)—Gives protection, absorbs negativity, and helps relieve grief or pain.

jade (comes in many colors, but most commonly green)—Serenity, inner peace and balance, and good fortune. Promotes the perfection of self and connection to Spirit.

jasper (red, brown)—Helps promote openness to new ideas and influences, and flexibility.

jet (black)—Sacred to Hekate. Jet gives protection, promotes mental and emotional clarity, deflects negativity, and helps to overcome sorrow or sadness. Traditional stone of mourning, now grown rare.

lapis lazuli (dark blue)—Promotes psychic opening and clairvoyance. Now grown rare.

malachite (green and black)—Malachite promotes success, whether in business or love. Prosperity, creativity, and fertility.

marlenite (red, red and yellow)—Also called "Philosopher's Stone." A very strong money stone, this synthetic stone is named for Marlena Berndt, famous metaphysical historian of gems and stones.

moonstone (milky white)—Protection and psychic opening. Absorbs negativity and promotes confidence.

mother-of-pearl (iridescent white)—Deepens emotional commitment. Draws marriage and long-term love.

opal (iridescent greenish white with orange or red)—Promotes psychic opening and development and sensitivity to spirits. Once considered unlucky by those who feared psychic phenomena.

pearl (white)—Peace, compassion, and love. Pearls are said to retain positive emotions incomparably well.

rhodochrosite (pink and gray)—Promotes sexual adventure, fertility, and pregnancy.

rhodonite (pink and black)—Helps healing of emotional pain, especially from loss of love or loss of a loved one. Helps requite grief and draw new love. Promotes reconciliations of parted lovers or friends.

rose quartz (pink)—Love, happiness, and self-esteem.

sodalite—Sodalite is very similar to lapis lazuli and is often used in place of it. Promotes psychic development and clairvoyance.

Lesson
XII

233

tiger's eye (gold and brown stripes)—Promotes popularity, eloquence, and persuasiveness. Helps improve communications. Also used for protection in traveling and for protecting mechanical vehicles.

turquoise (blue)—Protection, good fortune, and psychic opening. Considered very sacred.

• • • •

Exercises

If you have been doing your lessons regularly, your daily regimen should now include Exercises 7, 8, 9, 13, 14, 15, 16, 20, and 21. In addition, you should be doing Exercises 10, 17, 18, and 19 as needed.

At this point, you are ready to simplify your regimen again. Continue to use all of the exercises you have learned as you feel the need, but on a daily basis you will now substitute the two new exercises that follow.

Exercise 22

Begin as usual by clearing and releasing all excess energy. Then do Exercise 7, opening the chakras by visualizing a ball of colored light in each. Follow with Exercise 8, turning each ball of colored light into a ball of clear white light. Now go on to Exercise 9,

transforming each ball of white light to a ball of purple-colored energy.

At this point, you will deviate from the existing regimen. Follow Exercise 9 by returning to the root chakra. Focus on the ball of purple light you have opened here. Imagine that purple light being transformed into glittering silver energy, like that with which you have been working in Exercise 20. When this image is clear in your mind, move on to the second chakra and transform the ball of purple light you have opened there to a ball of sparkling silver light. Continue through all of the chakras till you reach the crown chakra. Then end by closing the chakras and clearing and releasing as always.

When you can open these balls of silver light in each chakra with ease, you are ready to move on to the next exercise.

Exercise 23

Exercise 23 differs from Exercise 22 in that after opening the balls of silver light in each chakra, you will now return to the root chakra. Transform the ball of silver light in the root chakra into a ball of golden light. Just as in the previous steps of this process, continue through each chakra until you reach the crown chakra. Then close them back down and clear and release as usual.

Remember that the silver and golden light differ from ordinary colored light in that they are not clear, but rather are composed of glittering, constantly swirling particles. This is an important distinction, as it makes a great deal of difference in the type of energy you are working with.

As this is the last lesson in this series, this is also the last set of exercises. As you go forward, you will want to continue to develop psychically. Use these exercises as a starting point, and allow your Higher Self to guide you in devising new exercises for yourself. Do not be afraid to play with them or to experiment. Just like with any skill you might develop with your physical body, this is a perfectly natural process. Do not push yourself or try to go faster than you are ready for, but take it at your own speed. Enjoy the process of growth, for that is part of the reason it is given to us.

• • • •
Spell for Lesson XII
Talismans and Amulets

In keeping with the subject of this lesson, our spell here is about the creation and use of TALISMANS and AMULETS. Talismans and amulets are magical items we use to help bring about changes in our lives or in specific situations. They can be carried on the person—in a pocket, for instance, or on a chain around the neck—or they can be put in an appropriate place such as under a pillow or on a desk.

A talisman or amulet can be made for any reason, though commonly they are used for such purposes as stimulating creativity, increasing prosperity, improving communication, expanding psychic receptivity, strengthening magical ability, drawing success either generally or to a specific endeavor, and overcoming general or specific problems.

The difference between a talisman and an amulet is this: a talisman is a natural object, such as a stone, that is used in its natural state or with minor augmentation, and an amulet is a specially created object made just for the purpose it will be used for. Over time, however, the meanings of these two words have blended together, and people often use them interchangeably.

A talisman may be made of just about anything. Found stones and other "lucky" objects are often used for talismans. Perhaps the best-known talisman of this sort is the four-leafed clover, which because of its scarcity is taken as an omen of and a talisman for good luck. A found penny, picked up for good luck, is another well-known and enduring example of a simple talisman. But a talisman need not necessarily be a found object. Many people purchase tumble-polished gemstones and carry them in a pocket or a small pouch; these

Color Chart for Amulets and Talismans

Color	Meaning
black	protection, safety, and grounding; also wisdom, guidance, and learning
purple	spirituality and psychism
indigo	psychic ability, clairvoyance, and spiritual guidance
blue	communication, focus, and willpower
green	healing, prosperity, fertility, growth, abundance, and money
yellow	pleasure, happiness, and success
orange	creativity and self-expression
red	strength, vitality, and passion; adds extra energy to any working
pink	romantic love, compassion, and nurturing
white	innocence, manifestation, unity, and purity; general purpose
violet	spirituality, connection to Higher Self, and the Goddess

Metal Chart for Amulets and Talismans

Metal	Meaning
gold	Gold is sacred to the sun, that is, the God generally, and especially in his form as the Lover or consort of the Goddess. Gold is used for physical success, fame, and personal achievement.
silver	Silver is sacred to the moon, that is, the Goddess generally, and especially in her form as the Great Mother. Silver is used for psychic opening, clairvoyance, and all manner of magical work.
mercury	Mercury is sacred to Mercury, that is, the God in his form as the Sorcerer. Mercury is connected to communication, speed, and movement—but as it is extremely poisonous, it is not generally used today. We recommend aluminum instead.
copper	Copper is sacred to Venus, that is, the Goddess in her form as the Maiden. Copper is connected to prosperity, fertility, and growth. It is also considered the metal most conductive to psychic energy, and therefore it is often used in the construction of magical tools.
iron	Iron is sacred to Mars, that is, the God in his form as the Hero. Iron is connected to strength, protection, and endurance.
tin	Tin is sacred to Jupiter, that is, the God in his form as the King. Tin is connected to expansion, joviality, and openness.
lead	Lead is sacred to Saturn, that is, the Goddess in her form as the Crone. Lead is connected to grounding, shielding, and protection; however, like mercury, it is extremely poisonous and so should not be used. We recommend pewter instead.

too are talismans, believed to impart the qualities of the specific stone to the user.

An amulet, on the other hand, is something we make. A stone carried in a pouch is a talisman. A stone set in a ring or augmented by a magical symbol is an amulet. Like a talisman, an amulet also can be made of almost anything and can range from the very simple to the extremely complex.

An example of a very simple amulet is a magical symbol, such as the Egyptian ankh, drawn on a piece of paper and worn or carried. This would impart the qualities of the ankh—life and vitality—to the user of the amulet. Pair the paper with a complementary stone, such as a carnelian, and put them in a small bag, and you have a more complex amulet. You might also add a complementary herb or other items that will also serve to stimulate the amulet's purpose.

Long lists of items and their correspondences exist that can help us in selecting what to use when making amulets. But ultimately whether an item "feels right" or not is the best way to decide whether to use it. The lists of herbs and stones that have accompanied this and the previous lesson, as well as the lists of metals and colors opposite, will go a long way toward providing inspiration for amulet making.

In making talismans and amulets, do not feel your efforts must conform exactly to what anyone else says. Remember that, like everything else in magic, the purpose of these items is for them to act as KEYS to stimulate powers within you. Even though the substances of which talismans and amulets are made have properties of their own, how you charge an item will greatly influence how those properties will be used.

. . . .

How to Charge a Talisman or Amulet

A talisman or amulet may be charged quite simply in basically the same way that you would charge anything else.

The easiest way to do this is to hold the item in your hands and visualize a ball of white light around it. As you do this, focus on the purpose to which the item is to be put. Concentrate on that purpose and imbue the item with that energy. In this way, you add greater energy to the item's native qualities. There are also more complicated ways to do this, such as the one described below.

Method 2

Begin by clearing and releasing all excess energy. Now place your hand over the item. Make three tuathail (counterclockwise) circles over the item, concentrating on removing any negativity from it. Say something to the effect of:

"Behold, I do cleanse and purify you, casting out from you any impurities that may lie within!"

Imagine yellow-white light pouring down from your hand into the item and forcing out all negativity.

Now make three deosil (clockwise) circles with your hand over the item. Say something like:

"And I do bless and consecrate you to this work!"

Visualize the item being filled with a clear, bluish-white light. Imagine the item filling with this light until it shines as brightly as if there were a blue-white sun within it. You have now cleansed and charged your object.

· · · ·

God for Lesson XII
Your Divine Body

The Goddess is not Greater than the God
Nor is the God greater than the Goddess
But Both are equal
And Neither is complete without the Other.

This simple piece of liturgy sums up much of the Wiccan attitude toward life and the Divine. As we learn in the *Vangelo delle Streghe*, the Goddess arose before all things—she is Spirit, the soul of the world

and of the universe. All things that exist are given life by her.

The Goddess created the God from herself. He is part of her: "Her Self and her other Self." As the Goddess is Spirit, the inner force behind all life, so the God is the outer form and process of living, through which Spirit expresses herself. Neither is complete without the other. Form without soul is dead. But soul without expression is stagnant.

Many people believe that the soul has more value than the body and that spiritual growth must come at the expense of the physical self. For this reason, ASCETICS have practiced self-denial and personal mutilation, in the hopes that they will be able to leave the physical world behind.

The Correllian, however, would say that the body is the vehicle through which Spirit is expressed, and thus is sacred and to be loved. We believe that it is through the union of Goddess and God—of Spirit and physical expression—that life goes forward. Neither is complete, and thus neither is happy without the other.

We began our regular god sections in these lessons with the Genius/Juno—your own, divine soul. We end it with your equally divine body. Your body, and the life you are living through it, is an expression of Spirit, of the Goddess. It is holy. The Goddess and the God come together in the

union of your soul and its physical expression. Therefore, honor it.

In the Great Rite, the athame is conjoined to the chalice. This represents the physical consciously uniting with the spiritual. You are yourself, in every moment of your life, the Great Rite personified. Your soul—your Higher Self—deserves your reverence, even as do the cosmic powers of Goddess and God, for you are part of them. Likewise, revere your body and your life path, for these are your most concrete expressions of the Divine and the way in which you can most affect the universe for the better. Do not underestimate the importance of this or take it for less than the miracle it is. All of existence, the Goddess and the God and all of the universe, has existed to bring you to this place, in this moment, in this body—the moment of creation is *now*. It is always now. And your physical expression, perfected to this point through thousands of lifetimes, gives you the capacity to take part in creation.

Hear, then, the words of Krystel Highcorrell, First Priestess and Paramount High Priestess of the Correllian Tradition:

Holy is my body and beautiful
Wise are its instincts and desires
Body, I honor your instincts
Body, I honor your desires.

Light a white candle to honor your body—your physical expression of your part of Divinity. Anoint your body with an anointing oil chosen for the pleasure of its scent. Repeat the wise words of Lady Krystel as an affirmation of your body's holiness, and remember: you are God experiencing herself.

• • • •

Glossary for Lesson XII

amulets—An amulet is a magical charm made for a specific purpose. Amulets can be very simple or extremely complex. A simple form of amulet is the famous rabbit's foot key chain. Another example is the practice of pressing a flower from a special event with the intention of giving that event success or permanence or stimulating a continuation of the positive emotion stemming from it.

ascetics—Ascetics use physical self-denial or pain to stimulate spiritual growth. Often, they do so in the belief that the physical world is bad, an aberration from a purely spiritual existence, which they believe would be better. In Wicca, however, we believe that the physical world is the expression of Spirit and is good and holy in its own right. We do not condemn asceticism and recognize that it has its place for those who need or choose it, but we do not believe that it is necessary to reject the physical in order to embrace the spiritual.

Higher Self—The Higher Self is that part of a person or other being that is usually referred to as its "spirit" or "soul." In Wicca, we strive to be more and more closely aligned to our Higher Selves, so that we may work from the highest part of ourselves for the highest good. Mechanically speaking, the Lower Self constitutes those parts of our being of which we are automatically aware: our physical self (our body), our emotional self (our feelings), our mental self (our ability to think and reason). Our Higher Self, which requires more work to access, includes our astral self (our ability to manifest things magically), our soul (the accumulation of the experiences of our many lifetimes), our monadic self (the part of ourselves that is at one with Deity yet can experience separateness), and our divine self (which is our ultimate point of connection to Deity, or All That Is).

keys—Keys, once again, are items, ordinary or extraordinary, that we use to stimulate the shift in consciousness that is necessary for the use of magic. By shifting consciousness, we connect to our Higher Self and work from the higher levels of our being, which are free from the blockages that often hold back our Lower Self.

occlusions—Occlusions are the markings and mottling within a stone that give it individual character. Like the wrinkles on a human brain, occlusions are developed as the stone takes on its individual character. Though an occluded stone varies from what is considered archetypically perfect for its type, these variations are often the very thing that makes the stone ideal for individual working.

stone's spirit—Each thing that exists, no matter how inanimate it may appear, is a manifestation of Deity—the Goddess—that has taken shape through the seven planes of existence and consequently has many levels to its own existence. Just as this is true for humans, this is also true for stones. And just as with humans, the stone's Higher Self is a clearer expression of its soul and of its ultimate connection to Spirit. Therefore, in working with stones and crystals, remember to connect with the item's Higher Self and you will have greater success.

talismans—When a natural object, such as a stone or plant, is used in its natural state or with minor augmentation with the intention of producing a metaphysical effect on or for the user, it is called a talisman. Talismans are used to bring luck, to stimulate success or prosperity, and for many other reasons. A common example of the use of talismans is finding and carrying a lucky stone. Another example is framing the first dollar a person's business earns.

vortex—A vortex is an energy center that exists naturally as a nexus point in the earth's energy or that has been specially created through magical means. For example, the energy construct known as the magic circle is an artificially created energetic vortex, used to augment the psychic or magical abilities of those within it. Because the energy in a vortex is especially strong, it will add power to any working performed within or through it. For this reason, natural vortex points are usually considered sacred and are often used as worship centers.

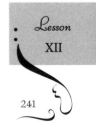

Study Questions for Lesson XII

1. How can stones affect people or places?

2. What sorts of things normally have auras? What sorts of things do not have auras?

3. Do synthetic stones have auras? Why or why not?

4. From what level do people commonly access stones? Are there other levels from which stones might be accessed?

5. Energetically, what is the difference between a clear stone and a stone with many striations or occlusions? Which one is better to use?

6. Can you name a stone that helps a person to connect to the Higher Self?

7. How would you visualize a stone's spirit? What might you hope to gain by doing so?

8. How might you cleanse a stone?

9. Can you name a famous stone from history? What do you think its special qualities are?

10. How might you select a stone to work with, if you were buying one?

11. What is the value of a found stone as opposed to a purchased stone? How would you go about getting a found stone?

12. What is a talisman? How does one use a talisman?

13. Name a popular form of amulet.

How These Lessons Came to Be

On Candlemas of 1579 Pisces (AD 1979), the Regent LaVeda, of beloved memory, convened the Correllian Council of Elders for what would prove to be a momentous meeting. This meeting ended the beloved LaVeda's regency and appointed her cousin Krystel High-Correll as the new head of the Correllian Tradition. The elders also appointed Lady LaVeda's son, Donald Lewis-Highcorrell, as co-head of the tradition.

Lady Krystel's first act as head of the tradition was to declare the tradition open to the public and to inaugurate a series of outreach programs. One of these outreach programs was to be a series of correspondence lessons in Correllian Wicca. Lady Krystel entrusted this project to her new co-head of the tradition, Reverend Donald, who began work on them at once.

Conclusion

Lady Krystel, Lady LaVeda, and Lady Gloria, then first elder of the tradition, all took part in the compilation of these first lessons.

The draft copy of these lessons was finished and presented to Lady Krystel for her approval by summer of 1586 Pisces (AD 1986), but little was done with them. Proposed revisions were delayed by the passing of key members of the tradition as well as the success of other tradition projects.

By the winter of 1590 Pisces (AD 1990), the revisions had been completed, and plans were made to produce both printed and videotaped versions of the lessons. A working partnership was established with Ed Hubbard (who had not yet entered the tradition) and his company, Psychic Services Incorporated, with a view toward producing and disseminating the material. In January of 1591 Pisces (AD 1991), filming began on the videotaped versions of the lessons, only to be halted when Reverend Don suffered a serious accident that would leave him bedridden for months and in recovery for several years. During the first priest's illness, the lessons were set aside, and by the time Reverend Don was able to again turn his attention to the lessons, it was decided that the original materials were outdated and needed a second revision.

Work began on the new revisions in 1597 Pisces (AD 1997), and the first of the revised lessons would be presented to Lady Krystel in 1598 Pisces (AD 1998).

The new lessons were much deeper and more thorough than the previous versions, with a stronger emphasis on the inner nature of Correllian teachings. After twenty years, the lessons in Correllian Wicca were finally completed, and these were presented to Lady Krystel early in 1599 Pisces (AD 1999).

The first Correllian cleric to be trained under this system was Cweord, of Chicago's Holy City Temple, who was initiated as a First Degree priest on November 11, 1599 Pisces (AD 1999). Cweord was the last Correllian initiated in the old century, and thus it is fitting that he should have been the first to come in under the long-awaited lessons.

In closing, we hope that you have enjoyed these lessons. Creating them has been a labor of love, which we gladly share with you.

• • • •

Some History of the Correllian Tradition

Correllian Nativist Wicca was founded by Orpheis Caroline High-Correll in 1479 Pisces (AD 1879). A woman of Scots-Cherokee ancestry, Orpheis Caroline is claimed by some members of the High-Correll family to have been a Scottish Traditional Witch. She was also a practicing psychic, spiritual healer, and herbalist, and she spent many years with the traveling circus she owned with her husband, John Correll.

In creating Correllian Nativist Wicca, Orpheis Caroline drew upon her Native American heritage as well as ideas from European Witchcraft, Spiritualism, and Hermetic thought.

The early history of the Correllian Tradition is somewhat unclear, as at that point familial and religious structures were wholly interconnected. The family followed a very formal matriarchal and matrilineal structure with roots in Cherokee custom; it is from these roots that the current offices of the Correllian Tradition derive their form.

Lady Orpheis called the tradition simply "Nativist," and this would remain the tradition's primary designation until the appellation "Correllian Nativist" came about in 1592 Pisces (AD 1992)—or, as we more commonly call it today, simply "Correllian." Lady Orpheis's Nativism was a highly political and deeply syncretic form of Pagan universalism, one which stressed the need for the world's Native (Pagan) religions to unite in the face of colonial Christianity.

Whether Correllian Nativism was originally a branch of what would later be called Wicca or not is a matter of debate. Correllianism's claim to Wiccan status rests both on Lady Orpheis's claimed Scottish Traditional lineage and on her Aradian lineage, which she acquired in 1504 Pisces (AD 1904) through a student of Charles Leland.

There have been many changes instituted in the tradition over the years, particularly in the Council of 1579 Pisces (AD 1979) and the Council of 1592 Pisces (AD 1992), both of which struggled with adapting the tradition's forms to the modern world and to the needs required for a public tradition.

• • • •

Current Structure of the Correllian Tradition

Outer Court

The term *Outer Court* refers to those members of the tradition who are not initiated clergy. The Correllian Tradition maintains a strong commitment to its Outer Court members. We believe that not everyone needs or desires to be part of the clergy, and we think that there is much the tradition has to offer to and gain from its Outer Court members.

Inner Court

The term *Inner Court* refers to the initiated clergy of the tradition. These are the people who have made a full commitment to the spiritual path, who have pursued and received initiation, and who thus form the tradition's spiritual core. It is the Inner Court that gives the tradition shape and structure. Inner Court members may be any of the following:

Dedicant: A dedicant is a person who has made a formal commitment to study for initiation into the First Degree of clergy. Usually this period of study lasts for a year and a day.

Postulant: A postulant is a person who has completed the requirements for initiation as a First Degree priest or priestess but has not yet received the actual initiation.

First Degree: The First Degree priest or priestess is the base level of the Correllian clergy. The First Degree priest or priestess should be familiar with the details of the Wiccan faith and have a thorough grounding in Wiccan philosophy and traditions. He or she should be able to answer most questions about Wicca on a practical (as opposed to philosophical) level. The First Degree priest or priestess should be able to take most roles in ritual with reasonable confidence.

Second Degree: The Second Degree priest or priestess should be able to take any role in ritual and answer most questions about Wicca, whether practical or philosophical. He or she should be able to manipulate energy in ritual and other settings with reasonable competence. The Second Degree priest or priestess should be familiar with most Wiccan rituals and techniques and should be able to undertake them without direct guidance.

Third Degree: The Third Degree clergy form the High Priesthood of the tradition. A Third Degree high priest or priestess should be able to answer all questions about Wicca and to facilitate all Wiccan rituals met with in the ordinary service of a temple. He or she should be competent in energy work and should be able to deliver an oracle or spirit message and perform the ceremony of drawing down the moon.

Director: A member of the temple's board of directors is called a director. Directors are involved in major decisions affecting the temple, leaving the daily administration of the temple to the temple heads. The temple directors, functioning pretty much as any board of directors might, decide questions of importance by vote.

Temple Head: The chief priestess or priest of the temple is considered the temple head. Temple heads may be nominated by the temple directors, but they are chartered by the head of tradition, who alone has the right to affirm or deny this rank. A temple head is responsible for the day-to-day running of the temple, as opposed to the directors, whose responsibility is not as specific. It is also the right and responsibility of the temple head to represent the temple in meetings of the Witan Council, which meets when needed to advise the tradition heads in matters of national or international importance. A temple may also have a co-head who shares the authority of head of temple; this is often the case when there is both a chief priestess and a chief priest. Unlike the head of temple, who may only be chartered by the head of tradition, a co-head of temple may be appointed directly by the temple head. The co-head of a temple is also considered a member of the Witan Council, but the temple will still have only one vote.

Tradition Leadership

Witan Council: The Witan Council is an advisory body that may be convened to advise the tradition heads on matters of national and international importance, and it plays an important role in matters of succession. The Witan Council is composed of the Correllian Tradition's temple heads from around the globe, elders, officers, and other notables, as well as the tradition heads themselves.

Elder: The Council of Elders is an advisory body made up of highly respected members of the tradition. It might be described as the "cabinet" of the tradition, as it is a council whose nonbinding opinion helps shape tradition policy. Recognition of elder status requires nomination by a member of the Council of Elders and confirmation by the tradition heads.

Chief Elder: The chief elder of the tradition is the principal advisor to the tradition heads, as well as to the tradition as a whole. The chief elder is chosen by the tradition heads and is the philosopher laureate of the Correllian Tradition. The current chief elder of the Correllian Tradition is Reverend Virginia Bitterwind Smith.

Tradition Heads: The First Priestess and First Priest of the tradition are the tradition heads. The principal responsibilities of the joint heads are (1) to form global policy for the tradition, (2) to facilitate international communication and networking within the tradition and with other traditions, and (3) to handle the day-to-day running of the tradition (such as the chartering of temples, affirmation of temple heads and elders, and so on). The first priest acts as chairperson for the Witan Council when it shall be invoked; he is responsible for coordinating relations between Correllian temples, for the tradition's relations with other Wiccan and Pagan traditions, and for maintaining the tradition's history, internal records, and publications. The first priestess is responsible for maintaining the sanctity of the Correllian Tradition and its connection with the ancestors and the Divine; the initiation of all priesthood, temples, and orders ultimately derive authority from this sanctity, and thus from the first priestess.

Chancellor: The chief executive officer of the Correllian Nativist Tradition is the chancellor. The chancellor is responsible for the day-to-day running of the tradition and the administration of all records and legal matters. The chancellor is the deputy of the leadership of the Correllian Tradition and represents its interests. The chancellor is the principal authority and the final court of ap-

peals for all matters relating to the administration of the tradition. The office of chancellor must be filled by one of the joint heads of the Correllian Tradition, but it may be filled by either the first priestess or the first priest. In the event that the joint heads cannot agree on which should act as chancellor, the matter will be resolved by a vote of the Correllian Council of Elders. Once filled, the office is understood to be held for life. The office of chancellor was established for the first time in the year 0 Aquarius (AD 2000).

• • • •

OK, Now What?

Now that you've finished these lessons, what do you do next? Well, that's really up to you. Successful completion of these lessons opens several options to you within the Correllian system. If you choose, you may apply for formal initiation, as outlined below, but you don't have to be initiated to play an active role in the Correllian Tradition. Correllian Wicca believes that everyone should be welcome to share in the joy of the Goddess and the God. Our initiated clergy hold a very important place in the tradition, but it is not the only place in the tradition.

You may also choose to forgo formal initiation and become an Outer Court member of the tradition instead. Initiated clergy form the Inner Court of the Correllian Tradition, while the Outer Court is formed of people who are considered full members of the tradition but who for whatever reason have chosen not to pursue clerical initiation—lay believers, if you will. The Correllian Tradition recognizes that not everyone has the time or inclination to follow the path of clerical initiation, and thus that providing a role for our Outer Court members is of great importance.

Of course, you may simply choose to take what you've learned from these lessons and continue on your own way with no further thought of, or connection to, the Correllian Tradition—and we honor that decision too, for those who make it. We have chosen to make these lessons easily available to seekers because we believe that the knowledge they contain is important and worthwhile, and we rejoice for any person who derives benefit from the lessons, whether that person will have any further connection to us or not.

• • • •

Outer Court Membership

You may be asking yourself, "If I wish to enter the Correllian Tradition but do not wish to become initiated clergy, what do I do?"

We welcome all people of goodwill. We believe that there should a place at the table for everyone. Our initiated clergy is important to us, but so are our sisters and brothers in the Outer Court.

Anyone can adopt Correllian beliefs at will and consider themselves to be Correllian in an inward sense. But to be *recognized* by the tradition you must do the following:

1: Register with the Correllian Tradition so that we will know who you are and may confirm your formal recognition.

2: Perform the Outer Court dedication ceremony. The instructions for performing this ceremony are in Appendix A. You may perform the ceremony for yourself, or, if you have access to other Outer Court Correllians or to initiated Correllian clergy, they can help you to perform it.

Recognition by the tradition makes you a formal member and means that should your membership ever be questioned the tradition will vouch for you. This is particularly important if you wish to attend members-only events or take advantage of members-only offers that may be made available by individual temples or by the tradition itself.

To register with the tradition, go to www.correllian.com and click on Applications. This will take you to an application form for Outer Court membership, which you can fill out. After filling out the form, you should hear back from the tradition, in general, on the next day. Once registered, you will receive confirmation by e-mail, along with a PDF certificate attesting to your status as an Outer Court member. And because you are registered in our membership lists, we will be able to vouch for your status even if you lose this paperwork.

Upon acceptance, you will be registered with the tradition and entered into our membership lists. These lists are strictly confidential and are used only by the tradition itself. Once registered, your name will be given to the first priestess, who will enter it into the Book of Life. The Book of Life, kept in the possession of the Correll Mother Temple, contains the names of all recognized members of the Correllian Tradition, past and present.

It must be noted, however, that we do reserve the right to refuse membership to anyone, although we rarely do so.

• • • •

What If I Do Want to Be Initiated?

These lessons have been made available with the expectation that most of the students taking them are ultimately seeking initiation. Completing the lessons is not, however, the only thing required for initiation. The tradition itself requires additional studies, notably courses in Correllian philosophy and Correllian ministry, as well as studying the Five Mystic Secrets. Also, individual Correllian temples often have further requirements of their own.

There are several formats under which these studies can be completed. You may study through a member temple or Shrine of the Tradition, or a recognized Correllian study group. You may study with an individual member of the Correllian High Priesthood, either in person or through correspondence courses, or you may study online through one of our teaching partners, such as www.witchschool.com. In any event, you will receive personal guidance from your teachers or mentors. When you successfully complete your studies, they will guide you through the process of becoming initiated.

Initiation may be accomplished through a self-initiation ceremony or through a real-time initiation ceremony at a local Correllian temple or at a Correllian gathering such as the Lustrations, which are held twice yearly. Many people who do not live near a Correllian temple will choose the self-initiation and then follow up with a real-time initiatory confirmation ceremony when they are able to get to a temple or event.

Self-Wiccaning Ritual

This is the ritual of Self-Wiccaning, or Entry to the Outer Court. In enacting this ritual, you are declaring yourself to be a Wiccan believer and affiliating yourself with the Correllian Nativist tradition of Wicca. Consider this well before you undertake the ritual.

In this ritual, you will use many of the skills you have learned in these lessons. You may enact the ritual alone or with others. It is best performed during the waxing moon. You will need the following materials:

- Altar candles, as many as desired
- Salt, sea salt if possible
- Water
- Matches or lighter
- Charcoal, if using powdered incense
- Incense, preferably powdered
- Athame
- Wiccaning candle, preferably purple
- Anointing oil

Appendix A

- Chalice with beverage of choice
- A libation dish

Notes: The Wiccaning candle should be a small, quick-burning candle. A votive or even a tea light is good. You may use any form of incense, but if you are not using powdered incense you will wish to substitute a candle for the charcoal to use in charging the circle.

· · · ·

Air/East: Opening

Begin as always by clearing and releasing all excess energy. Now prepare your ritual space for use by cleansing and charging it.

Bless the salt and water. Make three tuathail circles over the salt and send out of it all negativity or impurity, visualizing the salt flooding with yellow-white light. Declare the salt cleansed. Then make three deosil circles over the salt and bless it. Visualize the salt filling with blue-white light, raising its energetic vibration. Declare the salt blessed. Repeat this process for the water, and add three pinches of salt to the water.

Now use the salt and water to cleanse your ritual space. Make a tuathail circle aspersing the area, and visualize it filled with yellow-white light, sending away all negative and unfocused energy.

Now bless the fire and incense in the same way. The fire may be the charcoal on which you will burn your incense, or if you are not using a powdered incense, the

fire may be a candle. As with the salt, first cleanse and then bless the fire. Now repeat that process for your incense. Add three pinches of incense to the charcoal (or, if you are not using a powdered incense, wave the incense three times over the fire) to conjoin the energies.

Charge your ritual space by making a deosil circle around it with the fire and incense. Visualize the area filled with blue-white light, raising its vibrational rate.

Now take up your athame and cast the magic circle, surrounding your ritual space with an energetic barrier that will help to focus and strengthen your working.

· · · ·

Fire/South: Invocations

Now call the quarters. Move deosil around the circle, calling upon each of the quarters and asking them to aid your working. At each of the four quarters, create a pillar of white light. You are now ready to invoke.

Speaking from your heart, call upon the Goddess to be with you. Ask her for her guidance and her aid as you undertake this step of Self-Wiccaning and affiliation with the Correllian Tradition. Now call upon the God. Ask him to be with you too, to aid and help you. If you have a specific patron deity or patron deities, call upon those deities also.

Finally, and just as importantly, you must now invoke your own Higher Self and align with it so that you will be acting in accordance with the highest parts of your being.

. . . .

Spirit/Center: Ritual

Now take a few moments and look within yourself. Consider the step you are taking. Think about how you came to this place and the things you experienced in coming here. Think about what this ritual means in and of itself, and what it means to you. Through this ritual, you are making a commitment to yourself and to Deity: a commitment to continued spiritual growth, a commitment to honor Deity and self, and a commitment to the Correllian Tradition. The Correllian Tradition is not an exclusive tradition—you can belong to it and still belong to other traditions as well—but this ritual is still a commitment to honor Correllian teachings and ideas, to honor fellow Correllians as part of your spiritual family, and to honor and respect Correllian clergy and institutions. This is a commitment that can only be made by free will, and it should not be made without reflection.

When you have considered all of the above, take up the anointing oil. Imagine the oil filled with beautiful white light, which radiates out from within it like a sun. Place a small amount of oil on your fingertips.

Now take up the Wiccaning candle and dress it with the anointing oil. As you dress the candle, continue to reflect on the meaning of the ritual and your feelings toward the step you are taking. When you have finished dressing the candle, hold it before you.

Now light the Wiccaning candle. Look upon the candle. Look at the flame. Watch how it dances, how it sways. Behold its beauty, its strength, how generously the flame shares its light.

Know this: the flame that you are watching is but a pale reflection of another, greater flame—an Eternal Flame, a flame that burns within you, at the core of your soul. That Eternal Flame has burned since before creation and will burn throughout existence. It is your innermost soul, the Divine Spark of the Goddess within you.

Through that Eternal Flame, you are always connected to the Goddess, your source and the ultimate center of your being. Through the Eternal Flame, you are connected to all things that exist, from the smallest molecule to the greatest star—indeed, to the whole of creation—for the same Eternal Flame burns within all of these.

Through the Eternal Flame, you are always connected to the Goddess. Through the Eternal Flame, you may always call upon her. Through the Eternal Flame, you may always access her love, her strength, her powers. When you grow spiritually, the Eternal Flame burns stronger and your ability to access the Divine increases. When you deny your spirit, the Eternal Flame burns low—but it can never go out, not ever.

The Eternal Flame has always burned there within you, but now you know it and acknowledge it. You might say something like:

"Behold, it is not the light of this candle that lights my path, but the light of another, greater flame—the Eternal Flame that burns within me, and has burned within me since the first beginning. The spark of Divinity placed in me by the Goddess, which binds me to Goddess and God now and through all time. Through this inner flame I draw upon the divine energy that is always available to me in limitless quantities. I light this candle to remind myself now and forever of that Eternal Flame within me, and I shall never forget it again."

Stop and think about the Eternal Flame within you—your connection to Deity, the monad, which is the point of divine consciousness within you. See the flame and imagine it growing stronger and brighter.

Feel its strength and beauty, and feel the love of Deity within the flame.

Now speak the Oath:

"Behold, I, _____ , declare myself a spiritual child of the Correllian Nativist Tradition of Wicca. Acting from my Highest Self, and in accordance with the Sacred Flame that burns within me, I make this Oath of my own free will. I swear that I shall always respect the tradition's teachings and that I shall always act in accordance with the Wiccan Rede and the Law of Three. I call upon the Goddess and the God to witness my sacred Oath and to help me to make it as deep and full as possible. By my will, I will it so, so mote it be."

Now place the candle back upon the altar. If possible, it should be allowed to burn until it is completely gone.

Now take up the anointing oil to perform the ritual of self-blessing. Begin by blessing your feet. Place a bit of oil on your fingers. Use your index finger and middle finger together—this is the "blessing position." Touch the top of each foot and imagine a ball of bright white light around the feet. Say something like:

"Blessed be my feet, that I may walk always in the paths of Spirit."

Now take a bit more oil onto your fingertips, with which to anoint your knees. Place your fingers a few inches before the knees—it is not necessary to touch the knees directly, as anointing oil may stain a robe—and imagine a ball of white light around them. Say something like:

"Blessed be my knees, which shall kneel at the altars of the Ancient Ones."

Now take a bit of oil and bless your pelvic region. Again, you may hold the fingers a few inches before the pubic area and imagine a ball of white light there. Say something like:

"Blessed be my loins, which bring forth life, and joy, and creativity."

Now take a bit more oil with which to anoint your heart chakra—the center of your chest. Place your fingers a few inches before the heart chakra and imagine a ball of white light around it. Say something like:

"Blessed be my heart, which is formed in beauty, that I may give love and receive it."

Now anoint your lips. Again, you do not need to touch the lips directly (as anointing oil on the lips may burn), but rather place your fingers just before them and imagine a ball of white light to conduct the blessing energy. Say something like:

"Blessed be my lips, which shall speak the words of power in time to come."

Now take a bit of oil and touch your third eye, the center of your forehead. Imagine a ball of clear white light around the area. Say something like:

"Blessed be my eye, that I may see all things clearly."

And finally, take a bit of oil and anoint the very top of your head. Imagine a ball of white light here as well. Say something like:

"Blessed be my crown chakra, that I may receive always the messages of the Goddess."

Imagine a column of white light coming down upon you from above, going through the top of your head and into your body—a beautiful, clear white light. Let the light fill you, pouring into every part of you. Be one with the light and let it move through you. Let the light suffuse you for a few moments. Then release it: let it run down through your feet, retaining only what you need.

• • • •
Water/West: Offering

Now turn to your chalice. Take up the chalice and bless it. Imagine a ball of clear white light around the chalice, radiating out in all directions like a sun. Declare the cup blessed in the name of the Goddess and the God. You might say something like:

*"Behold, in the name of the
Goddess and the God may this
cup be blessed. We share it in
token of our love for them and
for one another. In perfect love
and perfect trust, so mote it be."*

Now take a sip from the chalice. If there are more than one of you, each person shall take a sip.

Now pour out a small libation and dedicate that to your ancestors, physical and spiritual, and to all your friends in Nature, seen and unseen. Then dedicate what remains in the chalice to the Goddess and the God. (After the ritual, the libations may be emptied outside or otherwise respectfully disposed of.)

• • • •
Earth/North: Closing

You are now ready to give thanks and close the ritual. Begin by thanking your own Higher Self and affirming your desire to move in harmony with it and fulfill your highest purposes. Now thank your patron deity or deities, if you invoked any, and give thanks to the God and to the Goddess.

Now go tuathail around the circle, thanking each of the quarters and taking down the pillars of white light you raised for each. Finally, take up your athame and, going tuathail around the circle again, take down the circle itself. You might say something like the traditional:

*"As above, so below. As the
universe, so the Soul. As without,
so within. Merry meet, merry
part, and merry meet again."*

And as always, conclude by clearing and releasing all excess energy.

If possible, the Candle of Dedication should be allowed to burn until it is all gone. If the candle cannot be allowed to burn down after the ritual, relight it at another time and let it burn down the rest of the way. You should not reuse it for any other purpose.

• • • •

Congratulations! After performing this ritual, you may call yourself Correllian. To be recognized as an Outer Court member of the tradition, follow the instructions given in the conclusion.

The Charge of the Goddess

The Charge of the Goddess is generally considered the most sacred piece of Wiccan liturgy. There are many versions of the charge, as different traditions and temples have adapted it to their needs.

The earliest form of the Charge of the Goddess appears in the *Vangelo delle Streghe*, to which we have so often referred. Here, it is given as the charge of the Maiden goddess Aradia to her followers. It is much shorter and less poetic than the modern charge.

The most famous version of the charge is the one written by the great Wiccan priestess Doreen Valiente, which expands the *Vangelo*'s charge with the "Words of the Star Goddess." Valiente's version of the charge is extremely beautiful and much more philosophical than its predecessor.

A portion of Valiente's charge is said to have been based on material from Aleister Crowley's *Equinox*, a major work of

Appendix B

the Ceremonial Tradition. There is much debate as to Crowley's proper role in Wiccan history—appropriate, considering the amount of debate on Wiccan history itself. Traditionally, Crowley is said to have been a Wiccan initiate of or through George Pickingill, and he left the Craft for the Ceremonial movement because he was frustrated with the power structure (matriarchal) and the time it was taking him to advance.

Many other versions of the charge have been created by Wiccan writers and leaders such as Starhawk and Grimassi, and these vary slightly or more significantly from Valiente's. Naturally, we too have our own Correllian recension, which is given below.

· · · ·

The Charge of the Goddess

*Hear now the words of the Great
  Mother
Who was of old called many names by
  the hearts of humankind—
Selv, Diana, Brighid, Laksmi, Yema-
  ya, Kuan Yin, and many others
Both known and unknown:*
Whenever you have need of
  anything
Once in a month and better it be
  when the Moon is full
Then you shall assemble in some
  sacred place

And adore Me, Who am the spirit
  of the Moon.
And you shall sing and dance, make
  music and make love
All in My name, Who am the
  Queen of all the Wise
And you shall be free from slavery
And as a sign that you are truly
  free, you shall be open in your
  rites.
For Mine is the ecstasy of spirit,
  and Mine too the joys of the
  senses
And My law is love unto all beings
Nor do I demand ought of sacrifice
For I am the Mother of All Living,
  and My love is poured out upon
  creation.
Keep pure this highest ideal, strive
  ever toward it
Let nothing turn you aside
For Mine is the cup of the wine of
  life
The sacred cauldron which is the
  grail of immortality.
On Earth I give knowledge of the
  Spirit Eternal
And beyond Death I give peace and
  freedom
And reunion with those who have
  gone before
For I am the Gracious Goddess,
  Who gives joy unto the human
  heart.

*Hear now the words of the Star
Goddess
In the dust of Whose feet are the
Hosts of Heaven
And Whose body encircles the
universe:*
I am the beauty of the Green Earth
and the White Moon among the
stars
And the Mystery of the Waters
I call unto your soul: "Arise and
come unto Me."
For I am the Soul of Nature, Who
gives life to the universe.
From Me all things proceed, and
unto Me all must return
Before My face—O beloved of
Gods and humankind—
Let your Highest Self rejoice
And be enfolded in the rapture of
the Infinite.
For My worship is in the Heart that
rejoices
And behold—All acts of love and
pleasure are my rituals.
Therefore let there be beauty and
strength, power and compassion,
Honor and humility, mirth and
reverence within you.
And you who seek to find Me
In the depths of the sea or the
shining stars

Know that your seeking will avail
you not
Unless you know the Mystery;
For if that which you seek you find
not within yourself
You will never find it
For behold—I have been with you
since the beginning
And I am that Which is attained at
the end of desire.

· · · ·

Along with the Charge of the Goddess,
there is also a Charge of the God. This
was created in recent years, and it too has
quickly developed many variations. Below
follows the Correllian recension of the
Charge of the God.

· · · ·

The Charge of the God

*Hear then the words of the God
In the crown of Whose head are the
millions of lives
And Whose body is the Great Dragon
of the universe:*
I am the forest, the field, and the
golden Sun
I am lightning and fire
I am the Lord of Time and Space
Who turns the Wheel and calls the
Dance of Life.

I am the Son of the Goddess, and
    also her Brother and Consort

But more than this I am her other
    Self

Obverse and Reverse are We

As the eternal cycle of Night and
    Day.

I am the radiant Sun Who shares
    his light with Earth

That all upon her may live

I am the fruitful harvest and
    verdant greenery

Offering My body that all who eat
    may thrive.

In life I am the Green Man

Spirit of life and freedom, Who
    spurs all on to growth.

At death I am the Stag King with
    his staff

Who guards the gate between the
    worlds.

If you would seek Me in the green
    field or the blue sky

Or the cry of the stag or the flight
    of the hawk

Know that your seeking will avail
    you not

Unless you know the Mystery;

For if that which you seek you find
    not within yourself

You will never find it

For I have grown with you from the
    beginning

And I am the attainment of desire.

• • • •
The Joint Charge

In addition to the Charge of the Goddess
and the Charge of the God, there is also a
combined form: the Joint Charge. In the
Joint Charge, lines from the Charge of the
Goddess and the Charge of the God alter-
nate, recited by the priestess and priest
respectively. The Joint Charge is generally
used in the Correllian Lustration.

Congratulations!
You have reached
the end of the
First Degree.

Llewellyn Ordering Information

Order Online:
Visit our website at www.llewellyn.com, select your books, and order them on our secure server.

Order by Phone:
- Call toll-free within the U.S. at 1-877-NEW-WRLD (1-877-639-9753). Call toll-free within Canada at 1-866-NEW-WRLD (1-866-639-9753)
- We accept VISA, MasterCard, and American Express

Order by Mail:
Send the full price of your order (MN residents add 6.5% sales tax) in U.S. funds, plus postage & handling to:

Llewellyn Worldwide
2143 Wooddale Drive, Dept. 978-0-7387-1301-4
Woodbury, MN 55125-2989

Postage & Handling:

Standard (U.S., Mexico, & Canada). If your order is:
$24.99 and under, add $3.00
$25.00 and over, FREE STANDARD SHIPPING

AK, HI, PR: $15.00 for one book plus $1.00 for each additional book.

International Orders (airmail only):
$16.00 for one book plus $3.00 for each additional book

Orders are processed within 2 business days.
Please allow for normal shipping time. Postage and handling rates subject to change.

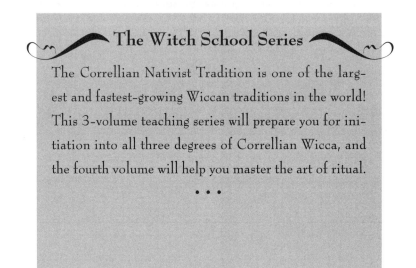

The Witch School Series

The Correllian Nativist Tradition is one of the largest and fastest-growing Wiccan traditions in the world! This 3-volume teaching series will prepare you for initiation into all three degrees of Correllian Wicca, and the fourth volume will help you master the art of ritual.

• • •

· ·

Witch School Second Degree

Lessons in the Correllian Tradition

Rev. Donald Lewis-Highcorrell

In twelve lessons, you'll learn about magical alphabets, energy working, and many topics that build upon the lessons from the first degree. The duties of second-degree clergy are also presented here. Every lesson features study questions, a glossary, and exercises to develop your psychic and magical skills.

978-0-7387-1302-1, 7½ x 9⅛, 480 PP. $24.95

· ·

Witch School Third Degree

Lessons in the Correllian Tradition

Rev. Donald Lewis-Highcorrell

Witch School Third Degree is for those who are called to Wicca as a vocation. This text explores Wiccan mysteries and spiritual concepts in depth and explains the responsibilities of the High Priesthood.

978-0-7387-1303-8, 7½ x 9⅛, 456 PP. $29.95

To order, call 1-877-NEW-WRLD

Prices subject to change without notice

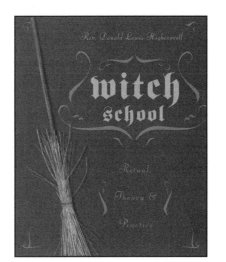

· ·

Witch School Ritual, Theory and Practice

Lessons in the Correllian Tradition

Rev. Donald Lewis-Highcorrell

From the Dance of Death for Samhain to fire jumping for Ostara, ritual is at the heart of religious devotion. Rev. Donald Lewis-Highcorrell, author of the Witch School series, is back with an in-depth exploration of ritual from the Correllian perspective. The Wheel of the Year is an ideal backdrop for mastering the art of ritual. Revolving through the sabbats, Lewis-Highcorrell examines every step of formal ritual—casting the Circle, invoking the quarters, acts of power, and so on—along with traditional Correllian practices. Encouraging improvisation and innovation, Lewis-Highcorrell also offers tips for keeping ceremonies fresh. There are suggestions for decorating, costumes, colors, props, and more. Sample ceremonies and dialogue are also offered as templates for creating your own ritual.

978-0-7387-1339-7, 7½ x 9⅛, 240 PP. $24.95

To order, call 1-877-NEW-WRLD

Prices subject to change without notice

· ·
To Write to the Author

If you wish to contact the author or would like more information about this book, please write to the author in care of Llewellyn Worldwide and we will forward your request. Both the author and the publisher appreciate hearing from you and learning of your enjoyment of this book and how it has helped you. Llewellyn Worldwide cannot guarantee that every letter written to the author can be answered, but all will be forwarded. Please write to:

Rev. Donald Lewis-Highcorrell
℅ Llewellyn Worldwide
2143 Wooddale Drive, Dept. 978-0-7387-1301-4
Woodbury, MN 55125-2989

Please enclose a self-addressed stamped envelope for reply,
or $1.00 to cover costs. If outside U.S.A., enclose
international postal reply coupon.

Many of Llewellyn's authors have websites with additional information and resources. For more information, please visit our website:

http://www.llewellyn.com